World Order and Religion

SUNY Series in Religion, Culture, and Society

Wade Clark Roof, Editor

World Order and Religion

Edited by

Wade Clark Roof

State University of New York Press

Published by
State University of New York Press, Albany

© 1991 State University of New York

For information, address State University of New York
Press, State University Plaza, Albany, N. Y. 12246

Production by M. R. Mulholland
Marketing by Fran Keneston

Library of Congress Cataloging in Publication Data

World order and religion / edited by Wade Clark Roof.
    p.   cm. — (SUNY series in religion, culture, and society)
    Includes bibliographical references and index.
    ISBN 0-7914-0739-X (alk. paper). — ISBN 0-7914-0740-3 (pbk. :
alk. paper)
    1. Religion and international affairs.   2. Christianity and
international affairs.   3. Religions—Relations.   4. Missions—
Theory.   5. United States—Religion—20th century.   6. World
politics—20th century.   I. Roof, Wade Clark.   II. Series.
BL65.I55W68   1991
291.1'7—dc20   90-45447
                                                              CIP

10   9   8   7   6   5   4   3   2   1

Contents

Acknowledgments

This collection had its origins in a conference on World Order and Religion, held at the Lord Jeffery Inn in Amherst, Massachusetts, in January 1989. All of the chapters contained herein were originally prepared for the conference. Funded by the Lilly Endowment, Inc., the project was part of a larger research agenda on religion and culture carried out at the University of Massachusetts from 1988 to 1990.

The editor is indebted to Jackson W. Carroll and William McKinney at Hartford Seminary for assistance in planning the conference and for arranging support for a dozen or so religious leaders to attend, to Jody McCarren who helped make the local arrangements, to Katherine Roof for assistance in the bibliographical search, to Kimberly Labor for editorial contributions, and to Bruce Greer who taped the conference proceedings. Special thanks are extended to colleagues and scholars who participated in the conference as discussants or contributed otherwise, including Madeleine Adriance, Jay Demerath, Robert Evans, David Heim, William Hutchison, Will Johnston, and Eleanor Scott Myers.

Introduction

Events every day remind us that ours is a global world. The crumbling of the Berlin Wall, student uprisings in China, the war in the Persian Gulf—all are happenings that seem perilously close no matter where we live. As the world has grown smaller, relations among nation-states have become much more complex. Drugs on the streets of Boston, Seattle, or Des Moines are embedded in a massive web of international relations extending across two continents. The opening of McDonald's in Moscow signals changing Soviet-American relations as well as the far reaches of multinational corporate structures across national and ideological boundaries. Increasingly terms such as *globalization* and *internationalization* are a part of our vocabulary, crucial to our thinking about what it means to live in a world that is shrinking into a single place.

In religious matters as well, we are forced to think more globally. Not only are we more and more aware of the millions of people around the world who believe differently than we do, but the reality of global politics and conflicting ideologies is impressed upon us in ways that easily provoke our fears. We see, hear, and read about how religion and politics are entangled in one tense spot after another, such as in Northern Ireland, South Africa, and the Middle East. Religion has become "politicized" and politics "religionized" in many quarters—what happens in any one of them bears directly upon us and the rest of the world in an age of potential nuclear destruction.

We cannot, in fact, adequately understand what is going on in the United States without placing events and trends in a broader context. Consider the nation's rapidly growing Muslim, Asian, and Hispanic populations. These new populations did not just come onto the scene but are themselves a reflection of the nation's shifting pattern of economic and political ties with other countries in the period since World War II. Political and ideological ties with the Middle East opened up possibilities for Muslim immigrants, many of whom have chosen to remain and settle in this country, thus making Islam one of the rapidly growing faiths in the United States. Large numbers of Cubans, Puerto Ricans, and Chicanos have entered the country during these years—an influx of people gradually reshaping American Catholicism as Hispanic culture and traditions are integrated into church life. Broadened ties with Asia, and especially with Japan, combined with American intervention in Vietnam, have resulted in a stream of "new immigrants" from many Asian countries. The United States' deep involvement in a global network of political alliances and trade relations over the past fifty years has created a new-style religious pluralism within its own borders — the global context of religions and peoples "writ small" on the nation.

A global network of political alliances and trade relations also creates its own vulnerabilities — potential shifts in a nation's power within the larger order. When the nation's niche in the larger system changes, cultural and institutional ramifications follow. The United States' standing as a world power, for example, has long sustained a sense of national purpose and patriotic pride, which, in turn, has helped to shape normative faith and the outlook of the American people. In times of national prosperity and of economic and technological advance, the American Way of Life as an ideology thrives; the mood of the nation is upbeat. In times of uncertainty and mounting threats to world dominance, however, the normative matrix of politics and faith — often referred to as "civil religion" — is easily transformed. Fears that the United States might be losing its hegemony in the world economy and a generalized loss of confidence in the nation's values and institutions as, for example, in the post-Vietnam years, parallel, not surprisingly, a loss of vitality and influence for the mainline Judeo-Christian traditions.

A World-Order Perspective

As these examples suggest, a more global perspective sheds insights on cultural and religious change. The advantages of such a perspective are more and more recognized in the social sciences. Theories of social and political change once cast primarily in terms of the internal dynamics of individual societies (e.g., structural differentiation, industrialization, modernization) are now increasingly challenged by more global perspectives. It is recognized that individual societies often are not the best context in which to examine change and that it is possible to identify transnational systems that better locate what is happening. Older notions of linear, evolutionary change over time within societies have given way to concerns with global systems, the relations among societies, and changing configurations of world order. Rather than theories of history of the sort advanced in years past by Spencer, Toynbee, and others, the newer paradigms posit systems of nation-states as power players and give attention to changes in the balance of power among them, as, for example, in historian Paul Kennedy's recent, best-selling *Rise and Fall of the Great Powers* (1987).

The newer paradigm goes by various names: world order, world systems, and international relations. "World order" and "world systems" are closely associated, but both are different from international relations as usually understood. Immanuel Wallerstein's work (1974, 1979), more than anyone else's, has shaped world-systems theory. As distinct from international-relations theory, which has looked upon the global system as a set of relationships among relatively separate entities, world-systems theory for Wallerstein posits the existence of a much more integrated entity with a logic and structure of its own. As a theory it stresses, first and foremost, a whole-to-parts mode of thinking that assumes *a priori* world social relations, and not simply among component parts, and it is in this sense a model of social order at the most generalizable level.

For Wallerstein, the focus of analysis is the modern capitalist world system emerging in the West in the sixteenth century. The term *world* does not refer to the globe but rather to boundaries of the capitalist division of labor. These boundaries are defined in terms of a hierarchical and territorial division of labor based on an exchange of commodities: high-wage goods are produced in the core of the system, and low-wage goods are produced on its periphery. The dominant core seeks to maintain its position of power and control over the periphery by means of effective legitimation and political and economic integration. The attainment and loss of hegemonic power is seen as resulting primarily from the operation of economic forces, and more specifically technological and organizational innovations that significantly alter the competitive advantages among nation-states. As such, the theoretical approach contains a distinct Marxist bias, thus tending to favor economic and material explanations while largely ignoring cultural and religious considerations.

Increasingly, though, scholars are recognizing that cultural factors need not be ignored and that including such factors might indeed enhance a world-systems perspective. Wallerstein himself seems to have moved in this direction, giving more attention in recent writings to "metaphysical presuppositions" and "organizing myths" that help in shaping the modern world system (see Robertson and Lechner, 1985). Roland Robertson suggests that the time has come to "go beyond" relatively simple models of world polity or world economy and to explore the "dynamics of global culture." His point is that globalization has a cultural dimension as well as economic and political ones, all three closely interwoven with one another. Whatever else it may be, the world system is, as Robertson says (1985), a "sociocultural system," the elements of which may be separated *analytically* but not in their actual dynamics. This is not to advance a cultural, or idealist, interpretation in place of others but to encourage a balanced perspective between determinism and voluntarism, and between materialist and nonmaterialist explanations. Thus, Robertson's plea is for a broadened approach to thinking about world order, and without resorting to reductionism of any kind, either materialist or idealist.

Relevance to the Study of Religion

Is a world-order perspective useful for religious studies? What are its intellectual advantages over other, more customary approaches for studying religion? These are pertinent and timely questions.

Surprisingly little attention has been given to global approaches in the study of religion. In the sociology and anthropology of religion, conceptual models remain limited largely to groups and structures *within* societies, such as Pentecostal migrants, Southern Baptists, middle-class churchgoers, New Agers, religious bureaucracies, and so forth; societies are viewed as systems made up of social classes, institutions, racial and ethnic groups, religious groups, etc. The religious life of whole societies is studied but typically as autonomous units, such as Japanese religion, American Catholicism, and British folk beliefs. Theories of secularization are cast largely in terms of macrosocietal trends, often laden with assumptions about unilinear and irreversible patterns of change, and almost always without concern for the wider relationships among societies. In religious studies more generally, historical and comparative methods of studying religion are the predominant approaches. Buddhism, Islam, Judaism, Hinduism, Christianity, and the other great world religions are treated as traditions or subtraditions encompassing beliefs, practices, values, and symbols extending over time and lands. Religions are compared, one with another, usually on the basis of their historical origins and development. Global considerations of power and exchange relations as a general underlying framework tend not, however, to be treated in any systematic manner.

A wider, global perspective would appear to offer many advantages for the study of religion:

One, by focusing upon the larger, transsocietal context, we are sensitized to the dominant patterns of change, which cut *across* societies and religious traditions. Much attention is given already in religious studies to the idiographic, or particular, characteristics of religions and cultures, but this approach overlooks the more generalizable features of continuity and change discernible today. Sorting out these features is essential to understanding the modern world and the relations of religion to modernity, and by establishing what is generalizable we can have a better appreciation of that which is truly particularistic. Religious responses to the common global influences vary enormously—from accommodation to protest —but to understand how and why responses vary, we need to know more about the larger contexts out of which they arise.

Two, a world-order approach offers a rich vantage point for examining trends in "establishment" religion. By virtue of their established status, such religions are closely aligned with political and economic institutions and ideologies. Historically, religious traditions have developed and expanded in ways closely related to trade patterns. The fate of all three institutions—political, economic, and religious—is linked to what happens in the larger global context. In nations experiencing ascendancy and dominance in the world system, establishment religion and ideology is more likely to flourish, while during periods of stagnation and decline, these suffer in popularity. Accentuated are the ebbs and flows, the dynamic rather than the static aspects of religious faiths and traditions.

Three, world order provides perspective on periods of religious unrest and dramatic religious change. Periods such as the 1960s in the United States, the early nineteenth and early seventeenth centuries in England, and the Reformation in the sixteenth century — all characterized by schism, sectarianism, and cult movements — can be viewed as transitional periods, as times of major realignment in the relations between domestic interest groups and world affairs. By exploring transitional periods, we gain insights not only on conditions underlying periods of intense religious activity but also on how to begin to compare watershed periods in religious history.

Four, a global framework forces upon us the concerns of people everywhere for survival and peace, for health and well-being, even for a sense of a common humanity. A nuclear age pulls the world together in a common fate. Indeed the possibility of a single world generates its own religious agenda: it poses new religious questions on the part of people bound together in new ways and encourages the rise of universal theodicies. What once seemed like insurmountable differences separating believers from one another and from nonbelievers, and which would have been in past eras, now diminish in the face of modern circumstances. We become, as Wilfred Cantwell Smith says, "heirs of the whole religious history of humankind."

Outline of Chapters

The essays in this volume cover a wide range of topics and explore many issues. Contributors were given considerable freedom in developing perspectives, the only major constraint being that the focus was on the Western world, or the cultural and religious developments in relation to the West. Because of the role of the United States in the modern world order, considerable attention was also given to the implications of such a perspective for American religion.

The papers are organized into five sections.

General Considerations

Section 1 includes two general essays, one by Robert Wuthnow and a second by James Davison Hunter and James E. Hawdon. In what was intended as a broad overview, Wuthnow argues for a global approach because of three major types of contributions. One is that such an approach draws attention to the more general dynamics of modern life in various societies—to features of a world culture, ranging from child-rearing habits and legal patterns to trends toward religious individualism and secularization. Organizational structures as well as religious and cultural styles are all shaped by the emerging conditions of a global existence. To overlook these patterns and trends is to fail to see modern life in its broadest context.

A second contribution is that we gain insight into the deeper changes underlying what appears to be more proximate influences on religion. He cites sectarianism as an example. Ernst Troeltsch's formulation has long been accepted as the classic statement on sects from the time of the Reformation to the end of the nineteenth century. Wuthnow observes, however, that the Protestant countries in which Troeltsch's sects were mainly located lay at the core of an expanding world economy. Economic expansion and industrialization made possible growth in population and a widening territorial division of labor, all of which created social upheavals generating potential recruits for sectarian movements. Their inclusion into an expanding dominant economy increased the likelihood of these movements gradually becoming established churches. Other types of world-economy conditions and dynamics might have produced patterns of sectarianism that are quite different. Thus, what may appear to be a universal characteristic of sectarianism, as some have argued, may be contingent on a particular set of historical and economic circumstances.

A third contribution is that a global perspective helps us to look at phenomena in quite a different way. One example he points to is American Protestant missions to the Third World. Mainline Protestant missionary efforts have scaled back in this century in favor of assistance to indigenous ministries, supplying social services and lobbying for social justice by political means. In contrast, evangelical and fundamentalist missions have grown and have continued to concern themselves primarily with conversions. Merely citing numbers of foreign missionaries can be misleading and minimizes the impact of the missionary enterprise as a whole. "Viewed from the American context," he writes, "it appears that mainstream Protestantism has suffered a serious decline in its missionary efforts. Viewed from a world-order perspective, the decline may be less serious than it would otherwise appear."

In a second general essay, Hunter and Hawdon are concerned with religious authority under conditions of advanced capitalism. With the expansion of the state and growth of the knowledge sector, religious authority has become marginalized from the structures of power in modern society. While religious leaders and influentials once played a dominant role in shaping public cultures, they do so no longer. This is not, as the authors suggest, because religious elites have withdrawn from the task but is, rather, a "consequence of their being structurally displaced." No longer enjoying a dominant cultural role, religious elites must now compete with secular elites to define the symbols of public life. They advance data showing that in the United States, Great Britain, Canada, West Germany, Switzerland, and France, the number of religious elites has remained relatively constant vis-a-vis the total population, while religious elites as a percentage of other cultural elites has dropped consistently and dramatically over the past century. The expansion of cultural elites in the contemporary world order is truly phenomenal and is crucial to understanding the fate of religious elites in Western societies.

The loss of cultural influence on the part of religious elites, however, has not resulted in their political solidarity. Hunter and Hawdon caution against a "new class" interpretation on the grounds of the diversity of political opinions among elites, both religious and nonreligious. A generally better explanation of ideology is the relative proximity of cultural elites to the mechanisms of profit making—the further removed from the market for their livelihood, the more likely to be critical. Among religious elites (especially Protestants and Catholics) they find theological orientation on an orthodox-progressive continuum to be a strong predictor of political views. The politically meaningful divisions among religious leaders, they conclude, are no longer defined by religious heritage but by how orthodox or progressive they are in theological outlook. The tendency of religious elites toward political polarization amounts to differing forms of posturing in the knowledge sector and strategies for regaining influence: progressives seek to form alliances with those who currently occupy the centers of cultural power, whereas conservatives challenge the legitimacy of powerful elites and seek to transform the center of power. Neither strategy, according to the authors, will likely restore religious elites to authority, given the basic structural realities of advanced capitalism.

Core and Periphery

Section 2 takes up a fundamental issue in world-order thinking — relations of core and periphery. So phrased, concern is with power structures and inequalities embedded in intersocietal relations. Essays here explore developments in various parts of the world in relation to world capitalism, with its core lying in Europe and North America.

Ninian Smart examines the historical experience of China, Japan, India, and Islamic states, and their differing trajectories of development and responses to the impact of colonialism and modern world capitalism. China has sought in various periods to combine Western science and Confucian values, and modern science and Marxism, with ideologies requiring that it abolish much of its past in the interest of either nationalism or socialist collectivism. By contrast, Japan has been successful in creating a vital synthesis between Western and nationalist values by importing Western models of education and by recasting its primeval Shinto tradition. In yet another pattern, India has been successful in its "grafting on" of Western values and modernization while at the same time retaining virtually all of its past, partly, as Smart explains, because of the "new" Hindu ideology, which was able to deal constructively with influences of Christianity, science, democracy, and nationalism. Islam has not fully worked out its independence of the West, and it has yet to produce, in the postcolonial period, a genuine new vision of itself as a faith and ideology. In each instance, the author interweaves political and economic factors with the religious and cultural, showing the impact of modern capitalism.

Smart's essay underscores that what we think of as religious traditions today are truly "inventions of the modern world." This is the case not just for the faiths of colonized lands but for the faiths of the colonizers as well. Christianity in Western countries, and especially liberal Protestantism in the United States, has successfully assimilated modern values such as liberalism, science, and democracy. However, as the author observes, because we are evolving towards a looser conception of core and periphery, the bonds between global capitalism and the United States will likely diminish. The new world order is seen as one in which both economic competition and individual human rights will be important, or as he says, an "order (that) will be 'liberal' in a classical way." His essay concludes with speculation about future trends: greater freedom of religion and corrosion of authorities, internationalism and diminished appeal of patriotism, pluralism of religious worldviews, and religions as transnational spiritual corporations.

Latin America and its relations with the United States is the topic of two papers. In his essay " 'God Damn Yanquis' — American Hegemony and Contemporary Latin America," Graham Howes examines the role of religious institutions in legitimating, mediating, and maintaining United States hegemony in contemporary Latin America. Three spheres of religio-political involvement are identified: radical subcultures within Roman Catholicism (Liberation Theology), conservative responses to this (Opus Dei), and the proliferation of fast-growing evangelical and fundamentalist Protestant sects. Linkages between the United States government and nation-states, and between the religious culture of the United States and its institutional counterparts in Latin America are closely examined.

The Catholic church up until the 1960s, he observes, legitimated the prevailing model of economic development—*desarollo*—which assigned a leading role to foreign capital, trusted in the military as a modernizing agent, and held out hope of sustained economic growth. In the period since, the church has been viewed as a less reliable ally of the United States, thus resulting in more covert involvement by the Central Intelligence Agency (CIA) and other United States government agencies in Latin American affairs. Aside from direct political intrusion, religious and ideological involvement ranges from efforts at turning public opinion against the "progressive" church to attempts at cultivating among intellectuals a right-wing, "revisionist" counterculture. It is among three Protestant constituencies — the Pentecostals, the fundamentalist sects, and the burgeoning middle-class evangelicals — that, as Howes says, "American missions and America's Mission are most clearly coincident." Utilizing the mass media and funded through bureaucracies based in the United States, growing numbers of Protestants are drawn to a faith possessing a mixture of theological conservatism and traditional anticommunism consonant with the interests of United States foreign policy. Paradoxically, as the Latin American case illustrates, a result of the efforts at using religion itself to try to induce approved political and ideological homogeneity has been the generation of greater religious pluralism.

Juan Carlos Navarro looks more specifically at liberation theology —its teachings and practice, and its implications both for Latin American politics and for Catholicism in the United States. He emphasizes that liberation theology is a dynamic religious force that will continue to evolve as a result of both internal developments and contextual modifications. He points to changes in the past twenty-five years, from the time of the Cuban Revolution to the Nicaraguan conflict: most notably the increased role of Catholic bishops, priests, and lay people in the revolutionary movements. He sees the recent process of democratization in many Latin American countries as in part a development to which liberation theology has made a contribution but also as perhaps "the most important challenge ahead." With repressive regimes being replaced by relatively open, democratic, but yet still capitalist, governments, have come shifts in thinking (revisions of "dependency theory," as he describes it) emphasizing internal, unexplored opportunities for economic development and general disillusionment with orthodox socialist solutions to social and economic problems.

Navarro views liberation theology as having a significant impact on Catholicism in the United States. He cites the concerns of the American bishops for the welfare of the poor and for distributive justice, and their emphasis upon the moral responsibility of rich nations for underdeveloped countries, as liberationist themes. While not expecting rank-and-file Catholics in the United States to fully endorse these themes, a more likely prospect, as he sees it, is "an increased awareness of Latin American problems in the United States coupled with a process of mutual enrichment of diverse Catholic traditions."

James H. Cone's "Martin Luther King, Jr., and the Third World" shows the reciprocal influence of the Third World on King, and of King on Third World people. He shows that especially in the latter period of his life, Martin Luther King, Jr. began to analyze more deeply the relationships of racism, poverty, and militarism in the policies of the United States government and in the international economic order. His focus on the global implications of racism in relation to poverty and war led him to the conclusion that the slums in American cities are a "system of internal colonialism" not unlike the exploitation in the Third World. King's global vision also helped him to see that the sociopolitical freedom of blacks was closely tied to the liberation of their sisters and brothers in Africa, Asia, and Latin America. Unless all were free, none were truly free.

King's impact upon the Third World was both symbolic and substantive. His symbolic influence was fourfold: (1) as a symbol of the black struggle for justice in the United States; (2) as a symbol of Third World peoples' struggles against colonialism; (3) as a symbol of the best in the American democratic and Judeo-Christian tradition; and (4) as a symbol of the struggle for world peace through nonviolence. Substantively, King's ideas and philosophy of nonviolence have prompted much debate among Third World leaders and inspired hope to millions throughout the world.

Mission and Ideology

A third set of papers focuses on Western Christian mission and related ideologies. The lead essay by A. F. Walls examines the spread of Christianity over the centuries, and particularly the shift during the twentieth century in the Christian center of gravity from the West toward the southern continents. In 1900 83 percent of Christians lived in Europe and North America; figures available for the late 1980s suggest that some 56 percent of the world's Christians now live in Africa, Asia, Latin America, and the Pacific. The "Christian heartlands are changing," as Walls says, and the concerns and priorities of people in these areas will likely shape the next phase of Christianity.

Walls sees this most recent shift in Christianity as related to the general impact of Western culture and hegemony on the southern world but notes that the relationship is not a straightforward one. Simple extension of territorial Christendom during the period of colonialism proved unworkable. The most important factor, he argues, was the simultaneous shift in the center of gravity within the West itself, that is, the Christianization of the United States and rise of the American missionary movement in the nineteenth century. Unlike in Europe where industrialization coincided with Christian decline, in the United States industrial transformation was accompanied by Christian growth. Energetic expansionism, resourcefulness, the application of business methods, the uninhibited use of money, the separation of church and state, and the creative use of voluntary religious societies all combined to give American missions a distinctive quality and momentum. These features have remained a mark of the American missionary movement even to the present, most notably among evangelical Christians.

Lamin Sanneh in "The Yogi and the Commissar: Christian Missions and New World Order in Africa" describes the impact of Christian missions in the indigenous African setting. Contrary to the view that missionaries were overseas agents of their imperial countries and the mission movement itself a source of major social and cultural disruption, Sanneh argues that missionary activity was neither terribly disruptive nor did it suppress indigenous creativity. He looks carefully at the accounts of missionaries themselves, noting that many were inclined to self-scrutiny about what they were doing and recognized the extreme ambiguity of European designs on Africa. Judged on the basis of actual missionary practices and effects in the field rather than on the motives of mission agencies or the intentions of some missionaries, he is inclined toward a generally benign view of the missionary's role in Africa. Thus, he would have us put to rest the political view of missionaries as the "religious surrogates of colonialism," so deeply built into the self-image of the West.

Sanneh proposes instead that the mission movement had a profound impact on the emergence of the new Africa. "If, in the light of the colonial takeover, we can speak justifiably of African capitulation, and, in that setting, of missionary assault on the old order," Sanneh writes, "we can, in the light of vernacular agency of missions, speak equally plausibly of African resistance to the forces of subjection, aided and abetted by missionary sponsorship of projects of cultural and social renewal." Of considerable importance in Sanneh's view was the development of vernacular resources and the promotion of African languages as complete and autonomous vehicles for conveying the Gospel to the people. Western missionary activity had the effect of promoting a sense of awakening and unity in many places. Also, he argues, such activity facilitated African exposure to the world and thus had positive long-run effects on indigenous development.

Michael A. Burdick and Phillip E. Hammond, in "World Order and Mainline Religions: The Case of Protestant Foreign Missions," explore the fit of a world-order perspective using religious data for Great Britain and the United States. They examine empirically the theory that periods of national dominance have been periods of religious florescence for the established churches catering to the middle and upper classes, and its corollary, that with a loss of dominance comes a decline in socially established religiosity. Although intuitively appealing as a theory, it should be revised, they suggest. First, they show that contrary to theoretical prediction, "establishment" church membership peaked in the United States before the United States *began* its world system ascendancy. Several major established denominations peaked in membership either in the nineteenth century or in the early decades of this century, suggesting, as they say, that "what was reached in the mid-1960s was not just the apex in sheer numbers of membership figures in churches serving 'middle and upper classes' but also the saturation of the religion market."

Data on missionary activity, however, provide the most severe challenge to the simple rise-and-fall thesis of national power within the world system. Foreign missions in the United States, more so than for Great Britain, fail to fit the model. Burdick and Hammond show that the rise and fall of mainline Protestant missionary activity occurs well before the ascendance and then challenge to America's hegemonic position in the world economy. A change of missionary ideology, seemingly independent of political and economic forces, occurred among the more liberal, mainline Protestants: from conversion in the nineteenth century to compassion in the 1920s, and finally, by 1970, to companionship with those to whom they ministered. Evangelical missionaries, in contrast, adhering to more traditional theological views, have grown enormously both in absolute numbers and in relative proportion of all missionary personnel. Evangelical missionary growth was most pronounced between World War II and 1968 — consistent with the world-order model — but the growth has continued to the present, contrary to what might have been expected. They suggest that if we look upon evangelicalism as becoming the "established" religion, then something of a world-order perspective on religious institutions would seem to be upheld.

American Religion and Civic Culture

Section 4 organizes themes pertinent to American religion and civic culture. In the first paper, George M. Thomas offers a "world polity interpretation of United States religious trends since World War II." Major trends identified include an increase in individualism, a growing liberal-conservative cleavage, and the politicization of religion. His approach to explaining these trends is to invoke the notion of "global density" (i.e., incorporation into global economic structures and nation-state involvement in the world polity) and to suggest that greater nation-state authority and status are the context of contemporary religion. A long-term increase in global density results in increased sociocultural heterogeneity and heightened competition and conflict over the nature of symbolic boundaries and the moral constitution of nation and citizen. He sees a concomitant intensification (resurgence, revival) of religious discourse and activity as an integral part of that reconstitution, conflict, and debate.

Because of the intensification of symbolic boundaries in the recent period, religious discourse took the form of social movements reworking those definitions. Thomas interprets the flurry of religious movements as liberal and conservative groups elaborating very different versions of individualism. Liberals stress personal choice, and conservatives stress personal conversion, yet both build on a subjective faith and value human happiness, self-esteem, and fulfillment. Generally, as Thomas says, the culture "defines the individual as a central unit of the nation-state, collective goals in terms of the well-being, happiness and autonomy of the individual, and rational moral action as the guarantor of progress. In short, both sets of movements are constructing the modern citizen and nation, albeit in significantly different ways." Different types of individualism are politicized largely around moral issues — concern about the breakdown of the family, abortion, prayer in schools, growing secularism. In the contemporary American context, conservatives are colorful and forthright, liberals are bland, but Thomas hints at the possibility that this difference might be short-lived.

Max L. Stackhouse, in his essay "Globalization and Theology in America Today," identifies three dimensions of globalization: deprovincialization, internationalization, and universality. Deprovincialization refers to a greater awareness of the larger world, internationalization to a growing interdependency and new levels of commonality, and universality to a basic "metaphysical-moral" vision of life. A theologian and broadly engaging theorist, Stackhouse seeks to weave into a single whole the social-structural aspects of globalization, a normative vision of universal truth and justice, and existential religious concerns of contemporary life. All are crucial, he believes, for creative theological reflection in America today.

His view of world systems reflects his broad orientation: "a modern rediscovery on this side of historical consciousness of what Troeltsch called 'relative natural law,' and what the theologians of old called 'orders

of creation,' now modulated by the results of both the contemporary
sense of change and new capacities to cross-culturally tabulate social-
scientific information." He is critical of American theology as narrow vision and provincial reflection and calls for a global theology based on
moral realities beyond private interest and beyond the privileged insights
of our unique historical experience. He draws parallels between global
order and what amounts to the ultimate theological affirmation: "the only
God worth worshiping liberates, but on the other side of liberation, calls
to order — to a universalistic order."

In her essay on "Realism, Just War, and the Witness of Peace,"
Jean Bethke Elshtain addresses what "just war" might mean in our time.
She explores the alternatives — pure war, or holy war if buttressed by ideology and doctrine, based on the rule of force and which sees the foreigner always as an enemy; and also, pure peace, or the Kingdom of God,
which holds out hope for a world of ongoing equilibrium, harmony, and
perfect order. Neither is satisfactory for one who "struggles to fashion a
world of relative order and stability that makes room for and accepts the
possibility of conflict." Ironically, as she notes, visions of pure peace often require their dialectical opposite, pure war, to sustain themselves.

Just-war thinking as a possibility, Elshtain insists, requires much of
us. It requires serious reflection about what our governments are doing,
but more than this it demands a sense of responsibility and accountability, or, as she says, a "morally formed civic character." Just war is not *just*
about war: it is an account of politics that seeks to be non-utopian yet to
place the political within a larger set of moral concerns and civic duties.
Thus, just-war thinking pictures the individual embedded within a framework of overlapping communities and loyalties: families, civil society,
state, and international order. The author welcomes a politics that offers
values for which one might die but not easy justifications for the need to
kill — a set of civic values embodied in a character she describes as the
"chastened patriot." The chastened patriot is committed yet detached,
compassionate yet critical, someone who recognizes that we have multiple ties and loyalties extending beyond our own nation. She calls for a reconstructed just-war tradition that "makes room for patriotism even as it
offers a critique of aggressive nationalism and imperialism, which makes
room for internationalism even as it offers a principled rejection of an
ideal of one world or one state."

Concluding Reflection

The final two essays were written in response to the other papers as
a general critique of world-order thinking in relation to religion. Both authors were asked to reflect broadly about the issues and approaches of
this perspective.

W. Barnett Pearce, a communications theorist, ponders whether the dynamics and trends within the world order can be satisfactorily understood using a vocabulary that names objective variables (e.g., economics, social structure) and excludes hermeneutics. His argument is that the act of representing world order as systemic is itself a crucial bit of data about the system. Representing the system in this way is a reflexive act and involves interpretive vocabularies and "stories" of the various component parts. In a complex cybernetic system such as a world-order system, Pearce argues that there must be not only narratives of the various parts but "narratives which describe the relation among other narratives." He proposes the term "eloquence" to direct attention to this more coherent, transcendent form of narrative.

His critique calls for a more rigorous pursuit of what kind of system is comprised by the world order. This will involve considerations of boundaries and structures using multiple vocabularies, of analyst and of analyzed, of the insider and of the outsider, of the core and of the periphery. Pearce argues that as human beings we live *in* discourse, that there are simultaneously multiple, incommensurate discourses, and that the way these discourses intermesh is crucial to understanding the lived experience of persons in the world system.

Rhys H. Williams examines world order as a paradigm for cultural and religious analysis. He dissects the various terms and meanings associated with the phrase *world order:* international, globalization, world system, and world order. His conclusion is that world order is the most appropriate construction because of its relative openness to interpretation and lack of association with a particular theoretical school. In a similar vein with Pearce, he observes that studies of economic, political, or social "order" typically portray that order as an end state rather than as a process, or collection of processes, and that they fail to give attention to the texture and multivocal nature of multiple discourses. Williams notes that a world-systems perspective, while obviously global, also emphasizes attention to local diversity, indigenous traditions, and cultural pluralism. There seems to be, as he says, "the simultaneous assumption that *both processes of core domination and peripheral resistance, are the primary locus of social vitality."*

The analysis of religion and culture, Williams emphasizes, cannot be divorced from questions of social power. He focuses attention, in the American case, on the debate surrounding the notion of the "public sphere." The issue is not simply who defines the public sphere at present, but also the changes that are developing in the way it is defined. He points to the role of global media and argues that it is essential to understand the differences between the "politics of imagery" and a public forum of viable motives and cultural resources in America today. Religious organizations have played, and continue to play, a crucial part in the formation of and commentary upon public issues, but there is a broadening cultural vocabulary on which to draw, a mixing of religious and nonreligious languages, and a need for greater clarity of how issues get defined and interpreted. An empirical task, he suggests, is to "understand how processes and events around the globe affect these resources for shaping our public sphere."

As is apparent in all five sections, many issues remain to be resolved before there can be any coherent world-order perspective on religion. No real consensus has yet emerged on how to approach the globalization phenomenon, on how to conceptualize what globalization is, or on what it might mean for religion. There is little agreement on basic terms, much less a full-blown vocabulary for intellectual exchange. Given that world order is still evolving as a conceptual approach and that it has received very little attention in the study of religion, this could hardly be otherwise. This volume is an attempt to contribute to this further development and to bring about more debate.

— *Wade Clark Roof*

References

Kennedy, Paul
1987   *The Rise and Fall of the Great Powers*. New York: Vintage.

Robertson, Roland
1985   "The Sacred and the World System." In P. Hammond, ed., *The Sacred in a Secular Age*, 347–358. Berkeley: University of California Press.

Robertson, Roland and Frank Lechner
1985   "Modernization, Globalization and the Problem of Culture in World-Systems Theory." *Theory, Culture and Society*. Vol. 2, No. 3, 103–117.

Wallerstein, Immanuel
1974   *The Modern World-System*. New York: Academic Press.
1979   *The Capitalist World Economy*. New York: Cambridge University Press.

Part I

General Considerations

1

International Realities:
Bringing the Global Picture into Focus

Robert Wuthnow

At no time in its history has the Judeo-Christian tradition been able to confine its interests within narrow ethnic, regional, or national boundaries. The Hebrew scriptures tell of a people forced to migrate beyond their own borders in search of food, displacing local gods with a God of the heavens, and recurrently finding themselves caught in the intrigues of warring empires. Jesus constantly ran into the limiting presuppositions of such boundaries in his day, and he repeatedly cut through them to enlarge his followers' vision. When the lawyer asked him for a definition of neighbor, Jesus pointedly told a story showing that compassion must extend beyond ethnic borders. He was crucified by Roman soldiers. When he commissioned his disciples, he admonished them to go into all the nations.

Over the centuries, the international dimension has been an integral feature of Western religion. By the end of the fourth century, Christianity had spread to nearly every corner of Europe as a result of the Romans' conquests. In 1095 the great crusades began, which pitted Christianity against the Muslim empire. By the end of the fifteenth century, Spanish and Portuguese explorers had taken their faith to the New World. In 1517 a wave of reforming zeal broke out in central Europe, which was to shape permanently the location of national boundaries and the strength of territorial sovereigns. By the end of the nineteenth century, the Western church was deeply implicated in the affairs of every continent as a result of missionary activity, trade, colonization, and war.

Today, as never before, the tender edges of our religious convictions are exposed to the wider world. Each day's headlines remind us that there are millions of people in the Far East, in the Soviet bloc, in Islamic

Robert Wuthnow

states who believe differently than we. Refugees arrive at our borders in a steady system, seeking better lives and fleeting civil unrest from governments kept weak by the policies of our own. They seek protection from our churches and force our attention to focus on the wider world. A third of the world languishes in hunger and poverty while the average American generates twenty-five pounds of trash a week. Questions of human rights and social responsibilities have never needed to be asked on a wider scale. Land developers burn forests in Latin America to feed the cattle that fill the cavernous appetites of fast-food chains in the United States — and the entire planet gradually warms, leaving even the experts in doubt about the future of our global ecology. Opinion polls reveal how closely our faith in ourselves is linked to the performance of the American economy. Yet, the performance of our economy is contingent as never before on foreign investment, shipping routes, exploitable pools of cheap labor, and favorable rates of currency exchange. If religion in today's world still supplies (in Peter Berger's words) the "sacred canopy" for our ordinary lives, it has surely become as precarious a canopy as the ozone layer of our world itself.

The images available in the social sciences for making sense of modern religion pay scant attention to these international and global realities. A few years ago, a comprehensive bibliographic guide listing more than 3,500 books and articles in the sociology of religion was published (Blasi and Cuneo, 1986). It provides a telling commentary on where the major theoretical and empirical emphases have been. Over 500 of the entries dealt with the social psychology of individual religiosity, and another 400 examined the beliefs and practices of individual believers. Seven hundred dealt with clergy and laity roles, and another 600 focused on the organizational characteristics of churches and synagogues, denominations, and sects. More than 200 dealt with religious movements, and an equal number presented abstract theoretical perspectives. Not a single section heading, subheading, or index item focused directly on the international or global characteristics of religion.

This is not to say, of course, that these characteristics of modern religion have been entirely neglected. One can scarcely read Durkheim without observing his concern for the tensions between religiously legitimated expressions of moral community and more universalistic orientations toward humanity in general. Studies of cargo cults, messianic movements, and Third World millenarianism, including widely read classics such as Peter Worsley's *The Trumpet Shall Sound* (1957) and Bryan Wilson's *Magic and the Millennium* (1973), have paid close attention to the effects of international relations on domestic religious developments. In increasing numbers, books have appeared on the religious situation in strategic parts of the globe, such as the Middle East and Latin America, and with growing frequency, articles on American religion refer to issues such as global consciousness, nuclear disarmament, and the effects of United States involvement in foreign affairs.

Among sociologists at large, the past decade and a half has also witnessed the development of a strong interest in so-called world-system theory (Wallerstein, 1974; Ragin and Chirot, 1984). Along with more conventional Marxist approaches and an eclectic array of studies concerned with "world conflicts," world-system theorists have initiated an important new line of inquiry focused specifically on the properties and dynamics of social configurations larger than the national society. This work has also contained a distinct Marxist bias, causing it to dismiss religion as epiphenomenal, while privileging studies of economic transactions, material inequality, and political structure.

It must be with humility, then, that the social scientist approaches the topic of religion from a wider, global perspective. The social scientist engaged in this pursuit is like the proverbial physicist struggling up the steep cliff of higher learning to discover the meaning of life, only to find upon reaching the top a humble guru who had been sitting there all along. The practitioners of religion have often been much more attuned to the international realities of the present world than their counterparts in the social sciences. They have had to be because their missionary and evangelization efforts have been truly international in scope. Nearly all the major denominations and faiths in the United States—Roman Catholics, Jews, Episcopalians, Presbyterians, Methodists—are themselves transplants to American soil and continue to be part of broader federations whose memberships span the globe. The universalistic normative concerns of the Judeo-Christian tradition have also forced its leaders to be attentive to such global issues as peace, hunger, poverty, and human rights. At least at these levels, the global concerns of American religion have simply been waiting to be discovered by social scientists.

The point, though, is not to engage in recriminations, but to advance in a positive direction. It is one thing to list such obvious topics as war and peace, poverty and prosperity, exploitation and social justice, and call for more studies and more understanding. It is quite another to move toward a more systematic theoretical perspective that links even the more mundane questions of religiosity and religious organization to broader concepts of world order. Indeed, the place to begin is to ask pointedly: What do we gain, if anything, from adopting a theoretical perspective that specifically attempts to take into account the forces of some social unit larger than the society itself?

Let us be modest at the outset; indeed, let us candidly admit that

many of the forces to which individual believers and their religious organizations respond are entirely local and operate at the microscopic level.
An individual parishioner loses a loved one and a member of the clergy
responds. An established neighborhood sees its population age, causing
a decline in the membership of a local church. Conversely, the pastor of a
suburban congregation finds herself increasingly torn between a dozen
committees as her neighborhood grows and the membership of her
church expands. We have social psychological theories about meaning
and belonging that help us understand what is happening in the first instance; demographic models for the second case; and studies of congregations and leadership roles for the third. It stretches the imagination to
say that world-order perspectives need to be added.

Beyond this, we can readily make a great deal of headway toward
understanding the social influences on religious organizations by focusing on familiar attributes of the national society. Suppose we do want to
understand aging and bereavement in a larger context. Then studies of the
age composition, family status, and health characteristics of the national
population are likely to be most revealing. Or suppose our interest lies in
predicting the impact of denominational loyalties and religious convictions on a congressional or presidential election. Clearly, societal data
and societal models are more relevant than studies of global dynamics.

Indeed, both the level of organization of our major denominations
and the method in which data are collected argue for societal models. Denominations are administered as national units, even if their constituencies are clustered in one part of the country more than another. When
they conduct research and when they consider the social environment
most relevant to their memberships, they think in societal terms. Standard means of data collection in universities, government, and private industry, such as the numerous surveys from which we infer trends in religious indicators, are designed to ensure national representativeness.

To ask what a global perspective may contribute to our understanding of religious establishments, then, is to ask about a marginal increment
in understanding, not a wholesale replacement of our standard theories
and methods of data collection. It is to ask whether the brute realities of
our increasingly interdependent world force us to consider religion from
more than an individual, community, or national level. In some cases, the
answer will clearly be yes; in other cases, parsimony would perhaps continue to dictate emphasizing more proximate factors, but seeing things in
context might argue for adding in less proximate effects in order to enhance our consciousness of global interdependence itself. Following are
some ways in which a global perspective might assist in gaining a clearer
understanding of the nature and dynamics of contemporary religious es-

tablishments. For convenience, I have divided them into three general types of contribution.

A Focus on Generalizable Patterns

One advantage we gain from taking a global or international perspective is that our attention is inevitably drawn to the more general dynamics of modern life. I begin with this because it is most familiar. It is, after all, what our theories and comparative studies, actual or implied, are supposed to provide anyway. They sensitize us to the generalizable, to representative or dominant patterns and trends, rather than the purely idiographic. Secularization theory provides a familiar example. It suggests to us that declining church membership rolls or the declining influence of religion in public life is not simply an idiosyncratic occurrence; these declines, our theories tell us, might be part of a global trend, a pattern associated with rising industrialization, affluence, the growth of cities, and increases in knowledge. A global perspective tells us to think big, to raise questions about dominant trends, to consider what plays, not in Peoria alone, but in Pretoria as well.

Theories of secularization, and more broadly, theories of modernization seem to have been useful in orienting our inquiries to these dominant patterns. Some of them, to be sure, are pitched decidedly at the societal level. The differentiation between religion and the state that is said to characterize modern societies, for example, focuses squarely on processes within individual societies. A closer reading of the argument, however, reveals that the pressures leading to this kind of institutional differentiation are understood in a transsocietal context. Institutional differentiation occurs, the theories argue, because societies must adapt to their environments, and they do so competitively with other societies. This competition makes the environment itself more complex, and those societies that differentiate their institutional sectors presumably gain a competitive edge in adapting to complex environments. In viewing processes of institutional change within American religion, such as the alleged differentiation of private piety from public policy, or the growing differentiation of secular education from its religious roots and the emergence of professional therapy as a distinct alternative to pastoral counseling, then, modernization theory suggests both that these might be bellwethers in advanced industrial societies generally and that they might be in some way influenced by broader international patterns.

Other influences are even more clearly global in origin. The effects of science on religion do not arise within narrow societal contexts. Neither Einstein's theory of relativity nor Heisenberg's principle of uncertainty was discovered in the United States; yet, both have apparently had profound effects on American theology. The iron cage of expanding rationality that exercised Max Weber's imagination has spread in more subtle ways. Religious organizations have borrowed rational procedures from the courts, from state bureaucracies, and from institutions of higher learning since the Middle Ages. These are part of a world culture that continues to have profound effects on contemporary religious organizations.

The list of such patterns and trends can be expanded greatly. It includes the growth of the modern state, about which I will say more later. It includes the growth of professionalism and what has been called a "new class" of knowledge workers and information specialists—growth that has, to say the least, occurred at the expense of the privileged position that clergy in past centuries occupied within the professions.

At present, much discussion has also focused on the nature and sources of individualism. While it may be true, as some have argued, that individualism has colored American religion in a particularly decisive way, others have pointed out that individualism is not only a feature of the cultural landscape between Boston and Los Angeles; it is reinforced in all advanced industrial societies, even in the Soviet Union, by the state's efforts to supply services and legal guarantees. It is reinforced by the workplace and by educational systems that attach credentials to the individual and encourage the individual to carry these credentials wherever he may go. It is also part of an ideological system that adapts to complex, heterogeneous environments by decoupling arguments and personalizing them to fit unique situations.

These are all features of a world culture. Studies of national constitutions, legal patterns, educational systems, child-rearing habits, and curricula in schools all reveal the extent to which such characteristics of modern societies have converged over time and the extent to which new societies imitate the patterns of more established ones.

They are also features of the environment to which students of religious organizations should pay heed. Where do the models come from that major denominations in the United States rely on to govern themselves and to conduct their business? Of course, from government and business: particularly since the end of the nineteenth century, denominational officials have looked to corporations and other bureaucracies to guide them along pathways toward greater efficiency. At the congregational level, boards of trustees often resemble, and sometimes are consciously modeled after, corporate management committees. If individual believers switch denominations and argue that their beliefs are their own, rather than the property of some ecclesiastical tradition, they are simply following patterns institutionalized in the marketplace with increasing intensity since the advent of a money-wage economy. None of these developments is unique to the United States; all, to one degree or another, are characteristics of a growing global culture that defines how organizations should behave and what it means to be modern.

It scarcely points in a new direction to suggest that sociological theories of this kind have often implicitly articulated a global dimension. Recent studies do indicate the importance of modifying standard theories to take international factors more explicitly into account. One such modification involves paying closer empirical attention to international influences and cross-societal convergences. Consider what might be learned from examining school curricula, for example. Standard theories of secularization might be interpreted to suggest that all societies would witness a gradual erosion of the place of religion in school curricula as they became more modern. If so, the prevalence of religion in school curricula across large numbers of societies should show a strong negative correlation with an indicator of modernization such as Gross National Product per capita or industrial contribution as a percent of Gross Domestic Product. In fact, these correlations are rather low. With a few exceptions, all societies have reduced the role of religion in school curricula, regardless of how advanced their economy is. The patterns suggest a developing global culture: a norm that says, in effect, legitimate regimes in the modern system of states should sponsor secular learning but not religious indoctrination (Benavot, et al., 1988).

Standard theories have also been modified in recent years for greater sensitivity to the *dynamics* of global patterns. In some formulations, theories of secularization, rationalization, and the like, seemed to posit only gradual, long-term, but inexorable tendencies in modern societies. Over the centuries, religion would become more clearly differentiated from the state, less influential in public affairs, and more characteristically individualistic and rational. Particular historical events—the Edict of Nantes, Bismarck's unification of Germany, or World War I—might have accelerated these trends, but the timing and severity of such events are treated as if they were exogenous to the system itself. More recent formulations try to offer more systematic accounts of these events and other short-term fluctuations. World-system theory, for example, has argued that economic cycles, called Kondrotieff waves, lasting approximately fifty years in duration can be identified over and above whatever secular economic trends might be at work. These cycles might be expected to have their own effects on religious organizations. World-system theory has also suggested that underdeveloped societies may be caught in permanent downwardly spiraling cycles of dependence. For this reason, reactions against modernization, including resurgences of religious tradition, might be expected rather than steady secularizing processes. Indeed, instances of religious fundamentalism in many parts of the world suggest there may be some validity to these arguments.

Even if the empirical questions that occupy one's attention are limited to changes in, say, Protestant denominations since World War II, then, the advantage of adopting a global perspective may be considerable. Linking such changes to arguments about world order provides a way of thinking about their place in longer-term historical patterns and their relation to trends in the wider system of societies.

A Focus on Deeper Changes

A second advantage of adopting a world-order perspective is that we sometimes stand to gain insight into the deeper changes underlying what seem to be more proximate influences on religion. Here I have in mind specifically those immediate social effects that can account for changes in religious establishments perfectly well by themselves. Often, though, these factors are in turn linked to broader patterns, therefore, gives a fuller understanding of what is happening. It is best to give some specific illustrations.

One topic that I believe can be greatly facilitated by understanding it in a larger context is the question of sectarianism. Discussions of church and sect have, of course, abounded in the sociological literature at least since Weber, and especially since Troeltsch. Even in recent years there have been new efforts to define the two, to create typologies of sects, and to discuss the evolution of sects into churches. For present purposes, it will suffice to say that one standard way of defining sects, and of distinguishing them from churches and cults, is to focus on their origins: sects arise as splinter groups through schisms from churches or other sects, whereas cults generally arise independently as autonomous organizations. Also relevant are two standard arguments about sects: they arise from some kind of organizational or societal strain, such as a catastrophe in the environment or a dispute over doctrines, and they gradually evolve into established churches. For questions about stability and change in religious establishments, then, these are relevant arguments indeed.

In a general way, the value of adding ideas about world order into the picture can be seen by relocating Troeltsch's classic discussion in its historical context. Troeltsch was thinking specifically about the origin and evolution of sects in Europe from the Reformation through the end of the nineteenth century. During most of this period, at least from the middle of the seventeenth century through the end of the nineteenth century, the world economy was expanding. The Protestant countries in which Troeltsch's sects were mainly located lay at the core of this world economy, especially Britain and Germany, and to a lesser extent, Scandinavia and the Netherlands. Economic expansion, moreover, was associated with two other dominant trends: one was growth in population, the so-called demographic transition that both facilitated and was facilitated by industrialization; the other was the geographic inclusion of previously isolated, local, and ethnic sectors of the population into the commercial and industrial labor force.

What some have taken as a universal characteristic of sectarianism, therefore, was contingent on a very particular set of historical circumstances. The inclusion of isolated population segments into the dominant economy created permanent disruptions in the moral economy of rural life — social upheavals that generated potential recruits for sectarian movements. Expanding population and material resources contributed positively to the numbers and variety of these movements. Their inclusion into the dominant economy increased the likelihood of these movements gradually becoming established churches. Certainly the Methodist case fits this trajectory. Other dissenting sects, brethren groups, and free churches seem to as well.

Given different dynamics in the larger world-economy, quite different patterns of sectarianism might be expected .Under more stagnant conditions, for example, social disruption may be present, but resources are likely to be lacking to transform dislocation into orderly social movements. Theories of world order also point to the importance of different patterns and rates of incorporation into the dominant economy. While workers were being drawn into the industrial labor force as individual breadwinners in Europe during the nineteenth century, for example, other workers in Europe's colonies were being drawn into a permanent state of dependence as producers of raw commodities: in mines and on plantations. Under these circumstances, as Eric Wolf and others have shown, religious movements were less likely to take the form of sects at all, and when they did, seldom followed the path of their counterparts in Europe in becoming prosperous middle-class churches.

This, of course, is to paint with a very broad historical brush. Some empirical rigor, as well as clearer applicability to the present situation in the United States, can be added by drawing on the results of recent research on sectarian schisms. Two of my colleagues, Robert Liebman and John Sutton, and I have recently developed a data set for 175 Protestant denominations in the United States from 1890 to 1980. The data cover all denominations having at least 1,000 members at some point during this time that were part of the four major Protestant families. They include fifty-five Baptist denominations, fifty Lutheran denominations, thirty-four Methodist denominations, and thirty-six Presbyterian or Reformed denominations. Among these denominations there were fifty-five schisms, all of which resulted in the formation of new denominations. Formally, the resulting organizations meet the definition of sectarianism, although for present purposes their actual conformity in substance to the definition of sect is unimportant. Thus far, we have examined only a small number of the potential explanatory factors that might be adduced to account for the occurrence of these schisms. Using a variant of instantaneous hazard analysis, we have, however, been able to rule out differences associated with denominational family and church polity type; i.e. denominations with congregational politics are no more and no less likely than denominations with presbyterial or episcopal polities to experience schisms. We were also able to show significant effects from four contextual variables. Rates of schisms were positively associated with size of parent denomination, negatively associated with membership in the National Council of Churches (and its predecessor, the Federal Council of Churches), positively associated with rates of failure among business organizations, and curvilinearly associated with the density of other schisms in the religious environment. Descriptively, these results produced rates of schisms that were highest in the 1930s and 1960s, although no decade in the past century was free of schisms (Liebman, et al., 1988; Sutton, et al., 1988).

None of these results bears directly on properties of the larger world order. This, then, is a case in which arguments about world order can at most enhance our interpretation of more proximate effects. Each of the four findings can, in fact, be interpreted in a broader context. The effect of denominational size, we know from other research, can be linked in turn to the effect of immigration to the United States, to competition among denominations and between Protestants and Catholics for members, and to the so-called baby boom that followed World War II. In other words, for the United States at least sectarianism has been associated with demographic expansion in the world system, just as it appears to have been in Europe in earlier centuries. The negative effect of the National Council of Churches (NCC) needs to be understood in relation to the history of the NCC itself, especially the extent to which it was modeled after the United Nations and was prompted by an interest in global religious concerns. Sectarianism, in this sense, has been reduced by efforts to create organizations aimed at better meeting the challenges of world society. Business failures, of course, occurred most widely during the Great Depression, which represented a major upheaval in the world economy at large and resulted in a permanent shift away from the monetary institutions on which the nineteenth century world market had been organized. Sectarianism, it appears, was at least modestly encouraged by this shifting of the gears in the world economy. Finally, the curvilinear relation with other schisms suggests a modified contagion effect: a few schisms tend to adapt to whatever strains have been present in the environment, but after this a large number of schisms generates an exponential increase in the likelihood of further schisms. Thus, during times of instability from economic downturns or other environmental strains, schisms are likely to become producers of further schisms, causing more turbulence in religious organizations than might be predicted otherwise.

These, of course, are highly speculative arguments. To be more credible, data on schisms in other societies and in other time periods would also be necessary. To the extent that they are valid, though, they suggest some of the ways in which religious establishments in the United States might have been affected by changing features of the broader world order during the twentieth century. Further population increase is likely to produce more schisms if denominations continue to grow in size. A major downturn in the economy could witness a new round of sectarian splinter groups.

A second illustration comes from considering the effects of rising levels of education on American religion since World War II. Rising levels of education, as we know, have had a number of serious consequences for American religion, both direct and indirect. An education gap exists in styles of religious commitment now that was not present as recently as the late 1950s. The better educated are less likely to participate in religious services regularly, less likely to believe literally in the Bible, more likely to have experimented with new religious movements, more likely to support social activism among clergy, and more likely to favor relativistic and androgenous images of God. A major shouting match, as we know, has also developed between religious liberals and religious conservatives, the two sides taking widely differing positions not only on theological orientations but also on social and political issues, and holding strongly negative views toward the other. Differences in levels of education are one of the strongest predictors of the cleavage between these two groups.

The effects of higher education on religious orientations can be interpreted entirely at the social psychological level or within the context of American society by itself. What were the less proximate forces behind this rapid expansion in higher education? To answer that question, it becomes useful to bring in arguments about changes in world order.

Specifically, the very rapid expansion in higher education in the

United States took place during the 1960s and it did so, not by some strange magic in the modernization process itself, but as a result of conscious planning and huge outlays by the federal government. Why, in turn, was the federal government suddenly interested in higher education? A major reason was the Cold War, and particularly the space race that developed with the Russians in the late 1950s. A second reason was that an increasing share of United States trade in the world economy after World War II came to be concentrated in high technology industries. A tertiary reason had to do with scaling down the armed forces after World War II and keeping veterans out of the labor force until it could expand sufficiently to absorb them. Beyond the sheer rate of expansion in higher education during the sixties, the fact that it took place when it did was extremely consequential. It took place during the buildup of the war in Vietnam, which in turn signaled a major realignment of world power between the United States and the Soviet Union and with China. In short, education was the proximate cause of religious change, but the timing of its expansion was closely linked with broader changes in world order.

The other example I wish to mention in this context concerns the effects of government activity on church membership. Clifford Nass and I have demonstrated a significant negative relation between government expenditures and rates of Protestant church membership in 1950 and 1980, taking states as the unit of analysis (Wuthnow and Nass, 1988). This effect appears to hold when other factors influencing church membership, such as religious composition, urbanization, region, and migration, are held constant. Over this period, government expenditures tripled, even taking account of inflation.

Was this increase simply the result of willy-nilly policies by spendthrift administrators? Or does it need to be understood in some broader context?

It was not simply a function of rising military and defense costs because we excluded those from our analysis. Rather, it was largely the result of the federal government shouldering increased responsibilities for entitlement programs, such as Social Security payments and workmen's compensation, for education, and for infrastructural services such as roads and hospitals. Government involvement in such activities has, however, been a global phenomenon, at least among advanced industrial societies. Partly again, it has been a function of imitation, beginning in the nineteenth century with Bismarck's social welfare programs in Germany. Partly it has been prompted by international economic competition, again starting in the nineteenth century, with national governments playing an increasing role in regulating and promoting all forms of economic activity.

A Focus on Alternative Interpretations

As these examples suggest, world-order perspectives can be of use in understanding changes in religious establishments even when more proximate factors may provide the most parsimonious accounts. The third possibility I want to focus on is that a global perspective may actually force us to interpret phenomena in a different way. The issue here is not one of gaining a broader understanding of what is going on, but of seeing that things may not have been what they seemed.

Let me illustrate this use of world-order theory with reference, first, to several examples that have nothing to do with religion but provide striking evidence of how one may be forced to draw new conclusions. An example from European history concerns the development and institutionalization of modern science in the seventeenth century. The fact that science flourished at all in this period is puzzling, for sociologists from Weber to the present have generally argued that decentralized political conditions are most conducive to intellectual innovation, and yet the seventeenth century was, as we know, the great age of absolutism. To make sense of this anomaly, sociologists and social historians did comparative studies—studies that tended to put England in a favorable light compared with France, and thus could be reconciled with received wisdom by pointing out that England was less absolutist than France, benefited from the Puritan work ethic, and so on. The only problem with this approach was that France, by most standards, had a pretty respectable showing in science as well.

Viewing Europe as a larger social entity—as a world system—provided a better solution. From this perspective, France and England (along with some of the German states) occupied structurally similar positions at the core of the world economy, and scientists themselves migrated back and forth, joined scientific academies as international members, carried on a brisk correspondence with other scientists across the continent, and when political pressures came simply moved on (or threatened to move) to more favorable contexts. From this broader perspective, Europe was in fact a decentralized polity of the kind that other theories predicted would be conducive to scientific development.

A more contemporary example comes from research on the effects of international relations on economic development. Both classical economic theory and more recent variants of modernization theory have predicted that international trade has a positive effect on economic development in Third World countries. It opens markets, provides jobs, encourages capital investment, and creates a more favorable trade balance. Viewed from the standpoint of individual societies, these arguments seemed to make sense. Third World countries would eventually become more modern, just like Europe and North America had, as they participated in industry and commerce.

When these relations began to be viewed from a more global or systemic perspective, though, other arguments rose to the surface. Part of the reason Europe and North America were modern, it was argued, was that they exploited the raw materials and cheap labor of the Third World. More international trade for the Third World meant being drawn into the world economy as a dependent partner. Resources actually flowed out of the country, rather than in, and the development of an export economy often proved disadvantageous for achieving a balanced and strong domestic economy. Much like the disadvantaged person who is forced into a workfare program, then, and as a result fails to ever gain any marketable skills, Third World countries suffered from incorporation into the world economy instead of benefiting. This, at least, was the argument, and some empirical research has supported it, although the final verdict is by no means in.

How might a shift of perspective of this kind lead to new ideas about the functioning of religious establishments? The dependent development case actually has a close parallel in religion. At the same time that policy analysts began rethinking the effects of foreign trade, religious leaders began to question standard assumptions about the role of foreign missionaries. Earlier arguments had, of course, presumed that carrying Christianity to the Third World was a good thing, not only spiritually but culturally as well. Indigenous peoples would learn Western values, become literate, and eventually modernize their own countries. With nationalism and anticolonial movements, however, these assumptions came into question. As a result, the missionary efforts of most mainline denominations in the United States have been scaled back considerably. Evangelical and fundamentalist mission agencies have grown in proportion, while mainline bodies have focused more on assisting indigenous ministries, supplying social services, lobbying for social justice through political channels, and even turning the cultural conduit around by sponsoring reverse missionary programs. Viewed from only the American context, it appears that mainstream Protestantism has suffered a serious decline in its missionary efforts. Viewed from a world-order perspective, the decline may be less serious than it would otherwise appear.

A second example involving religion comes from thinking about America's position in the world economy over the past half century or so. How we perceive ourselves as a nation plays an important role in shaping the content of what has been called our civil religion, and our civil religion in turn influences what we think of our churches and what we feel they should be doing. One interpretation of America's position has focused on its exceptionalism: its deep (or at least widespread) religiosity, its afflu-ence, its democratic traditions. In this view, America has been the leader of the so-called free world: flying higher and moving faster than all its al-lies, pulling them along, and protecting them from Communism. This ver-sion is not exactly unmindful of international realities. But it primarily takes a diachronic view of history: at one point, the Roman Empire dom-inated; more recently, the British empire; and now, the United States. Its religious implications coincide well with arguments about American mil-lennialism and the relation between religion and national strength. Our ascendancy is often associated with the Christian heritage in popular dis-course, and evidence of economic or military stagnation is referred to in rhetoric calling for deeper commitment to the churches.

The alternative view is more synchronic. It emphasizes the multi-lateral nature of contemporary world order rather than American hege-mony. If the United States emerged from World War II as leader of the free world, this view suggests, it nevertheless emerged with partnership commitments to western Europe and Japan, and in competition with a strong Soviet bloc. In this scenario, core power in the contemporary world has remained divided to a much greater extent than it was, say, dur-ing the nineteenth century under British rule. At least three iimplications follow for the analysis of American religion. First, the qualities of Amer-ican civil religion must be seen in terms of their boundary posturing func-tions in relation to other dominant world powers. That is, civil religion not only reflects our past and serves not only (as Durkheim might have ar-gued) to promote domestic cohesion, but also to differentiate ourselves from our competitors and buttress our identity within the wider global culture. Second, the universalistic aspects of American civil religion must be understood and emphasized in order to reckon with the pluralism of world power, rather than assuming that American culture is simply generalizable to the rest of the world. Third, religious establishments are likely to be influenced more by the placement of their constituencies in relation to the heterarchic structure of world order than by simple up-swings or downswings in the American economy.

This last point needs greater explication. In an upswing-downswing scenario, the fate of religious establishments, it is likely to be argued, will depend chiefly on the countercyclical functions of religious compensa-tions. During downswings, fundamentalist commitment is likely to grow; during upswings, liberal religion and/or secular humanism is more likely. There is, incidentally, little convincing evidence that either supports or refutes these arguments.

In the multilateral world power scenario, a dual economy is envi-sioned: one part depends more on domestic markets, autarky, and pro-tectionism; the other part depends more on international markets, stable diplomatic relations, and free trade. The composition of these two sectors, of course, varies constantly, as does the relative prosperity of the two, because of shifting currency rates and foreign competition. Nevertheless, sociopolitical attitudes are likely to be rooted in one set of interests or the other, and modes of religious identification will at least partly reflect these attitudes and interests as well.

For example, sectors of the population whose prosperity is linked to protectionist, domestic, or autarkic policies may well emphasize traditional morality, American particularism, and the localistic-familial values of Protestant fundamentalism. Specific groups in this sector might include the petty bourgeoisie or small merchant class, farmers (insofar as protection against foreign competitors, but government policies aimed at selling freely in protected overseas markets are relevant), members of the military, and workers in threatened industries such as steel and heavy manufacturing. In contrast, sectors of the population linked to international trade, occupying a dominant position in world markets, and depending on open diplomatic channels might well find themselves more in sympathy with lower defense budgets, higher education outlays, cosmopolitan values, and liberal religious institutions whose theologies favor universalism and whose moral teachings favor relativism and discretion. Specific groups in this sector might include scientists, employees of multinational corporations and the international service sector, media and entertainment specialists, and persons with advantageous levels of education.

Little has been done to test these ideas either, it should be noted. They would, however, buttress the argument that the important development in American religion in recent decades has not been simply the rise or decline in religion generally, nor the relative rise of fundamentalism and the relative decline of liberal mainline institutions, but the consistent and widening gap between liberalism and conservatism itself. Neither side is so consistently related to America's position in the larger world economy that its progress depends on the policies of a particular administration. For example, religious conservatism during the 1980s may have grown partly through reinforcement from a regime that championed strong military defenses, the protection of domestic markets through low taxes and, therefore, meager social services, and the values of small-town America, even though it was in other ways an administration firmly committed to free trade and international markets.

The point, though, is that both sectors are integral features of the American economy, and that the multilateral shape of world order is such as to necessitate continuous realignments of policies favoring one or the other. The religious orientations associated with the two, therefore, are each likely to gain periodic reinforcement from government and, at the same time, divisions of opinion in the wider policy arena are also likely to reinforce the tensions between these orientations.

Conclusion

Clearly, more research needs to be done to assess the merits of arguments such as these, but more theorizing is also needed to guide this research. How we think about world order, and how we view the United States' position in the world order, will greatly affect the kind of theorizing we do.

The gains from thinking about religion from a broader global perspective accrue, not only to the academic researcher in pursuit of recondite problems to study but also to the practitioner of religion and to those whose interest in world affairs resides simply at the level of informed citizen. It does so partly by tempering the ways in which we think about assertions that frequent the public realm. These assertions often do not differ markedly from the kinds of theoretical and explanatory arguments prevalent in the social science literature. They do, however, serve as rhetorical appeals aimed at shaping the way we think about our world, the ways we vote, and the policies we support.

For example, the arguments advanced by public officials, and especially by candidates during political elections, often invoke causal statements aimed at influencing our assessments of public responsibility. These assessments in turn influence how we think and vote, and indirectly provide support or conflict with the positions taken by our religious leaders. When Republicans, for instance, damn Democratic leaders for high prices and inflation, we can blame the Democratic Party and vote Republican, despite misgivings about Republican preferences for the wealthy at the expense of the poor. Or we can look at the turmoil in the Middle East during the 1970s that was more responsible for high prices and inflation in that period than a Democratic administration. Similarly, when Democrats take credit for promoting higher education through tuition credits and payback plans, we can deflate their rhetoric by recognizing the pressures world affairs place on both parties to advance science and technology. There is no simple relation between this kind of analysis and one's political or religious preferences, but it provides a broader context in which to speculate about responsibilities and the constraints of social circumstances.

The other practical implication comes from recognizing that responsibility itself is closely linked to the ways in which we understand sovereign authority, and our understandings of authority are closely linked to ways of experiencing the divine. When there is no higher authority than man, it has been said, man becomes God. Similarly, when there is no sense of any unit more powerful than the nation, national sovereignty becomes divine. However, when individual and national authority are understood — and relativized — in the context of social relations that affect all of humanity, then a broader, more encompassing, and even more transcendent sense of the sacred becomes necessary. This sense of the sacred may encompass nothing more than a triumphal vision of humanity itself, but it may also point toward a sacred dimension that is even more powerful than the global order we have inherited.

References

Benavot, Aaron, David Kamens, Suk-Ying Wong, and Y. K. Cha
1988   "World Culture and the Curricular Content of National Educational Systems: 1920–1985." Unpublished paper presented at the annual meetings of the American Sociological Association, Atlanta.

Blasi, Anthony J. and Michael W. Cuneo
1986   *Issues in the Sociology of Religion: A Bibliography.* New York: Garland.

Liebman, Robert C., John R. Sutton, and Robert Wuthnow
1988   "Exploring the Social Sources of Denominationalism: Schisms in American Protestant Denominations, 1890 – 1980." *American Sociological Review* 53:343–352.

Ragin, Charles and Daniel Chirot
1984   "The World System of Immanuel Wallerstein: Sociology and Politics as History." In Theda Skocpol (ed.), *Vision and Method in Historical Sociology,* 276–312. Cambridge: Cambridge University Press.

Sutton, John R., Robert Wuthnow, and Robert C. Liebman
1988   "Organizational Foundings: Schisms in American Protestant Denominations, 1890 – 1980." Unpublished paper presented at the annual meetings of the American Sociological Association, Atlanta.

Wallerstein, Immanuel
1974   *The Modern World-System: Capitalist Agriculture and the Origins of the European World-Economy in the Sixteenth Century.* New York: Academic Press.

Wilson, Bryan R.
1973   *Magic and the Millennium.* London: Herder.

Worsley, Peter
1957   *The Trumpet Shall Sound: A Study of Cargo Cults in Melanesia*. London: MacGibbon and Kee.

Wuthnow, Robert and Clifford Nass
1988   "Government Activity and Civil Privatism: Evidence from Voluntary Church Membership." *Journal for the Scientific Study of Religion* 27:147–174.

2

Religious Elites in Advanced Capitalism: The Dialectic of Power and Marginality

James Davison Hunter and James E. Hawdon

How are we to understand religious authority in the contemporary world order? Anecdotal evidence alone makes clear that neither the presence of religion has lessened nor its quest for power substantially weakened, particularly on the American scene. The ancient philosophical and scientific dogmas predicting the political enfeebling of religion, if not its complete disappearance (as almost everyone has pointed out), no longer provide a satisfactory explanation. Yet those who now completely reject the secularization hypothesis, contending that religion is just as prevalent and vibrant today as ever—that religion and the authority it wields has not substantially changed through its encounter with the contemporary world order—would seem to be equally untenable. Religious authority is not epiphenomenal to the course and conduct of public life but neither is it always, or even very often, commanding in that sphere, at least in the way that it has been in the past or the way it potentially could be. One can quickly see, then, that the problem of understanding the nature of religious authority at the end of the twentieth century is infinitely more complex than the current debate in social science would indicate.

Yet, the conceptual shortcomings are only part of the problem with coming to terms with the nature and fate of religious authority in our time. The empirical scope of most efforts to sort out the answers to this query are very narrow—treating religion, for all practical concerns, as an autonomous reality, with little or no relation to a larger historical or structural context. The clergy studies of the past two decades, for example, are notorious for being ahistorical and noncomparative, but the context is always key.

In our own time the setting within which religious authority exists is defined principally by the institutional configurations of advanced capitalism. The expansion of the state in national and world economies is perhaps its fundamental characteristic, but a related, and perhaps more relevant feature, is the historically unprecedented expansion of the knowledge sector (Machlup, 1962; Rubin and Huber, 1982). The significance of these social and historical developments for religious institutions, the elites that serve them, and the authority they aspire to, has been momentous and multifaceted. The most important consequence, however, has been their marginalization from the structures of power in modern society.

The Impetus Toward Marginalization

The marginalization of religious authority from the structures of power is a complex reality deriving from several sources. One dimension of this tendency can be seen in the contraction of organizational influence — a fundamental displacement of religious institutions in their various public roles by different agencies of the state. Another dimension of this can be seen in the estrangement of religious authority from the laity. On the surface this means there has been a decline in popular regard for the activities and pronouncements of religious institutions and a decline in the popular status of religious leaders. More importantly there is a decline in the ability of religious authority to compel action on the part of the laity.

There is a third and arguably more important way to conceive of the marginalization of religious authority. This is in relation to the structures of cultural power—the power to create and maintain a definition of public reality. Everyone participates in the construction of their own private worlds. Yet the development and articulation of the more elaborate systems of meaning, including the realm of public culture, falls more or less exclusively to the realm of elites, and in particular, intellectuals or cultural elites. They provide the concepts, supply the language, and define the parameters and content of public discussion. They define and redefine the meaning of public symbols.

The relevance of this cultural approach to the phenomenon of marginalization is clear. Religious elites, in Weber's generic use of the concept, were the archetypal intellectuals who dominated the realm of symbolic discourse. Even through the period of liberal state-building from the late-eighteenth century to the mid-nineteenth century, religious elites and the institutions they served played a formidable role in shaping the parameters and content of public culture. In this they played a significant role in the process of state-building. This they did through engineering the expansion of the common school and later the public school movement; through the management of large-scale public philanthropy not only in the administration of various Poor Laws but in the overseeing of hospitals, almshouses, and a myriad of charitable institutions; and through the championing of moral reform, particularly in the international temperance movement. Even more significantly, religious institutions provided a wellspring of moral authority for the expanding state structure and its myths, perhaps the most critical sources of national identity and national unity at that time. While religious institutions once played a dominant role in shaping public cultures, they no longer do. This is not, I would argue, because religious institutions have submissively withdrawn from the burden of this task; it is, rather, a consequence of their being structurally displaced. In other words, where at one time there was little or no serious competition to define the symbols of public culture, there is now an overwhelming competition.

All of this is suggested by intuition but illustrated graphically in labor statistics from North America and several countries in northern Europe. (See figure 1. For further details, consult the appendix to Chapter 2.) In virtually all of these countries, the number of religious elites has remained relatively constant vis-a-vis the total population—the ordinary people whose spiritual needs they serve—in some cases for over a century. In the United States, there has been no appreciable change for 130 years. In Great Britain, Canada, and France the ratio remained relatively constant until the 1950s but soon after began to decline quite sharply. Though the data is less complete, much the same trend appears to have taken place in West Germany and Switzerland as well. Through the same period, the number of religious elites as a percent of other cultural elites (symbol specialists who also contribute to the definition of national public culture) has dropped consistently, dramatically and, as much as the findings can tell, uniformly through all of the countries. The drop was particularly dramatic in the post-World War period. The reason, of course, has to do with the expansion of the ranks of secular cultural elites, once again, particularly since mid-century. Interestingly, nowhere has this expansion been greater than in the United States.

The point is also illustrated by the historical tendencies in cultural production. Across national boundaries, religious book production has increased in absolute terms just as knowledge production more generally has expanded. Yet as a percent of the total production of books in each country, the ratio has declined. (See data in appendix to Chapter 2.) In the United States, religious book production in 1980 was half of what it was in 1890. In France in 1972, it was half what it was in 1941. In the Neth-

FIGURE 1.

Trends Among Religious & Knowledge Workers

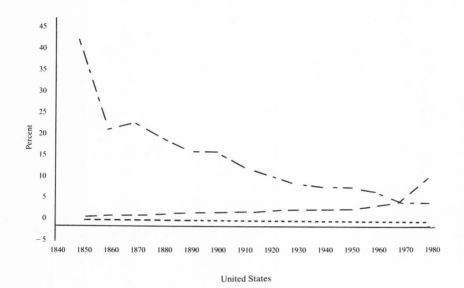

United States

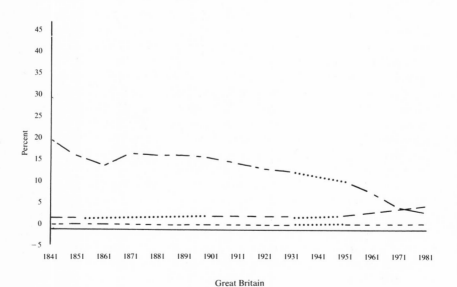

Great Britain

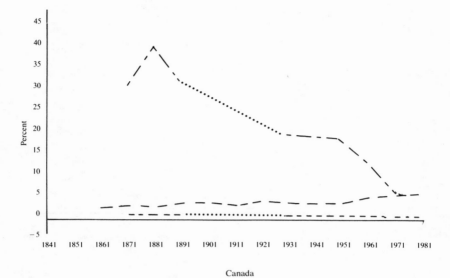

Canada

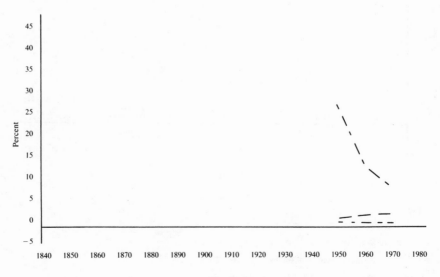

West Germany

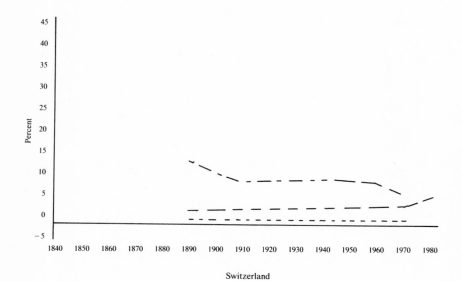

Switzerland

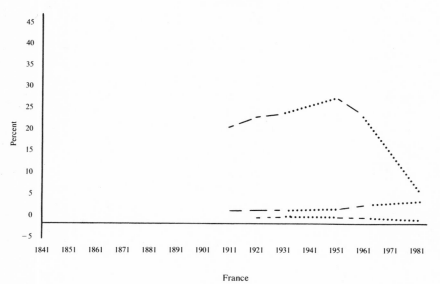

France

—·—·— Religious Elites as Percent of Cultural Elites

— — — Cultural Elites as Percent of Total Working Population

- - - - - Religious Elites as Percent of Total Population

erlands and West Germany, religious book production in 1980 was roughly three-fourths of what it was in the 1950s. The same pattern is seen in the publication of religious newspapers and periodicals in America as well. Cultural production has declined significantly relative to the production of all such publications — from 7.6 percent in 1850 to 2.6 percent in 1984.

Cumulatively the evidence is indicative of trends that go back in history long before the mid-nineteenth century. In many respects the historical findings presented here only catch the end of a longer trend. Having once dominated the knowledge sector, religious elites have in the modern age now become only a small part of the knowledge sector. In the post World War II period (especially in the United States), that tendency has even intensified. Religious elites and the knowledge they promote has been structurally displaced.

Coping With Marginality

Not surprisingly, the effects of this structural marginalization are reflected, in some measure, in the attitudes and opinions of the elites themselves. This became especially clear in the 1987 Religion and Power Survey.[1] (See table 1.) A substantial majority of the academic, media and religious elites surveyed in the United States, Great Britain and West Germany agreed that "leaders in the news and entertainment media pay little or no attention to religious values in their work."[2] Virtually the same sentiment was expressed by these elites in agreeing (though with slightly less intensity overall) that "writers, academics and other intellectual groups pay little or no attention to religious values in their writings and pronouncements."[3]

The marginalization of religious influence from knowledge-based occupations is perceived widely by both religious and secular knowledge workers. This perception also extends, in many respects, to a sense of its marginalization in the larger social order. With the exception of rabbis and other Jewish elites in America, the overwhelming majority of Protestant and Catholic elites in these three countries agree that "the influence of religion (in their respective countries) is too low."[4] The contrast in opinion with their secular counterparts is interesting. With the exception of the United Kingdom, less than a third of the academic and media elites surveyed shared that perception.

The majority of religious elites in the United States and Great Britain and a substantial plurality of religious elites in West Germany also recognize that the status of the clergy has decreased in recent years.[5] Though media and academic leaders in the United States are not, as a

TABLE 1
Perceptions of the Marginalization of Religious Elites (Percentages)

% Agreeing that:	United States					Great Britain			West Germany			
	Academic	Media	Protestant	Catholic	Jew	Academic	Media	Anglican	Academic	Media	Protestant	Catholic
	N=199	90	531	172	88	171	109	129	136	116	138	126
*Leaders in the news and entertainment media pay little or no attention to religious values in their work.	75	81	76	68	78	75	75	62	60	87	65	75
*Writers, academics and other intellectual groups pay little or no attention to religious values in their writings and pronouncements.	64	66	65	56	65	67	64	50	52	48	40	50
*In general, leaders in politics, business, academia, news and entertainment should pay more attention to religious values.	26	43	89	95	84	37	37	91	44	31	87	94
*The influence of religion in this country is too low.	15	29	77	74	41	38	41	91	16	10	63	75
The status of the clergy has decreased in recent years.	43	57	68	71	53	61	71	61	60	47	47	46
The influence of the clergy has decreased in recent years.	29	28	58	55	40	54	61	48	44	40	48	68
Compared to other professionals the contribution of the clergy to society is of marginal or no importance.	42	21	7	5	10	50	39	11	43	42	2	2

*Included in marginality index

Source: 1987 Religion & Power Survey

whole, willing to concede the point, roughly half of all religious elites in all three countries (slightly more in the case of American Protestant and German Catholic elites) believe that the influence of the clergy has also decreased in recent years.[6]

Interestingly, the survey shows vast disparities in opinion among religious and secular cultural elites over what the role of religion and of the clergy in society should be. Roughly nine out of ten of the religious leaders in all three countries agree that "in general, leaders in politics, business, academics, news and entertainment *should* pay more attention to religious values."[7] Of the academic and media leaders, less than one-half (and on average only about one-third) share a similar view. Roughly the same pattern holds when assessing the value of the contribution of the clergy in society. Never more than 11 percent of the religious elites (and as low as 2 percent of the Protestant and Catholic leaders in West Germany) agree that "compared to other professionals, the contribution of the clergy to society is of marginal or no importance."[8] Yet more than 40 percent of the academic elites, and between 21 percent and 42 percent of the media elites in these countries do agree with that assessment.

These last figures suggest more than occupational self-interest on the part of religious elites — the desire to be taken more seriously in society as a whole and by the secular intelligentsia in particular. They also point to a latent structure of anticlerical opinion among at least a significant minority of secular intellectuals and media elites. Again, this is not only true in two European countries but in the United States as well.

What does all of this mean? Consider the structure of the knowledge sector in terms of the organizing logic of center and periphery. Insofar as they provided one of if not the dominant influences in defining public realities, religious elites historically held the center. There were few if any other knowledge-based occupations that enjoyed the special patronage and protection of the state. There were few if any knowledge-based occupations large enough — with the critical mass or resources — to credibly challenge the symbols promoted by the religious establishment. All of that, however, has changed with two simultaneous developments. The first is that the patronage of the state has shifted away from religious knowledge and ecclesiastical authority toward secular knowledge production. At the same time, the expansion of the knowledge sector in the nineteenth and twentieth century (made possible, in large part by that shift in state patronage) had the effect of intensifying the competition of opposing definitions of public reality. That competition has not only intensified but it has become overwhelming. The consequence is that religious institutions and elites have been, in effect, pushed to the periphery of the knowledge sector. The attitudinal data suggests that religious elites have not just migrated passively to the periphery of the knowledge sector but have even been banished there by virtue of the anticlericalism of those who have come to occupy the center: secular cultural elites.

Religious Authority and Political Judgment

What of religious authority in this context? Caught between the City of God and the City of Man, the authority wielded by religious institutions and elites is concerned with both spiritual and secular affairs. By its very nature, then, the secular authority it asserts is political in character. The positions taken by ecclesiastical authority can be located within the larger field of secular political discourse.

It is not immediately clear whether the perception of their own marginalization has any direct effect on the political judgments of religious institutions or elites. Clearly, within this context religious institutions express nothing even close to political solidarity. This is reflected in survey data but is most clearly seen in the institutional life of religious organizations. Even a casual perusal of the *Encyclopedia of Associations* makes clear that one can find organizations within the Catholic, Jewish, Methodist, Episcopalian, Presbyterian, Baptist, Lutheran, and Mormon confessions (among others) on every side of almost every issue: abortion, American involvement in Central America, church and state relations, gay rights, nuclear energy and nuclear weaponry, women's rights, the family, and on down a very long list.

Accounting for Political Ideology

The lack of political unity among various religious institutions and elites presents an interesting theoretical and interpretive problem. How is one to account for that uncompromising diversity? According to recent theories about the political orientation of knowledge workers, one would predict that all religious elites would be adversarial not only toward capitalism but toward other institutions of bourgeois culture. Protestants, Catholics, and Jews may differ slightly as a consequence of historical factors relative to their own traditions and heritage, but they would all express a fundamental hostility toward the structure and culture of free enterprise and its related institutions.

One version of this argument maintains that in the transition from industrial to post-industrial economies a "new class" of knowledge workers has emerged, which is preparing to wrest control of society from traditionally dominant groups. Although rooted in the structure of advanced capitalism and dependent upon its economic expansion, the new knowledge class undermines the interests, delegitimates the authority, and challenges the values of the old capitalist class. Following this logic, the knowledge class possesses a common set of interests, which is reflected in a relatively homogeneous worldview, one that is essentially hostile to capitalism. Individuals and groups that make up this class may or may not be self-conscious about their collective interests (as a "class-for-itself"), but by virtue of their similar position in the social structure, they do operate within a similar structure of interests and express them through common values and opinions (as a "class-in-itself").

The difference in attitudes among elites in the Catholic and Protestant communities, however, are much more pronounced. Catholic elites, on the whole, were considerably more liberal in their general political orientation, notably more in favor of the state intervening in the market, and significantly more critical of America's role in the world economy, than Protestants.

Beyond this ecclesiastical factor, one can also see where religious elites stand vis-a-vis traditional (bourgeois) family values and moral values is also a strong predictor of political variation.[14] The more one is committed to a traditional sexual ethic and family arrangement the more conservative they were likely to be toward the workings of the market.

Yet while there are political differences among major religious traditions and political differences explained by other cultural and demographic factors (such as race and family income[15]), the most consistent and powerful predictor of political variation on all of these measures is found in the respondent's theological orientation—where religious leaders locate themselves on an orthodox-progressive theological continuum. Overall, the more orthodox the theological commitment, the more conservative the respondent is likely to be, and vice versa.

The problem with this explanation, of course, is that the empirical data describing the political opinion of individuals who work in the knowledge sector does not fit. Instead of homogeneity there is tremendous ideological diversity (Ladd and Lipset, 1975; Bell, 1979; Brint, 1982). Such diversity provides ample grounds for rejecting the term class as descriptive of the phenomenon.

A much more nuanced version of the argument maintains that the highest levels of "upper white-collar dissent" varies according to relative autonomy from profit making. The degree of opposition to bourgeois values on the part of knowledge workers is directly related to the distance of an occupational category from the institutional mechanisms of profit making (i.e. business ownership, management, sales and applied technology, etc.) and market enhancement (i.e. banking and finance). Those whose livelihoods are less dependent upon the institutions of profit making are in a structural position in which it becomes possible not only to challenge the legitimacy of the market system, but all other forms of bourgeois authority as well.[9] Because religious elites do not directly depend upon the market for their livelihoods and because their occupational skills and activity do not contribute to capitalist production and distribution, they are in a position to be highly critical. Much the same can be said for university-based intellectuals. Elites in the communications media, however, because the distribution of news takes place in a competitive market, which depends upon attracting subscribers, television viewers, and generating advertising revenue, would tend to be less adversarial than academics and religious leaders. Engineers and other technicians would tend to be even less adversarial. So goes the logic.[10]

At first blush, the evidence would seem to bear out this latter line of reasoning. The data come from an earlier analysis of the 1987 Religion and Power Survey (see Hunter, et al., 1988). The focus of this effort was to examine the relationship among economic elites and three categories of cultural elites (media, intellectual and mainline Protestant religious elites) in their attitudes toward three distinct dimensions of capitalism: the evaluation of capitalism, the extent to which the state should intervene in the market, and the role of America and American market forces in the Third World.[11] The setting was the United States and Great Britain. In a comparison of group means for both the United States and Great Britain, the elites lined up as one would predict. The media elites, being closer as an occupation to the mechanisms of profit making than either the academic or religious elites, did not express tremendous ideological affinity with economic elites over the workings of capitalism. However, the ideological disagreement between themselves and the business elites was far less than it was among the other cultural elites. It is difficult to say which group of elites — academic or religious — is further removed from the mechanisms of profit making than the other, but arguably they are both further removed than media elites. As it turns out, both groups are not significantly different from each other, but they do maintain an ideological posture that is significantly more inconsonant with that maintained by both the economic and media elites.[12]

This analysis was limited for it only considered the attitudes of mainline Protestant elites. The plurality of religious profession in both the United States and Great Britain renders the situation far more complicated and interesting. The anomaly is this: with the exception of a few television evangelists, religious elites of nearly every calling (pastors, pastoral counselors, denominational administrators, and theologians) are all roughly the same distance from the mechanisms of the market. What, then, accounts for the broad political diversity.

The complexity of the situation is illustrated when considering the relationship among the three principal religious bodies in America: Protestantism, Catholicism, and Judaism. A comparison of groups means (see figure two) reveals no clear pattern across the traditions. That is, religious persuasion does not account for the disparity in political convictions among these religious elites. (In all of this, it should be noted, it is the elites representing entire Protestant community, not just its main-

FIGURE 2

Differences in Means on Four Dependent Variables by Elite Type

Political Orientation	Mean	(SD)	Elite	(N)
	0	(98)	Economic	155
********************************	− 165	(111)	Academic	198
****************	− 84	(109)	Media	90
**********	− 53	(123)	Protestant	536
*********************	− 111	(94)	Catholic	172
*********************	− 110	(111)	Jew	89

Market Autonomy	Mean	(SD)	Elite	(N)
	0	(75)	Economic	155
****************************	− 143	(91)	Academic	198
****************	− 88	(101)	Media	90
*******************	− 97	(98)	Protestant	536
********************************	− 161	(61)	Catholic	172
************************	− 128	(78)	Jew	89

Evaluation of Capitalism	Mean	(SD)	Elite	(N)
	0	(78)	Economic	148
***********************	− 120	(103)	Academic	177
**************	− 71	(95)	Media	85
****************	− 84	(96)	Protestant	508
*********	− 47	(84)	Catholic	165
****************	− 83	(94)	Jew	81

American Hegemony	Mean	(SD)	Elite	(N)
	0	(51)	Economic	150
**********************	− 116	(103)	Academic	185
*************	− 66	(95)	Media	86
**************	− 72	(100)	Protestant	519
**********************	− 117	(92)	Catholic	167
********	− 42	(87)	Jew	83

line.) The complexities of the problem are too great for a bivariate analysis; however, multivariate analysis can help illuminate the situation.[13]

First, it would appear that there are no significant differences between Protestants and Jews in their general political orientation or in their overall attitudes toward modern capitalism. The only exception is in their respective views of the role of American and American market forces in the Third World. Jews, on the whole, were more conservative than Protestants.

The Importance of Theological Commitment

Given the relatively conspicuous role of theological inclination among religious leaders as a whole, it seemed appropriate to explore the ways in which it "interacts" with religious affiliation. Not only does this allow one to see the dynamic of theological commitment *within* each religious tradition, but it also allows one to more accurately compare its relative strength to effects of religious tradition.

Indeed, the "interaction" of theological inclination and religious tradition is both statistically and substantively consequential.[16] The most striking effect of this interaction can be seen in the relationship between political alignment and religious tradition. For example, when the theological orientation of these religious leaders is held constant, the original political differences between Protestants and Catholics disappear. That is to say, theologically liberal Protestant elites and theologically liberal Catholic elites have, for all practical purposes, identical political sympathies. Likewise, theologically orthodox Catholics and Protestants (evangelicals/fundamentalists) also share comparable political convictions. The one exception is that the Catholic community overall remains more critical of America's position in the world economy than the Protestant community.

Interestingly, holding theological orientation constant has the opposite effect in the relationship between Protestants and Jews: these communities are, in fact, significantly different in their political alignments (in general and toward capitalism). Jews are, on average, considerably more bullish than Protestants in their attitudes toward capitalism. The theological inclination of rabbis (orthodox to progressive) works the same way as it does in Protestantism and Catholicism, yet it is much less influential there than within the Christian communities.[17] In other words, there is something about being Jewish other than theology that creates political solidarity on these issues.

The importance of theological inclination for Anglican elites in Britain is less obvious. In a statistical sense, theological orientation does effect the way in which they identify their general political orientation but not how they posture themselves toward the workings of the market (and America's role in global market). Its lack of prominence is probably due to the relatively small size of the sample. Yet even in this group of Anglicans, theological inclination works in the same way as it does in America.[18]

In sum it is fair to say that on both sides of the Atlantic, the relative proximity of various types of cultural elites from the mechanisms of profit making is enormously consequential in shaping their political ideals. Yet within the boundaries of one bloc of cultural elites, religious leaders, theological conviction has strong, independent, and mediating consequences. This is especially true on the American scene evident in the attitudes of the religious leadership but especially visible in the activities of religious institutions. Indeed, as a few have suggested (Hunter, 1987, 1989; Wuthnow, 1988) the politically meaningful divisions among religious elites (and particularly Christian elites) in the American context, are no longer defined by their religious heritage but by how orthodox or how progressive they are in theological taste.

Posturing in the Knowledge Sector

There are probably strong independent reasons why the theologically orthodox are inclined toward political conservatism and the theologically progressive are inclined toward political liberalism. Historical factors are undoubtedly at play. Morphology (the cultural affinities between religious conservatism and social preservationism on the one hand and between religious liberalism and social reform on the other) is also at play. Yet there is arguably another reason why this is so—a reason having to do with the relationship between religious authority and marginality.

Religious elites and the institutions they represent appear to be just as earnest about playing a strong and formative role in public culture as they have in the past. (There are good theoretical reasons for maintaining that there is an intrinsic relationship between religious experience and the quest for power.) Nevertheless, because of their location on the margins of the knowledge sector, they are structurally hindered from actually pulling it off. One could speculate, then, that the tendencies toward political polarization among religious elites represent relatively distinct strategies for regaining the center. Political ideology and activism, then, can be seen as a form of posturing in the larger knowledge sector. For the theologically progressive, political liberalism and even radicalism represent the effort to form alliances with those who currently occupy the centers of cultural power in advance societies, the strata of secular cultural elites. For the theologically orthodox (and especially the evangelicals), political conservatism and even reactionism represent the effort to challenge the legitimacy of the center—to fundamentally transform the center of cultural power. Why else would evangelicals, for example, establish over 1,300 radio stations, over 220 television stations, over 400 periodicals and over 17,000 day schools if it were not that they felt so estranged from the center and desired so passionately to transform it with an alternate system of cultural symbols.[19] The same can be said, to a lesser extent, for Orthodox Jews and conservative Catholics. Each is actively engaged in creating its own alternative institutions of reality definition as mechanisms for preserving what they value most highly.

Yet, at the end of the day, given the basic structural realities of advanced capitalism in the contemporary world order, neither strategy is likely to succeed in restoring religious elites and the institutions they serve to positions of real authority, especially to positions of authority in the knowledge sector. This is not to say that they are or will become completely irrelevant to shaping the course and outcome of public life in our day, but it probably does mean that political frustration and disappointment may be the only certainty in their future.

Notes

1. This research is based upon data gathered from a survey fielded in the United States and Great Britain in early 1987. Respondents in the American survey were randomly selected from various sample universes: economic elites (*Who's Who in Business and Finance*), religious elites (*Who's Who in Religion*), academic elites (*The National Faculty Directory*), and media elites (a comprehensive list of news editors and journalists in national and regional newspapers, television stations, and opinion magazines). In the American case the data was collected by means of a mail questionnaire. After three mailings, the overall response rate was 61 percent. In the end the total number of respondents was 730 — 155 business elites, 199 academic elites, 286 religious elites, and 90 media elites.

In Great Britain, the data was collected by means of telephone interviews. Respondents were similarly sampled from appropriate sample universes: economic elites from a national list of senior managers of manufacturing and finance, religious elites from *Crockford's Directory* of the Church of England, academic elites from a list of the teaching staff at all major English, Welsh, and Scottish universities, and media elites from a list of national and regional television and newspaper journalists and editors. A total of 550 respondents were surveyed—99 business elites, 152 religious elites, 171 academic elites, and 109 media elites.

In both the American and British surveys, three of the samples were further specified. Economic elites were located in the highest echelons of manufacturing and finance and not, for example, in the knowledge sector such as the communications industry. Academic elites were selected from Ph.D.-granting universities and highly selective private colleges. (Community and vocational colleges were not included.) In the sample of religious elites, the plurality of faiths were sampled in the American cases but in the British case, only Anglican clergy were sampled. For the sake of comparability, then, only mainline Protestants elites were isolated for analysis.

2. This is a rough paraphrase of the original question, which was, "How much attention do you think well-known people in the news and entertainment media pay to religious values in their writings and pronouncements—a lot, some, only a little, none at all?"

3. This too is a rough paraphrase of the original question. It was originally asked as, "How much attention do you think writers, academics, and other intellectual groups pay to religious values in their writings and pronouncements — a lot, some, only a little, none at all?"

4. This question was originally posed as, "Do you think the influence of religion in this country is too high, too low, or just about right?"

5. The original question was, "Do you think that the status or prestige of the clergy has increased, decreased or stayed about the same in recent years?"

6. This too is a rough paraphrase of the original question which read, "Do you think that the influence of the clergy in the affairs of the community and the larger society has increased, decreased or stayed about the same in recent years?"

7. The question was originally posed as, "In general, do you think leaders in academics, news and entertainment paid more attention to religious values, less, or do you think they pay about the right amount of attention?

8. "Compared to other professionals, how important is the contribution of the clergy to society — very important, somewhat important, marginally important or unimportant?"

9. This argument can be framed in less abstract terms. It has been argued that economic elites legitimate their right to exercise power by appealing to the institution of private property and the political rights and material benefits that are assumed to derive from it (cf. Schumpeter, 1942). The authority of knowledge workers, by contrast, is derived from other sources. Certainly it is derived from their specialized expertise (Rueschemeyer, 1986). Perhaps more importantly, it is based in their appeal to what Gouldner (1982) calls self-grounded rational discourse—the justification of assertions solely on the basis of arguments adduced. The degree to which knowledge workers actually justify their own claims to authority in this way, is the degree to which they would be disposed to challenge the authority grounded in the market, in patriarchy, in traditional morality and traditional ecclesiastical dogma.

10. See J. D. Hunter, et al. "Cultural Elites and Political Values," unpublished manuscript, University of Virginia, for an elaboration of this logic.

11. *Dependent Variables.* From the survey data indices were created to measure three distinct but interrelated dependent variables: "market autonomy" (MRKTAUTN), "market performance (MRKTPERF), and "American economic power" (AMERIHEG). [For their construction, see Hunter et al. 1989] "Market autonomy" measures the degree to which the respondents approve or disapprove of private enterprise free of state intervention. Practically, it examines the degree to which the respondents favor or oppose governmental regulation of business and moderation of the economic effects of the market (i.e. reducing inequalities in wealth or income). "Market performance" measures the respondent's perceptions of the superiority or inferiority of a market economy as compared to other socioeconomic systems. The range of response varies according to the degree to which the elites surveyed believe that a market economy provides superior life chances and a higher material standard of living for the populations of both the first and the third worlds. The third variable, "American economic power" is concerned with assessing the respondent's attitudes towards the role of the United States in the world economy. This index measures the degree to which the United States (as an economic actor) and United States-based multinational corporations play an economically and morally beneficial role in the world economy (but particularly in the economics of the Third World states).

The dimensionality of these dependent variables was verified through factor analysis. The results of these factor analyses for both the American and British samples are found in the appendix to Chapter 2. In every case the principal components analysis indicates that the indices account for at least 50–60 percent of the variance in the component variables. From these results, it is clear that the structure of the variables within each index supports their usefulness in further analysis. The appendix also describes the distributions of the dependent variables for each of the elite groups. Note that these indices have been standardized and, therefore, they have means of zero and standard deviations of one hundred units.

12. The observable differences that do exist between the academic and religious elites is not statistically significant, except when considering evaluations of capitalism (MRKTPERF) among the British elite.

13. Multiple regression analysis was performed, including two blocs of variables: theoretical and demographic. The theoretical variables included were theological inclination, traditional family values, traditional morality, and a series of "dummy" variables (Catholic and Jew — Protestant was the reference category). Demographic variables included were age, race (American sample only), educational attainment, number of employees, and total family income.

14. The only exception to this general pattern is for attitudes towards America's role in the world system. Here, traditional family values is slightly more important than theological inclination (*BETAs* — $-.290$ and $-.280$, respectively).

15. Three demographic variables produce significant effects; yet, no demographic factor is as influential as any of the variables of theoretical interest. Race significantly affects attitudes towards governmental intervention and evaluations of capitalism. Blacks are more likely to favor intervention and are more critical of capitalism than are whites. Total family income significantly affects one's evaluations of the market economy. The more one earns, the less critical of capitalism they tend to be. The number of employees in the respondent's organization influences their perceptions of America's role in the world system. The more employees, the less critical of American foreign involvement.

16. The R squares increase significantly for each case. More interestingly, the $BETA$ coefficient for theological inclination is increased in all cases. The relative importance of the other explanatory variables is slightly decreased.

17. In fact, the effect of theological inclination is reduced by between 44 percent (on general political values) to 89 percent (on evaluations of the market economy) relative to its effect for Protestants.

18. Again, though statistically insignificant, theological inclination was typically the most influential variable and consistently supported the basic argument. For attitudes toward state intervention ($BETA - -.13$), evaluations of capitalism ($-.27$), and American hegemony ($-.15$) theological inclination had predicted effects. The equations also explained 15 percent of the variance in attitudes toward governmental intervention in the market, 19 percent of the variance in evaluations of capitalism, and 13 percent of the variation in attitudes concerning American economic hegemony.

19. Not insignificantly, a marginality construct was created from some of the items in table 1. This, as it turns out, is positively correlated with theological orthodoxy. Though direction is not specified, it is fair to assume that the more orthodox, the more marginalized they feel, and therefore, the more politically conservative they will be.

References

Abstract of British Historical Statistics, 2nd edition, 1971.

Annual Statistics of Switzerland, 1970: 1980.

Annvier Statstique a le FRANCE, 1961: 1973: 1986.

Bell, Daniel
1979   "The New Class: A Muddled Concept." In *The New Class?* B. Bruce-Briggs (ed.) 169–190. *New Brunswick: Transaction Books.*

Brint, Steven Gregory
1982   "Stirrings of an Oppositional Elite: The Social Bases and Historical Trajectory of Upper White Collar Dissent in the United States, 1960–1980." Unpublished doctoral dissertation, Harvard University.

Canada Year Book, 1922: 1932: 1942: 1952: 1962: 1972: 1985.

Census of Canada, 1861–1921: 1931: 1941: 1951: 1961: 1981.

Census of Great Britain, 1841: 1851: 1861: 1871: 1881: 1891: 1901: 1911: 1921: 1931: 1941: 1951: 1961: 1971: 1981.

Census of Switzerland, 1960: 1970.

Gouldner, Alvin
1982   *The Future of Intellectuals and the Rise of the New Class.* New York: Oxford University Press.

Historical Statistics of the United States Colonial Times to 1970.

Hunter, James Davidson
1987   *Evangelicalism: The Coming Generation.* Chicago: University of Chicago Press.

Hunter, J. D., James Tucker and Steven Finkel
1988   "Religious Elite and Political Values," unpublished manuscript, University of Virginia.

Hunter, James Davidson, John Herrmann, John Jarvis
1989   "Cultural Elites and Political Values," unpublished manuscript, University of Virginia.

Hunter, J. D., James E. Hawdon and James Tucker
1989   "Cultural Elites, Political Values and Advanced Capitalism," unpublished manuscript, University of Virginia.

Ladd, Everett Carl and Seymour M. Lipset
1975   *The Divided Academy,* New York: W. W. Norton and Company.

Muchlup, Fritz
1962   *The Production and Distribution of Knowledge in the United States.* Princeton: Princeton University Press.

Rubin, Michael Rogers and Mary Taylor Huber
1986   *The Knowledge Industry in the United States, 1960–1980.* Princeton: Princeton University Press.

Rueschemeyer, Dietrich
1986   *Power and the Division of Labor.* Stanford: Stanford University Press.

Schumpeter, Joseph
1942   *Capitalism, Socialism and Democracy.* New York: Harper and Brothers.

Swiss Yearbook 1931: 1951: 1971: 1981: 1986.

Historical Statistics of the United States Colonial Times to 1970.

W. Kohlhammer-Verlag
   Statistik Der Bundersrepublik Deutschland, Book 12: 19: 37.

Wuthnow, Robert
1988   *The Restructuring of American Religion.* Princeton: Princeton University
   Press.

U.S. Department of Commerce, Bureau of the Census, *Historical Statistics 1798
   —1945.*

U.S. Department of Commerce, Bureau of the Census, *Statistical Abstracts,*
   1951: 1981: 1985: 1986.

Appendix to Chapter Two

TABLE 1

Religious Elites as Proportion of the Total Population

Year	U.S.	Great Britain	Canada	West Germany	Switzer-land	France
1840		.13				
1850	.12	.13				
1860	.12	.16				
1870	.11	.16	.22			
1880	.13	.16	.28			.24
1890	.14	.17	.34		.15*	
1900	.15	.18			.14	
1910	.13	.16			.13	
1920	.12	.13			.13	.27
1930	.12	.13	.24		.13	.27
1940	.11		.23		.14**	
1950	.11	.12	.22	.14	.14	.30t
1960	.11	.12	.18	.12	.14	.34tt
1970	.11	.08	.11	.08	.11	
1980	.12	.07	.13			.11

Though reported at the turn of each new decade, the census for Great Britain, Canada, and France were taken in the year immediately following (1841, 1851, etc.) with the following exceptions: *–1888; **–1941; t–1946; tt–1962.

TABLE 2

Religious Elites as Percent of All Cultural Elites

Year	U.S.	Great Britain	Canada	West Germany	Switzer-land	France
1840		20.7				
1850	43.3	16.5				
1860	21.9	14.1				
1870	23.8	17.3	31.3			
1880	20.1	16.8	40.7			
1890	17.2	17.0	32.4		14.5*	
1900	17.0	16.3			11.5	
1910	13.5	14.9			9.4	21.6
1920	11.5	13.6			9.7	24.1
1930	9.5	12.9	19.6		9.7	24.9
1940	8.7		19.2		10.0**	
1950	8.8	10.4	18.7	28.3	9.6	28.9t
1960	7.5	7.9	13.0	13.1	9.1	24.4tt
1970	4.8	4.2	5.5	8.0	6.3	
1980	4.7	3.1	4.9			6.8

Though reported at the turn of each new decade, the census for Great Britain, Canada, and France were taken in the year immediately following (1841, 1851, etc.) with the following exceptions: *–1888; **–1941; t–1946; tt–1962.

TABLE 3

Cultural Elites as Percent of the Total Working Population

Year	U.S.	Great Britain	Canada	West Germany	Switzer-land	France
1840		1.65				
1850	.8	1.70				
1860	1.6		1.79			
1870	1.5		2.39			
1880	1.9	2.17	2.11			
1890	2.2		3.16		2.32*	2.30
1900	2.3	2.39	3.30		2.58	
1910	2.4	2.37	2.52		2.91	1.96
1920	2.6	2.19	3.60		2.83	2.00
1930	3.2	2.19	3.24		2.91	2.04
1940	3.1		3.10		2.98**	
1950	3.1	2.44	3.08	1.1	3.20	2.28t

Year	U.S.	Great Britain	Canada	West Germany	Switzer-land	France
1960	4.0	3.28	4.74	2.0	3.33	3.36tt
1970	5.7	3.87	4.91	2.3	3.68	
1980	11.0	4.56	5.34		5.88	3.72

Though reported at the turn of each new decade, the census for Great Britain, Canada, and France were taken in the year immediately following (1841, 1851, etc.) with the following exceptions: *–1888; **–1941; t–1946; tt–1962.

TABLE 4

Religious Book Production as a Percent of Total Book Production

Year	U.S.	West Germany	Switzerland	France	Netherlands
1890	10.2				
1900	7.9⁻				
1910	8.3⁻⁻		8.3'		
1920	6.0		5.7		10.1^
1930	8.3		8.0		10.7
1940	7.4		6.7"	6.7t	10.2
1950	5.7	7.4*	7.4	7.7	10.2
1960	6.5	6.7	8.3'''	6.6	9.0
1970	3.6	6.0	6.4	3.6tt	7.6
1980	4.8	5.7	7.6		7.2

Though reported at the turn of each new decade, the census for Switzerland was taken in the year immediately following (1841, 1851, etc.) with the following exceptions: ⁻–1899, ⁻⁻–1909; *–1951; **–1941; t–1941; tt–1972; ^–1926; and ' –1917, "–1946, '''–1965.

TABLE 5

Religious Newspapers and Periodicals as a Percent of All Newspapers and Periodicals (U.S. Only)

Year	U.S.	Year	U.S.
1850	7.6	1930	3.8
1860	6.8	1940	3.1
1870	6.9	1950	3.3
1880	4.9	1960	3.4
1890	3.9	1970	3.1
1900	3.9	1980	2.9
1910	3.6	1984	2.6
1920	3.9		

Part II

Core and Periphery

Old Religions and New Religions: The Lessons of the Colonial Era

Ninian Smart

In this paper I shall examine the experience of China, Japan, India, and Islam during the period of the formation and elaboration of the modern world order. The ways in which these cultures responded, religiously and ideologically, to the impact of colonialism and modern world capitalism is instructive. Various strategies can be used in the path to a realignment of cultural identity in the face of profound political, social, and economic changes. We may view these strategies within the perspective of the notion of a world order. The consequences of the replacement of an older mercantile system by free trade and emerging world capitalism, with its core in Europe and America, are that we now live in a single interacting global organism. Thus, changes here will affect life there: and changes there will affect us here. While world-order theory, as advanced by Wallerstein (1974), has made economic and material factors central in analysis, the approach of this paper has more to do with the symbolic interactions of different political and economic systems. The two levels of analysis are, of course, tightly interwoven.

The world system we are primarily considering is that established during the colonial period. The question here is how well did peripheral cultures react to the challenges constituted by the ideas and symbols of the center (as well as to the economic forces at work). We are now emerging into a postcolonial order, which has somewhat diverse characteristics from the older order. We have seen, because of the development of faster means of travel and communication, a very tightly knit global network; and because of economic transformations, the concepts of center and periphery need to be modified. This is because we are seeing a world capitalist system where the major corporations are becoming disconnected from national-states and imperial powers, through the strategy of creating transnational entities, which can be of no fixed address. In the new world order the dominant economic power is still northern, but it has expanded into new countries, such as Japan, Korea, Singapore, etc. Gradually the core is becoming a network, which covers a globe, which contains an underlying peripheral network at a different level of economic development. Maybe South Africa is a good model in one way: as it is said, a First World economy embedded in a Third World country. Moreover, the Second World of socialist countries is loosening up somewhat, in order to create wealth through something resembling a market economy: in doing so it is merging with the capitalist order, rather than existing as islands of centralization within a sea of relatively free and decentralized markets.

Clearly, nationalisms are not really relevant any more to the emerging world order. Nevertheless, nationalist sentiments and ideologies remain powerful, and my analysis of India, China, and Japan relates to the blending of religion and/or ideology with nationalist and connected themes. The creation of countervailing strength ultimately was in part dependent on spiritual and intellectual forces.

In the concluding section I shall relate these wider world patterns to the religious situation in the United States.

I

The reactions of China and Japan to essentially similar Western incursions were indeed diverse. The process of dissolution set in earlier in China, particularly through the first Opium War (1893–1842) and its aftermath. This amply demonstrated British and European military superiority. It eventually led to heavy Western control of Chinese customs, the establishment of ninety extraterritorial concessions in various cities, and the opening of China to capitalist penetration. In due course Maoist communism took charge of China, with disastrous results to its traditional and literary culture and to its old and complex religious weaving together of Taoism, Buddhism, and Confucianism. In order to reform socially and politically and to acquire the strength and morale to stand up to the Western powers, China in effect sacrificed its past. By an irony, the triumph of Maoism, so adept at war and consolidation, was a prelude to deep economic problems, which called in question Maoism itself and posed the problem of whether one could have Western technology without some sacrifice of Marxist principle. Ironically it was the same question as a century earlier; only then the question was about Confucianism.

Let us trace the story from the Opium Wars through to the Cultural Revolution. Naturally, I simplify: but we can pick out some major movements and moments.

After the peace of 1842, the first major convulsion was the so-called Taiping rebellion—some say revolution—(1850–1864), led by the visionary Hung Hsiu-chuan (Shih, 1967). He had been exposed to Protestantism and saw himself, as a result of visions, as the younger brother of Jesus. He was bitterly against the Manchu dynasty: it was a foreign, Manchu, imposition, and it had been weak in face of the West. The uprising was in many ways a typical Chinese peasant rebellion, but it had a mythic ideology to sustain it and direct it. In 1851 Hung proclaimed himself as the Heavenly Emperor of the Great Peace (T'ai P'ing). It became an immensely successful movement, capturing the southern capital of Nanking. It was only suppressed with difficulty and with foreign help, in 1864. The chaos and bloodshed surrounding the rebellion killed some twenty million persons.

The movement in effect blamed China's predicament on the Confucian tradition, meshed in with others. The movement smashed idols, destroyed temples, and trampled on tradition. It advocated land reform, the use of vernacular forms of Chinese, the emancipation of women, shared communal wealth, and other social programs. All this hinted at the later, more or less identical, reforms undertaken by the Communists about a century later. Because of the element of Protestantism in it, opinions were divided, among Westerners, as to whether the rebellion should be supported. The fear that it might create a stable and forceful government in Central China alienated official circles, however. Moreover, it was more analogous to independent African Churches of this century than to anything orthodoxly Protestant (Barrett, 1968). Its ultimate lack of success was in part due to the fact that though it may have had mythological appeal, it had no more sophisticated doctrines with which to appeal to the intelligentsia. It must have seemed peculiarly barbarous to traditional Confucian scholars and bureaucrats.

It was a kind of blind, and to begin with, greatly successful, reaction to foreign incursion. It often happens in the encounter of colonialism that the other cultures produce an experimental reaction to start with, but not based on a worldview sufficiently persuasive to intellectuals to have permanency. For generally it is by a rebellion of the masses led by people with a theory of how the world is and what to do that revolutions are born.

Obviously something had to be done. Apart from the loss of twenty million lives and the disruptions caused by the T'ai P'ing affair, there were dread droughts and floods, such as the famine of 1877–1878 in Shansi, Shensi, and Honen. China was unable to make any real economic progress, and the menace of opium entered the vitals of Chinese society. Anti-Christian riots helped to express antiforeign sentiment. Industrial plants were beginning to be created but on a narrow basis. For the failure of the Taipings almost inevitably drove Chinese thought inwards and gave rise to a differing tack: the Self-strengthening movement, which, as one of its exponents averred, should make "use of the barbarians' superior techniques to control the barbarians." A politer slogan was that "foreign knowledge was for use, and Confucian tradition for values." As both these sayings indicate, there remained a pride in the immensely superior philosophical and aesthetic basis of the two cultures, something like a fusion of them, such as Japan was performing during the last four decades of the twentieth century.

Part of the problem lay in the nature of government, and partly in the shape of China's ideologies. The Manchu government was still perceived as a foreign one: of this the pigtail was a symbol. This created hostility, which left the imperial family defensive and not really apt for bold new initiatives. Also, the Chinese bureaucratic structure, based on the examination system, was highly conservative. The very beauties of Confucian literature were an obstacle to new ways of thinking. The ideology was thoroughly Sinocentric: it still saw China as the central country, the focus of world civilization. Confucianism could be represented as the worldview of the civil service, and its priests were gentlemanly mandarins. As for the other religions of China, Taoism as the representative of popular culture was insufficiently adaptable to modern scientific and technological thinking and practice, while Buddhism has too much of withdrawal about it to underpin a militant nationalism.

The lack of impact of the Self-strengthening movement led to the only major attempt at a fusing of Chinese and Western tradition, at least during the late nineteenth and early twentieth centuries, namely the thought of K'ang Yu-wei (Kung-chuan, 1975). His was a remarkable combination of ideas. He employed Buddhist principles, as well as Western historical example, to show that change was necessary. K'ang (1858–1927) saw history as having three ages—one of chaos, another (the present age) of emerging peace, and a final era of great unity, in which the perfect society would be realized. This was characterized in ways that brought East and West together: K'ang's philosophy looked to technological development, material riches, and moral perfection, in which humans would be equal, free, and rich. He derived the ideas of the three ages and great unity from the Confucian and Taoist traditions.

K'ang was an influential reformer and persuaded the Kuang-hsu Emperor in 1894 to promulgate a whole program of political and educational reforms. After 100 glorious days, however, the dowager moved against the emperor and dismantled the program: K'ang escaped to Japan. He traveled widely promoting his ideas and was later to return to China after the revolution of 1911. His career, however, was essentially a failure, and though the Kuomintang later achieved some reforms, these were based rather on the rather watery ideology of Sun Yat-sen. A genuine restructuring of China was needed, and the chaotic times of the warlords, civil war, and Japanese invasion were not to be propitious.

K'ang's instincts had been right: there was a genuine need for a worldview which could fuse Chinese and Western ideas. For as others were to discover, it is not possible to modernize without education, and that implies a more open society. *Glasnost* is important both for scientific training and for the creation of wealth. After 1917 Chinese intellectuals debated the issue of whether science itself could form the basis of a way of life: the fact that they did so is a testimony to the lack of a fusion of Confucianism and modern science in a genuine synthesis. Moreover, many Chinese, especially in the Kuomintang between the wars, looked on religion as a relic of feudalism, which was what the revolution had overthrown. In any case, Confucian ideology was under a cloud. Meanwhile, the most distinguished Buddhist reformer, who did much to revitalize and purify Buddhist values, T'ai Hsu (1890–1947), was essentially a Buddhist modernist, aiming to revitalize the tradition, but not more directly aiming at Chinese national revival.

By the thirties of this century, China was still looking for a world view that could strengthen and reshape Chinese society and restore its independence. The Cultural Revolution of May 4, 1919, was a response to the shock of seeing the effects of the infamous Treaty of Versailles, which gave German concessions in China to the new imperialists, the Japanese. It was an ominous signal of Chinese humiliation in the concert of nations.

Every nation in distress had the option of taking over, wholesale, Western ideology. Ataturk had taken over the model of modern Western capitalism, but the trouble was, for many countries, that capitalism was woven into the fabric of oppression. The piecemeal domination of China was largely in the interest of trade. Moreover, though some of the new leadership, notably Sun Yat-sen and Chiang Kai-shek; and his wife, were Christian, Christianity had the disadvantage of foreignness in its symbolism. However, there was another Western ideology, Marxism, which had various appeals. It was the revolutionary counterideology to the Western establishment ideology. It was militant (which Buddhism, for instance, was not) and a good vehicle for national reawakening to struggle. It was collectivist and so could promise a kind of socialist reaffirmation of the identity of the Chinese people as a whole. It was also—or claimed to be—scientific. Mao, of course, adapted it to the Chinese condition, he brought peasants into the forefront of the revolutionary process, along-side the rather small proportion of urban workers. He could also lure the intellectuals, because Marxism was and is a very intellectual sort of religion. He could also, through leading the Long March, create a myth which was important in mobilizing national sentiment. His devotion to combat against the Japanese was also in line with national feeling. After the struggle before, during, and after World War II, and after he had become master of China, he reorganized the country in a way that gave it national strength and independence.

In a way, Mao's goals were more clearly seen in the Cultural Revolution — the Great Proletarian Cultural Revolution — of 1966 onwards, a name echoing the (bourgeois) Cultural Revolution of 1919. It marked the high point of collectivism and showed the vast price China had to pay for national independence. Unlike India, which hung on to virtually all of its past, China abolished the past. Reading was restricted to a few rather elementary Marxist texts, and to the Little Red Book, more like a manual of devotion than a serious anthology. The whole of the wonderful literary and artistic past was wiped off the face of China, together with the religions, so far as was possible. Temples were destroyed or turned into housing and offices. Priceless statues were smashed. Socialist realism and concrete party headquarters replaced the graceful products of the past: Western-style anti-Western propagandistic ballets dominated the theaters. In brief, China junked nearly all its heritage, for the sake of the ideology that had helped it to win national independence.

It was a bad deal, as far as the restoration of cultural identity went. Moreover, it has left China in exactly the same position as it had been in 100 years before. Then, as we have noted, the debate was whether China could have Western science for use and Confucianism for values. Now it is whether China could have modern science for use and Marxism for values. The new cloth-capped mandarinate has an ideology of being scientific and marveling at Maoist pigs and Stalinist steel mills. Beyond that, can China cope with the postindustrial age while retaining control of thought? Again it is a question of the need for Western semicapitalist values if China is to benefit from the various scientific and technological revolutions currently under way.

Japan makes an extraordinary contrast partly because of the difference of social and political conditions in the middle of the century, when the shadow of Perry's black ships stretched far beyond Tokyo Bay, and partly because of its very economic success today.

The three religions of China, transmuted, were part of the fabric of Japanese civilization, and most notably the Confucian and Buddhist worldviews. In addition there was the old, rather loose, tradition of the *kami,* integrated somewhat into Buddhism (Anesaki, 1970). Its myths were specially connected to the imperial family, but this family now, at the end of the Tokugawa period, had no power. Shoguns ruled. The system was a blend of the feudal and the mercantile. The revolt of the young samurais, possessed of a strong antiforeign sentiment and the intuition that Japan had to absorb some of the features of Western government, education, and organization, paved the way for the restoration of the rule of the emperor in 1868. The *bukafu* or shogunate was dismantled. Indeed, the whole samurai class was virtually dissolved and given other tasks than those of medieval warriors. They were to be the basis of a new professional class devoted to the slogan *fukoku kyohei*, "Rich country, strong arms": a similar strategy to that of modernizing Muslims. Under the Emperor Mieji, Japan underwent an amazing revolution, especially during the period from the Restoration (1868) to the Constitution (1889). In 1890 the Imperial Rescript on Education laid down Confucian and Shinto values as governing national identity and the new ethos. Higher education and indeed the rest of the system would be modeled on Western examples, but ideologically education must embrace a national, Japanese sense of values. The dominant partner in the Shinto-Confucian alliance was reorganized Shinto. While freedom of religion was guaranteed by the constitution, Shinto was declared not to be a religion. Buddhism, which had suffered severely in 1870–1871, during and after the forcible separation of Buddhism and Shinto, was in effect demoted.

In this way Japan westernized and attained an apparent pluralism of religion which was not truly tolerant because all religions were ultimately subjected to the overarching sacred system of Shinto, and concretely to the emperor. Shinto was a symbol of the sacralization of Japan: all this prepared the way not merely for Japanese imperialism but also for renewed self-confidence rooted in what were taken to be traditional values. It was an ingenious way of importing large draughts of Western thought and practice while maintaining the final authority of the sacred emperor as incarnating Japanese history (Holtom, 1970).

Though Buddhism suffered in the transition, some of its forms were important as expressing, paradoxically, the spirit of chivalry, which took on new forms in the Japanese armies created out of the Meiji revolution and which were to prove to be so successful in the Russo-Japanese War of 1904–1905, and during World War II and its preludes in Manchuria and China. Buddhism also took forms easy to reconcile with modern scientific thinking. In these various ways, religions took part in the framing of a vital synthesis between Western and traditional values (Kishimoto, 1956).

This synthesis was even further improved by the Japanese collapse at the end of World War II. It was fortunate that Japan had such an understanding ruler as Douglas MacArthur (Woodard, 1952). It was possible to fuse democratic values with the spirit of national identity by further modifying the institution of the sacred monarch. Defeat in war substituted the pursuit of economic wealth for force of arms, putting Japan now in a highly powerful position in today's world. We can no doubt expect a continued revival of patriotic self-satisfaction, and perhaps a more aggressive role in the politics of the Far East.

The educational system, a major key to Japan's success, still stresses the virtues of duty and obedience, in the Confucian manner, and respect for the *kokutai* or national essence. The patriotism is muted, however, and overtly Shinto does not quite play the role which pre-war State Shinto occupied, but dormant beneath the scurrying surface of modern Japan lies the feeling for duty and the national essence, which Confucianism and Shinto respectively represent.

We have seen in all this the way in which Japan and China have dramatically diverged—China towards the abolition of its past and socialist collectivism, Japan towards capitalist traditionalism, which fuses the values of East and West. By the criterion of how much of its past Japan has managed to salvage in the vicissitudes of the modern age, it lies between China and India. To put the matter in terms of what I have called position theory, Japan during the imperial phase went back to an interesting kind of neofoundationalism, reverting to what society conceived of as its primeval tradition, the gods of the ancient past. This Shinto was cast in a new way, as being the crown of a modernized set of values for ordering society. Whether one counts this as a kind of fundamentalism depends, of course, on your view of Japanese religion. If you think of it as consisting in separate traditions, then my analysis does not work so well: if you think of it as a congeries with Shinto, Taoist, Confucian, and Buddhist elements, then it makes more sense, for the most primeval and basic of these values is that which came first, namely the *kami*. Whether there is such a thing at the earliest stage of Japanese history as what came to be called Shinto is not relevant: for in these matters perception is everything, and in Meiji times Shinto was seen as a primordial basis of values. It blended, too, with the idea of the *kokutai* or national essence. So a foundationalist position was adopted, which helped to express a very powerful modern nationalism.

When this position was smashed by World War II, a retreat had to be made, and Japan retreated to a position like that of other modernizers, a secularist emphasis. By this time it was feasible to blend into it elements from the past — Buddhist, Confucian, and so forth. The emperor, however, still remains a figurehead as befits a democracy, but trailing little clouds of sacrality nonetheless, perhaps preparing Japan for a new phase of Shinto nationalism. Meanwhile Western fashions and values are there too, in a new synthesis.

India has, as I say, been much more successful in its grafting on of Western values and modernization because it has retained virtually all of its past. This is in part due to the new Hindu ideology, which so gracefully dealt with the challenges to tradition of Christianity, science, domocracy, and nationalism. It was not the reversion to a neofoundationalism (the Arya Samaj tried that), but rather a neoclassicism in which India drew on the multiple resources of its classical period, above all Shankara's Advaita Vedanta suitably adapted and updated. India did not have to turn its back on its classical and medieval past, but rather used it in a fresh way in the struggle against the British. It also no doubt had the advantage of being conquered by one power, which stimulated a joy in the rediscovery of the great Indian past.

China was less happy. For reasons we have hinted at, the options of the past were not so healthy. In modernizing, the attempts to shape a new Confucianism came too late, and were vitiated by the association of Confucianism with an old and smug bureaucracy. In China's way forward, a secular position seemed necessary: but the ideal of a pluralist and liberal democratic revolution was hard to realize because nationalist sentiment ran in a contrary direction, against a bourgeoisie that had for the most part cooperated with foreign trade and exploitation. It was at least superficially attractive to opt for the Marxist position because this could revolutionize decadent Chinese society and at the same time incorporate (it was thought) modern values. As it turned out this ideological position was fruitful in nationalist terms and fatal in terms of modernization. Totalitarianism runs counter to science, and so to the whole process of economic development.

Of all the cultures we have looked at briefly, Islamic culture remains the most unproductive, on average. It has not solved the problem of real independence of the West. On the other hand, nothing stable has emerged in the swings between the secular position and neofoundationalism. The question of the future of Israel has not been settled, after forty years. All this is in part a failure of the intellectuals of Islam in trying to express, in the postcolonial period, a genuine new vision of Islam and its place in the contemporary world. Because it has on the whole turned its back on classical Islamic civilization, there is wanting a recasting of the thought of those times, such as the Hindus have achieved. In the religious impulse to point fingers at the cause of the decay of Islam, one of its most creative aspects, Sufism, is no longer taken up to provide a framework of Islamic thought that will be both traditional and modernizing. Maybe we await some new developments for the future along these lines. Meanwhile, there is restiveness that modernist blends such as in Egypt have been so unsuccessful. There seemed a time when Nasser was on the brink of great things, it was thought, at least on behalf of Arab nationalism, but Arabism is now in as bad a state as is Islamic resurgence. Yet welling up from below there are signs that radical neofoundationalism, aiming at the creation of Islamic states, will increase in power. The immediate future lies in such radicalism. Its force will be seen, I suspect, in Egypt, Syria, Iraq, Tunisia, Morocco, and elsewhere: even here and there in the Gulf states. There is restiveness among neotraditionalists in Pakistan, Malaysia, Indonesia, and elsewhere.

The ultimate need for a Sufi revival springs from another source than the impulse towards a modern religion. It springs too from the need of the diverse faiths to live together in a single globe. Their traditional theologies of exclusion need to be reshaped. In this the modern Hindu ideology is something of a pioneer. They require rethinking because of the fact that not only is bitterness between religions undesirable, but because traditional exclusivist theologies have largely been built on ignorance. You could not expect a person sitting by the Nile or the Ganges in the old days to know anything about distant alternatives. Confucius meant nothing to such people, and Buddhism, little. The world has changed so much in bringing far peoples and faiths together, and this challenges all faiths to rethink their ideas. Sufi notions drawn from the great classical period of Islam have much to offer in a more open attitude to other cultures. Maybe a neoclassical position will be a better place to occupy during the revival of Islam.

Here the importance of diaspora Islam is not to be neglected. Many forward-looking Muslims from South Asia, the Arab world, and elsewhere have emigrated to the West. There they are bound to be infected with individualism and a kind of eclectic mind: it is in such conditions that a revival of Sufism may flourish and be carried from the diaspora to the heartlands of the religion.

So long as the completion of the postcolonial phase of Islam is postponed, however, the more rampant will be anti-Western values. For Muslims on the whole, Marxism has no appeal because of its atheism. In the immediate future a revived Islam is most likely to be the revolutionary ideology that animates the next phase of development in Muslim countries.

Meanwhile, what of the West itself? There are also worries in traditional Christian countries about the effects of liberal modernism, which itself has penetrated so deeply into both neofoundationalist Protestant and Catholic forms of the faith. Backlashes are evident here and there, combining with the forces of nationalism, but the democratic West has managed very successfully to evolve a new over-arching pluralism, which meshes well with liberal Christian values. Despite the fact that in certain ways liberal Protestantism looks somewhat insipid, its power remains because its values have spread to Catholicism and much of Judaism. It now provides the basis of a new democratic, capitalist order, which sets up a humanist umbrella beneath which the varied religions and ideologies can shelter. It is only in Marxist states that the old intolerant principle of *cuius regio eius religio* applies.

There is restiveness with it. Some intellectuals in the West use the Marxist route to social criticism; others have a nostalgia for virtue or civil religion. A tolerant society, though killing some strong faith with kindness, does give everyone a chance to practice most of their traditional religions. It is a better bargain than theocracy, which gives one religion or worldview 100 percent of what it wants, and the rest considerably less.

Meanwhile there is an aspect of religions and their adaptation to the modern world that should give us deep concern. The world has been shaped by nation-states, and nationalism remains the most potent force in the organization of human beings. Worldviews tend to get bent on its demands. Furthermore, often religion is one mark, sometimes the most essential mark, in the definition of ethnicity. Religious ethnicity is a most powerful and heady brew. Behind it lies Buddhist nationalism in Sri Lanka, Cypriot and Turkish ethnicities in Cyprus, the division of Northern Ireland, conflicts in Israel, civil strife in the Southern Philippines, unrest in the republics of Armenia and Azerbaijan, the war between Iraq and Iran, battles in Afghanistan. In short, it is a widespread and dangerous phenomenon. Liberal religion of the old sort has failed to deal with these problems, as for that matter has liberal politics. We need new and creative religious and political initiatives if this new disease in the world is to be quenched.

It is not of course merely in divided countries where these problems exist, but also, as the world migrates hither and thither, in many of our cities in the West and elsewhere. There is ethnic friction in France and Britain, in Frankfurt and Los Angeles; such friction is sometimes amplified by religious differences. All this needs thinking about if strife is to be diminished.

Intellectual and political liberalism has been weak on these fronts because it does not heed sufficiently the emotional forces built up around ethnic identities. This is one area where religions often blind themselves to the strength of our new religions—the variety of nationalisms. The reason why they are blind is in part at least because of lack of insight and analysis. By thinking of only some of the rituals and ideas of the world as being religious and others as secular, religions have failed to see that forms of nationalism are the most powerful religions of today (Smart, 1983). Our myths are American or British or Indian history; our doctrines are those of democracy or Marxism or Fascism; our priests are high school teachers and soldiers; our sacrifices are those of blood and martyrdom in battle; our rituals embrace saluting the flag and national anthems; our religious experiences are the joys of patriotism and feelings of awe before the sacred past and the holy territory; our organizations and churches are states; our ethics are those of a good citizen. By binding ourselves into thinking that these arrangements are "natural" and not religious, we are preventing the insight that so many of the manifestations of modern religion are blends or syncretisms with nationalism and the problems of pride and identity.

As we have seen, profound transformations have occurred through modernity and colonialism. Not a single faith is unaffected. What we think of as our traditions are inventions of the modern period. How much of the past can you retain and be modern? The Indians have done best, and we are all in search of psychic deals, which give us our identities while allowing us to take advantage of the splendors of modern living.

II

In the time since World War II, some of the themes that we have seen to be operative in the wider world, in coping with the stresses of change, have been present in America. Of course, as in other Western countries, the United States did not have to deal with foreign conquest and domination, and so issues of national identity and nationalist struggle were at the most muted, but they were not absent. Partly because the ethos of being American is rooted in the Constitution and so has an ideological basis (in a way which is much less true of being an Italian or a Pole, for instance), the existence of a counterposed ideology, that of Communism, was seen more as a threat to national identity than would otherwise have been the case. The relative success of Marxism during the postwar period was itself due to its position as a possible anticolonial nation-builder. With the perception of an emerging tightly bound world order, it was easy, too, to see the issue of capitalism versus Communism as being central to the domination of the future global civilization. On such a worldview we can see how McCarthyism was built—identifying ideological anti-Communist rectitude with American patriotism. Now this phase of American life is not usually seen as a religious struggle because in the West we have a rather constricted definition of religion: undoubtedly McCarthyism represented a symbolic worldview that had many of the properties of a religious commitment.

The new global situation had other challenges. Notably there were the great religious traditions outside of Christianity and Judaism, and especially those of India and Japan. The mainstream Protestant ideology had successfully coped with modern values — liberalism, science, democracy, but its establishmentarian connections (its very success in laying the groundwork of modern American values) left it exposed to criticism. Such criticism came, during the sixties and early seventies, from a variety of directions — from other religions, from some strands of Marxist ideology, and from a new individualism manifested through the drug culture, sexual liberation, and self-exploration. Religiously, this stimulated the growth of new syncretic movements, blending Eastern and Western themes (such as unificationism and transcendental meditation), and the flourishing of certain Eastern religions — notably, varieties of Buddhism, the Hare Krishnas, and among blacks the Nation of Islam.

More recent interest in civil religion may point up a question that the new world order poses to American national identity. Because we are evolving towards a looser conception of center and periphery, the bonds between global capitalism and the American nation will obviously diminish. The new religions mentioned above are in some ways a recognition, albeit in a somewhat obscure way, that we are now all citizens of the world. Governments' economic roles will diminish, perhaps to become above all unions which bargain with the world system for a decent cut for their members. The new world order is increasingly seen as one in which both economic competition and individual human rights will be important. In brief, that order will be 'liberal' in a classical way, but its transnational character holds a challenge to patriotism. This may help in part to explain the religious backlash against some aspects of such liberalism. The historic relation between American nationalism and capitalism leads the religious right to react against other elements of the liberal mix — historical and critical views of the scriptural texts, an individualism that corrodes larger groups of which the family stands as chief symbol, and a generally critical attitude to received institutions, including capitalism itself. At a milder level, there is a nostalgia for a civil religion, which will unite Americans through a revival of some of the traditional values.

It seems, however, that the new world system will impose a determinate set of values upon us, which are different from those of traditional faiths, though perhaps congruent with them to some degree. First, individual freedom of religion and worldview will corrode authorities. Second, the transnational character of world civilization will diminish the appeal of patriotism, but the notion of world citizen will become more dominant. Third, pluralism is a necessary outcome of the fact of competing and different worldviews. This is especially important for minority groups, such as non-Christians in Europe, the classical African religionists of the southern Sudan, and Muslims in Israel. Fourth, the major religions will function as transnational spiritual corporations, drifting together and coalescing into large blocs; yet each one however large will see itself as a minority in world culture. Mutual toleration will become more and more necessary as different cultures live side by side (though no doubt backlashes of intolerance are to be expected, too, because groups regard others of differing customs often as threats). These values — individualism, internationalism, pluralistic toleration — are already will entrenched on the American scene because of the very genesis of the nation and its development. One would expect, therefore, more individual experimentation and eclecticism, together with greater solidification of the major religions (for instance, let us note how in effect the Roman Catholic Church has joined the liberal camp). Clearly, nontraditionally American religions, like Buddhism, are likely to make further progress, too, as civilizations increasingly penetrate one another.

This suggests that those who hark back to a quasi-Protestant civil religion will be looking to something obsolete. Spiritual search and choice within a plural framework, cemented by genuine toleration, are the more relevant values: they do not need specific doctrinal or ritual content (beyond the rituals of the democratic State), and such content already begins to verge on intolerance. America is a fortunate place for such values to be promoted because they can be plausibly found in the history of the nation.

References

Anesaki, Masaharu
1970   *History of Japanese Religion*. Rev. Edition. Tokyo: C. E. Tuttle.

Barrett, David B.
1968   *Schism and Renewal in Africa: An Analysis of Six Thousand Contemporary Movements*. Nairobi: Oxford University Press.

Holtom, D. C.
1970   *Modern Japan and Shinto Nationalism*. 2nd Edition. Chicago: University of Chicago Press.

Kishimoto, Hideo
1956   *Japanese Religion in the Meiji Period*. Tokyo: Obunsha.

Hsiao, Kung-Chuan
1975   *A Modern China and a New World: K'ang Yu-wei, Reformer and Utopian, 1858–1927*. Seattle: University of Washington Press.

Shih, Vincent Y. C.
1967   *The Taiping Ideology*. Seattle: University of Washington Press.

Smart, Ninian
1983   *Worldviews: Crosscultural Exploration of Human Beliefs*. New York: Scribner's.

Wallerstein, Immanuel
1974   *The Modern World-System*. New York: Academic Press.

Woodard, William P.
1952   *The Allied Occupation of Japan, 1945–1952, and Japanese Religions*. Leiden: Brill.

4

"God Damn Yanquis" — American Hegemony and Contemporary Latin American Christianity

Graham Howes

This paper examines Latin American religious developments from a world-order perspective. It offers some provisional reflections by a British social scientist—with a long-standing interest in religion—on the relationship between contemporary American realpolitik and contemporary Latin American Christianity. It rests heavily, and selectively, upon secondary sources[1] reinforced by six weeks study leave in Peru during the summer of 1987.

Even such a limited exercise as this is not without its dangers. One is to generalize on behalf of two continents, each of which is in fact a complex mosaic of political, social, and economic realities. Another is to accept too readily the functional interdependence of Christianity and economic and political hegemony, especially when, in the case of Protestantism in the British Empire, and of Catholicism in the Spanish and Portuguese empires, the historical evidence appears so persuasive, and religious and secular triumphalism appear to be so self-evidently interdependent.

A third danger is, of course, to treat major institutions — empire, church, state, governments — as unitary monoliths, and their ideologies — whether evangelical Protestantism, liberation theology or the Reagan doctrine — as mere stereotypes. It is in any case difficult to establish the precise interrelationship between domestic religious trends in the United States — especially the religious right (both Protestant and Catholic) — United States foreign policy, and United States-derived missionary activity in Latin America. We also have to establish whether the increasing po-

larity between the radical left and conservative right among American
Catholics and the unresolved tensions between mainline Protestantism
and the fundamentalist sects are themselves mirrored and acted out
south of the Rio Grande.

Yet Latin American Christianity is more than a test-bed for sociological theory and research. It already possesses its own political dynamic. At a personal level one does not have to spend long with United
States-trained Catholic priests and nuns in Peru before learning of an
acute conflict of interests between their sense of Christian mission and
their awareness of America's mission, and then meeting with Protestant
missionaries for whom there is no such conflict at all! The broad dynamics of hegemony are, of course, formally articulated on both sides. An
early North American expression of it can be found in Vice President Nelson Rockefeller's conclusion, in his 1969 memorandum to the Nixon administration that "the Catholic church has ceased to be an ally in whom
the United States can have confidence" (*DSB*. 1969:16). Similarly the
Santa Fe Document of 1980 affirms that "America's global power projection has always centered upon a cooperative Caribbean and a supportive
Latin America . . . U.S. foreign policy must begin to counter (not react
against) liberation theology as it is utilized in Latin America by the liberation theology clergy" (*SFD*. 1980:II).

In Latin America itself America's role in religious affairs is perceived not merely as an extension of foreign policy, or as part of the traditional burden of a client state. It also forms part of a normative anti-
Americanism, which embraces more general charges of exploitation and
cultural imperialism. For example, in December 1988, the Central American bishops equated "the loss of cultural identity among our people with
the process of Americanization" (*LP*. 5 December 1988). Similarly Brazil's Roman Catholic hierarchy recently associated the growth of fundamentalist sects with "U.S. geopolitical strategy" (*LP* 7 September
1987), while in Peru such groups are still popularly, and significantly,
known as 'Reagan cults'). These are the views not only of the Catholic
left but also of the Protestant center. Indeed at the important ecumenical
meeting in Cuenca, Ecuador, in November 1986 both groups explicitly
denounced "the manipulation of religion as a new device used on behalf
of economic or political ideologies and interests" (*Cuenca*. 1986:9). The
difficulty is not only to identify and analyze this process but to set it in the
context of world order and religion. We shall describe the Roman Catholic
and the Protestant cases, before turning briefly to some more theoretical
reflections.

Catholicism

Since the Hispanic conquest, the Catholic church has served historically and culturally as the chief source of moral legitimacy for secular authority in Latin America. Institutionally and ideologically it has remained integral to American policies of supporting existing military and civil elites.

It also, until the 1960s, legitimated the prevailing, United States-derived, model of economic development—*desarollo*—which assigned a leading role to foreign capital, trusted in the military as a modernizing agent, and promised take-off and sustained economic growth for all social groups. At the same time the Vatican's high profile in the Cold War, its hostility to communism and its antipathy to socialism also brought it into active if not always smooth alliance with the United States, while the direct plea—at the first Conference of Latin American Bishops (CELAM) in 1955—which Pope Pius XII made to Catholics in the developed countries of the West "to send resources and personnel to Latin America to combat communism" (*RA* 1985:27), led directly to an increase in United States Catholic personnel in Latin America of nearly 65 percent between 1958 and 1964. Also Cardinal Spellman's increasingly interventionist role in Latin American church affairs over three decades not only made the North American Catholic Church a power as well as a presence in Latin American affairs, but also symbolized and articulated the positive role of domestic Catholicism in United States foreign policy.

Finally, there was the well-attested evidence of CIA collaboration with the Vatican in the face of what both acknowledged as a common enemy. Such collaboration dated back to 1945 when the CIA's predecessor, the Office of Strategic Serivces (OSS) worked with the Curia to help defeat the communists in the Italian elections. Indeed the man who later became Pope Paul VI, Montini of Milan, had no hesitation in turning over the Italian bishops' files on activist parish priests, for use by the CIA during the Italian election of 1960.

With the new political direction of the Vatican under Pope John XXIII, and when some Latin American bishops began themselves to criticize the region's rightist governments—Spellman's friends—for blocking reform, an apparently special relationship seemed clearly threatened. In 1962 a CIA report concluded that the Vatican was becoming a less reliable ally. The agency felt compelled to express its concern formally about the Vatican's leftward drift, and CIA director John McCone made a special visit to Rome to inform Pope John of President Kennedy's concern about his overtures to the Soviet Union and his support for critics of United States allies in Latin America. By 1964 the CIA and other United States government agencies were heavily funding the Chilean Christian Democratic party of Eduardo Frei in its electoral campaign against Allende's Socialist party. Between five and ten million dollars from American sources (including the Agency for International Development as well as the CIA) was allocated for expenditure on Catholic housing schemes and lay training programs as part of the effort to build a Christian Democratic power base.

By the Medellin Conference in 1968 the proportion of military regimes throughout the continent had increased, eliminating political opposition and leaving the church and especially the "base communities" as the only possible outlet for radical organization and activism. At Medellin itself Latin American Catholics and their church seemed to sense, institutionally, the crisis in their society, the failure of *desarollo,* and the need for "liberation." "We wish to emphasize" the conference document stated, "that the principal guilt for the economic dependency of our countries rests with powers inspired by an uncontrolled desire for gain which leads to economic dictatorship and the international imperialism of money" (Cleary 1985:109–110). In Peru, for example, the 1973 Pastoral Letter of Msgr. Burke, Bishop of Chimbote, urged "the Church to be identified with the people's struggle against exploitation, hunger, poverty, humiliation, inhuman treatment and injustice." (Klaiber 1976:78).

Official United States responses to post-Medellin Catholicism are well documented and do not need to be reiterated here. They are not untypically encapsulated in the *Santa Fe Document*'s allegation that, in Latin America, "Marxist/Leninist forces have utilized the church as a political weapon against private property and productive capitalism by infiltrating the religious community with ideas which are less Christian than communist" (SFD 1980). Less officially, but no less typically, the *Wall Street Journal* still saw liberation theology four years later as "part of the communist effort to destabilize the entire Latin American continent" (12 December 1984).

The operational response, if overt in its intentions, was often covert in its execution. This, too, is well documented. Lermoux, in an accessible and well-informed account, outlines the relatively subtle efforts, throughout the 1970s, of Cardinal Baggio, president of the Pontifical Commission for Latin America, and Lopes Trujillo, general secretary of CELAM, to stitch together, with major support from the DeRance Foundation of Wisconsin, a coalition of international financial agencies, Curia members, and Latin American conservatives to acquire permanent control over the structure and content of Latin American theological debate. She also reminds us of the 1975 Banzer Plan and numerous other—often

CIA-inspired — efforts to turn public opinion against the progressive church in many Latin American countries. Lermoux gives full, if slightly sensationalized details of the "black propaganda" projects undertaken in Ecuador, Brazil, and Chile, and how in Colombia the agency also penetrated a church-run literacy program on the radio, with half a million peasant listeners, with a view to injecting a strong anti-communist message. A more recent and widely reported instance of such covert activity is perhaps the alleged funding, between 1985 and 1987 — via a Cayman Islands account—of Cardinal Obando and Bravo of Managua by the CIA and its surrogates, and possibly also from Oliver North's rogue operation in the White House basement (*Newsweek* 15 June 1987).

Equally significant have been the efforts to foster among Latin American Catholics the growth of a right-wing, revisionist counterculture. The degree to which this is State Department policy or the result of pressure from influential United States Catholic clergy and laity who seek firmer ties between the United States government and the Latin American church remains problematic, and needs more systematic research (Reichley 1985:chapter 6). In Brazil, for example, the CIA funded the long-established and ultraconservative "Tradition, Family and Property" group, whose neo-McCarthyite methods have included publishing lists of subversive clergy and taking out advertisements in the local press calling certain individuals unpatriotic. Finally, and less easy to substantiate, would be formal backing for Opus Dei, whose North American support, like that in Latin America, has long been buttressed by wealthy Catholic laity. In Peru Opus Dei has an unusually high profile. In 1989 it already had six Opus Dei dioceses and seven Opus Dei bishops who, supported by their conservative colleagues in Germany and the Papal Nuncio in Lima, are currently lobbying Rome for one of their own number to succeed Ricketts as the next cardinal archbishop of Lima. More consonant with conservative North American Catholic expectations is the substantial bid that Opus Dei is making through its university in Piura (whose registrar told me of its "fruitful affiliation" with Georgetown) to secure the ideological loyalties of Peru's next administrative and business elite. Opus Dei is also investing heavily and for the first time in building secondary schools in four predominantly working-class areas of Lima.

This account is, of course, overcompressed and oversimplistic. It is also, perhaps, a little overconspiratorial. It is also what happens when British academic prudence encounters American plenitude in the shape of the data released by a viable Freedom of Information Act, but like all the best data it has implications far beyond itself.

One is the convergence of presidential and papal, secular and ecclesiastical world views — the new Protestant right and the traditional Catholic one. Like former President Reagan, and presumably President Bush,

Pope John Paul II sees the world ultimately in terms of theological geo-politics, of totalitarianism versus Christianity. For both, it is clear that the Latin American church is more than a symbol of the overall global conflict between traditionalism and modernity within Catholicism. Both seek more than doctrinal orthodoxy and the restoration of a pristine pre-Vatican II or pre-Ortegan world nucleated around authority and tradition. Just as the Vatican seeks to combat secularism and restore the role of the Roman Catholic church as the sole mediator of human interaction with the world, so the State Department seeks to fashion what Dr. Mark Falcoff of the Hoover Institute describes as "an inter-American community of which, at least implicitly, the U.S. is the leader" (Kirkpatrick 1988). Both have made it a priority to delegitimize currents of Christian — or secular-political — inspiration beyond their control and thus their offensive against liberation theology has taken on a global dimension with both the papal redefinition of the so-called social project and the theology of reconciliation, and the new presidential emphasis upon "humanitarian" and "security" assistance (SDA 1985:847–54).

Secondly, in their Latin American context there is also some evidence of cultural crisis within both systems. Just as the United States is, in the words of the *Santa Fe Document,* "helping to preserve Hispano-American culture from sterilization by international Marxist-Materialism" (SFD 1980), so the Vatican feels itself instrumental there in preserving Christendom against secularism and Marxism. It is, above all, in this tradition of cultural Catholicism and Catholic nationalism that the lay and clerical counterattack against liberation theology has found its inspiration. Its leading political figures such as Alberto Ferre (who is in charge of the CELAM Department for the Laity) place special emphasis upon what they call "the Christian vocation of the Latin American peoples,"[2] and on the very special place of Latin America in the history of the church. Like the moral majority, their own continent remains, in their eyes, the sole repository of pre-Enlightenment Christian values and as such is the great hope for a Christendom assailed by secularism. In such a context it is important to remember that the preindependence period in Latin America marked the incorporation of Latin America into Christendom, a body of cultural beliefs that is primarily concerned with the idea of where authority is derived from and how it is legitimated, rather than with the tenets of Christianity itself. In colonial Christendom secular and religious authority were integrated and the church grew accustomed to serving the civil power in order to accomplish its mission of evangelization. It is this historico-cultural assumption that resonates strongly with North American presumptions of the Catholic church remaining as the guardian of empire and a buffer state against communism. It also helps to explain the elective affinity—some might call it an unholy alliance!—between the Catholic and Protestant right in the United States on Latin American issues. It also shows that there is more afoot than a right-wing plot managed by wealthy Catholic lay organizations throughout the world.

In this sense, paradoxically, Catholic liberation theology, for all its neo-Marxist conception of the poor as the collective agents of revolutionary and religious change, presses very close to its institutional *alter ego* — American Protestant fundamentalism—in its insistence on the sinful nature of structures as well as the sinful nature of individuals, in its emphasis upon personal salvation, and in its strong biblical orientation.

Protestantism

Forty-five years ago Kenneth Scott Latourette in his "History of the Expansion of Christianity" could write that "Culturally Latin America and the United States were separated by a vast gulf ... the United States was suspect in Latin America as a potential aggressor, especially after its territorial gains at the expense of Mexico and its policies in Central America and the Caribbean ... That, under these circumstances, the Protestant Churches of the United States inaugurated extensive enterprises among the Roman Catholics of Latin America ... was not due to political or imperial commercialism. It came about through the missionary purpose of these churches which regarded the entire human race as their field" (Latourette 1943.V:115–6).

Today in Latin America it is not hard to find North American Protestant missionaries who at the very least recognize the cultural and religio-political barriers that they face and are quite capable of seeing themselves in the vanguard of North American interests. Many are consciously mounting what Nelson Rockefeller called "an extensive campaign with the aim of propagating Protestant Churches and conservative sects in Latin America" (*DSB* 1969:17). It is likewise a strategy that is clearly perceived by many of those towards whom it is theoretically directed. It is, as the Argentinian liberation theologian Jose Miguez-Bonino describes it "outside interference of a most insidious form." It is "the massive and growing presence of a religious message brought by groups tied to the system that fosters Latin American political and economic domination," message that "legitimizes the situation of oppression" (*LP* 24 July 1986). Yet evolved Protestantism in Latin America is a highly complex phenomenon. Historically it too is well-documented. During the sixteenth and seventeenth centuries it was largely confined to small enclaves of Calvinism among Dutch and French settlers, and by the early nineteenth century had been extended by European and American missionaries and European Protestant migrants. Indeed the exodus of Spanish priests at the time of independence, and the lack of an indigenous clergy to replace them may have left Latin America in a kind of spiritual vacuum in which Protestant activity came almost to be regarded as primary evangelization. Through this process it became increasingly identified with liberalism, free trade, scientific and technical progress, democracy, and capitalism. In short it was a vehicle for, and a symbol of, modernization.

In the early twentieth century (and especially throughout the economic changes of the 1920s) while the historic Protestant churches continued to minister to German- or English-speaking populations (and even attracted some middle class Catholics) the main Protestant growth point became — and indeed remains — indigenous Pentecostal movements among the urban or semiurban poor. Today about 80 percent of Latin America's practicing Protestants are Pentecostal. More than 20 percent of all Guatemalans, and 50 percent of the Indian population belong to the Pentecostal sects, and, combined, they may constitute a majority by the end of the century. Some 15 percent of Panama and Chile are adherents, as are 10 percent of Brazilians. In Brazil the religious reality may be that the Pentecostals constitute twenty-five million "practicing" Christians as compared with twenty million "observant" Catholics.

In recent years, in addition to para-Christian groups such as the Jehovah's Witnesses, Mormons, and Moonies, two significant trends have emerged. One has been the emergence of evangelical, often charismatic movements among conservative, predominantly middle-class churches. The other — the most widely and sometimes adversely publicized — are ultraconservative, fundamentalist sects, usually of North American origin, whose main work has been among indigenous tribal groups, as well as in the cities.

Today Latin American Protestantism is a complex phenomenon, and the relationship between the four main groupings — historic churches, Pentecostals, evangelicals, and fundamentalist sects — remains intricate and shifting. Furthermore, the theological or ideological positions held by a denomination in one country cannot necessarily be presumed to be the same in another. Yet the overall taxonomy not only reflects a similar configuration and process within North America itself (with, for example, historic Protestant churches losing members to fundamentalism on both continents), but each also displays a marked degree of ideological affinity and institutional linkage across the two Americas.

In any case most non-Catholic churches (we are talking of about 3 percent of all church members who are nominally Protestant or *"evan-*

gelista") are perceived as having North American roots, and as purvey-
ors of American values and norms. Indeed America's present doctrinal
diversity and toleration sometimes obscures for Americans—but not for
their hosts—the fact that they are seen elsewhere as integrally a Protestant nation, insensitive and vaguely hostile to the sociological and psychological foundations of a Catholic society. In Latin America, this perception of American Protestantism as culturally alien can lead to a crude
equation. Anti-Protestantism equals anti-Americanism and vice versa
among both radical and conservative Catholics. Even some historic,
mainline Protestants, while tacitly identifying themselves with the social
and political status quo, have also begun to make what Trevor Beeson has
called "the traumatic realization that Protestantism . . . has allowed itself
to become a vehicle for what can only be descirbed as alien cultural penetration and domination" (Beeson 1984:42).

This guilt by association is not only often reinforced by the North
American dress, lifestyle, verbal mannerisms, and managerial style of
much Protestant leadership but also by some identifiable institutional
links. For example, the historic Protestant churches—Methodists, Lu-
therans, Presbyterians, Anglicans, and Episcopalians, although with
smallish, long-established and inward-looking memberships—still retain
close ties with their parent organizations in the United States and Europe. Some para-Christian groups, too—notably the Jehovah's Witnesses and the Mormons (the Moonies are perhaps a separate case) are
not only perceived as expansionist American entities — "Gringo
churches"—but are presumed, correctly, to be extensively and directly
funded from North American sources.

Among the three remaining Protestant groups—the Pentecostals,
the fundamentalist religious sects, and the burgeoning middle-class evangelical churches — American missions and America's mission are most
clearly coincident. Although the Pentecostals — the fastest growing
group numerically (the Assemblies of God have been especially successful in making converts among the poor)—are, in their theology, more visibly linked to the African independent churches than to American charismatic movements, they also possess not only a transnational network
for religious leadership groups within Latin America and other parts of
the Third World, but also operate one which extends back and forth from
Latin America to the United States. In Peru in 1987 they publicized their
somewhat tenuous formal links with Jimmy Swaggart, whose program
was broadcast on the nation's largest private television network at 5:30
a.m. every morning, at a time when the majority of viewers were likely to
be peasant farmers and *campesinos,* a major segment of the Pentecostal
constituency.

Other fundamentalist missionary sects, and the middle-class evangelical churches, such as the Allianza (the Christian and Missionary Alliance), are also spreading and growing. In Peru 431 of the former and twenty-seven of the latter were officially recorded in 1987, and the former have recently been the subject of some scholarly, ecclesiastical (CONEP 1987) and much journalistic attention.[3] While it is clear that the missionary activities of both groups are directed mainly by bureaucracies based in the United States and that their presence may serve in many cases as what Jorge Alvarez Calderon described to me as "a channel for the hegemonic interests of the United States," it still remains difficult to demonstrate any *direct* involvement by United States government agencies in the promotion of fundamentalist sects for secular political ends. The ideological rationale for this—a global offensive against communism—is undoubtedly there, but as yet the evidence for the official use of Protestant missions as a form of low intensity operation is not as conclusive as one would wish. Despite some earlier, historical evidence of United States government links to Protestant missions — such as CIA involvement with missionaries in Brazil, Chile, and Bolivia in the 1950s and 1960s — it is difficult to find firm proof that there are any evangelical movements that are now actively engaged in political resocialization.

It could, in any case, equally well be argued that the present boom in United States-derived fundamentalism has its own internal dynamic and does not require covert manipulation to support United States interests. Such groups, in their middle- and working-class, rural, and urban variants, may already possess a mixture of theological conservatism and traditional anticommunism entirely consonant with the interests of United States foreign policy. These factors may probably be more critical in sustaining hegemony than either direct CIA manipulation or right-wing funding of the electronic church.[4] It could also be argued that an equally plausible explanation for growing working-class sectarianism lies through a serious analysis of the social, economic, and historical problems burdening Latin America's poor. In most countries the rural areas remain solidly Catholic, but over the last quarter century the cities have swollen with peasants seeking work or fleeing guerilla warfare. Uprooted from families, living in slums, politically and socially powerless, many of the poor turn to the sects in fellowship and hope. Many Pentecostal congregations are hardly bigger than an extended family and within these circles the dispossessed find a very personal Jesus. It is, of course, sometimes suggested that Latin American Catholicism has such strong cultural roots, is so much part of personal identity, especially among the poor, that leaving *the* church is not just leaving *a* church; it also means leaving one's culture and fracturing one's social identity. For many Catholics joining an *evangelista* sect requires no such break with the past. Like the Japanese, many Latin Americans have become practiced pluralists, who retain their folk Catholicism (whose saints, if prayed to will still protect them) while relocating their primary Christian allegiance within the new sects. The new, and phenomenal growth of middle- and working-class fundamentalism in Latin America is not wholly explicable in terms of economic deprivation, electronic or dollar imperialism, or even simply because American hegemony remains deceptively strong. There is a fourth explanation. It seems incontrovertible that in Latin America there is clearly a growing challenge to United States national hegemony. Hence, powerful institutions and interest groups (both public and private) in the United States are committed to ensuring that the sects prosper on their behalf. In Peru, for example, the Allianza tend to be almost exclusively middle-class charismatics, while many converts to the New Tribes Mission are predominantly an indigenous and highly marginalized rural proletariat. Both tend to eschew political involvement if only because their members are likely to see personal "salvation" as the only meaningful goal. Both are also precisely the same social groups as those who are judged, in Washington, as well as in Rome, to be highly vulnerable to liberation theology in a religious context and leftism in a political one.

Conclusions

It must be recognized that since Roman times, imperial powers have always used Christian missionaries, converts, movements, and institutions for purposes other than the communication of the Gospel and its liberating power. In Latin America the intrinsically fissile and fragmented nature of many Protestant churches makes them especially vulnerable to an America — and its client states — that increasingly seeks Protestant legitimation as Catholic support appears to waver. They find it as, in their turn, Protestant leaders and their flocks (in a spurious application of *Romans* 13.1) accept or court legitimation from the government of the day.

There are, in any case, three stronger linkages. Institutionally, one notes the connections some of the fundamentalist groups operating in Latin America have with extreme right-wing groups in the United States rather than with United States Government, per se. A tight-knit network of right-wing political, religious, and humanitarian organizations provide the main private support for hard-line economic policies. The main channels of communication — and funding — have been through such "religious transnationals" as World Vision, Campus Crusade for Christ, and

Club 700. Such transnationals tend to be interrelated and have connections with such United States-based fundamentalist bodies as the Moral Majority, the Religious Round Table, the Religious Voice, etc. These are the identifiable core of the so-called religious right and are financed by state organizations, major trusts, and wealthy individuals in the United States, and to a lesser extent by donations from grass-roots American fundamentalists. Most continue to campaign alongside the new (political) right, which supported the hard-line policies—both internal and external —of the Reagan administration. In Latin America and especially Central America, some missionary sects are directly supported by funds from politically conservative television preachers from the United States.

Secondly, in strictly ideological terms there is a clear elision between conservative Protestantism and political conservatism. There is a commonly held core of new right ideology. There is an unreconstructed anticommunism. There can be no accommodation between East and West. There are only two worlds, the communist world represented by Russia, which is socialist and atheistic, and the capitalist world, which is Christian and democratic. This overpolarized, dualist, and ultimately Manichean view of world politics also has an offensive dimension. "The United States must seize the ideological initiative . . . the war is for the minds of mankind" (*SFD* 1980:16). One must fight back. In this sense Rockefeller's 1969 call for an "extensive campaign in Latin America with the aim of propagating Protestant churches and conservative sects" prefigures subsequent and current attempts—such as by the Institute on Religion and Democracy—to use Christianity as a primary mechanism for turning broad political philosophy into effective political strategy.

Finally, such ideological reductionism carries with it at least three sources of ready-made theological legitimation. One is that among many American mission personnel there is an effortless identification of the capture of souls "for Christ," with conquest of "hearts and minds" in the name of Western-style democracy and freedom. As an earnest Adventist couple put it to me in Lima, "For us this is a war for souls, on both fronts." Or in Falwell's own phrase, "Get them saved, baptized and registered."

It is also that beneath the missionary emphasis on the primacy of personal religious experience and on the subjective and existential content of that experience there is, as Max Weber observed long ago, a hard-headed and occasionally hard-hearted core of secular individualism. The third source of right-wing legitimation is the Protestant propensity to explain existing structures as the will of God rather than in terms of the economic relations that they perpetuate. This not only encourages political quiescence but also makes it difficult for individuals to apprehend poverty or unemployment as a structural problem. Instead they tend to presume (as part of a pervasive conviction in new right circles) that it is the "conversion" of the individual rather than the actions of the state that can lead to the solution of collective economic problems. In this sense, as in Thatcherism in Britain, the established, normative structures of development and dependency are consciously displaced by those of personal autonomy and Protestant individualism. Such a mutation is likely to encourage and legitimate the growing intrusion of American-sponsored fundamentalist organizations into Latin America. Not—pace Latourette — because of their missiological imperatives but because they are precisely consonant with a military strategy of low intensity conflict and because they provide an identifiable solution to a hegemonic dilemma — namely that the social and economic fissures within Latin America now increasingly compel the United States to choose between its desire to enhance democratic rights and its wish to defeat Marxism.

Notes

1. J. Lloyd Mecham, *Church and State in Latin America—A History of Politico-Ecclesiastical Relations*, Chapel Hill, University of North Carolina Press 1966, was a useful starting point, followed by the valuable collections of essays edited by Daniel H. Levine "Church and Politics in Latin America," London: Sage, 1979, and "Religion and Political Conflict in Latin America," Chapel Hill: University of North Carolina Press, 1986. The Catholic Church seemed well served by Eric O. Hanson's "Catholic Church in World Politics," Princeton, N.J.: Princeton University Press, 1987, Frederick Turner's "Catholicism and Political Development in Latin America," Chapel Hill: University of North Carolina Press, 1971, and by two excellent monographs — Brian H. Smith's *The Church and Politics in Chile*, Princeton, N.J.: Princeton University Press, 1982, and Daniel H. Levine's *Religion and Politics in Latin America: the Catholic Church Venezuela and Colombia*, Princeton, N.J.: Princeton University Press, 1981. Philip Berryman, *The Religious Roots of Rebellion*, London: SCM Press, 1984, and Edward Cleary *Crisis and Change*, Maryknoll: Orbis Books, 1985, were useful for the theology of liberation.

Protestantism is much less well-served. Rubem Alves' article "Protestantism in Latin America — Its Ideological Function and Utopian Possibilities" in *The Ecumenical Review* XXII No. 1, Jan. 1970, is full of insights, as is the essay by J. M-Bonino in S. Shapiro (ed) "Integration of Man and Society in Latin America," Notre Dame: University of Notre Dame Press, 1967. C. Butler Flora *Pentecostalism in Latin America*, Rutherford, N.J., Fairleigh Dickinson University Press, 1976, is a useful study.

Other sources are as cited under references.

2. Dr. David Lehmann of the Centre for Latin American Studies, University of Cambridge, has a full critique of "cultural Catholicism" in his forthcoming study of ideology in Latin America. I am indebted to him for the quotation from Ferre.

3. David Stoll's *Fisher's of Men or Founders of Empire,* London: Zed Press, 1982: a detailed, if polemical, critique of the Wycliffe Bible Translators' operations in Latin America.

Also Tom Barry et al. *The New Right Humanitarians* (n.p.) and *Report on the Americas* op. cit. Vol. XVIII, no. 1 "The Salvation Brokers — Conservative Evangelicals in Central America" pp. 2–36.

4. It is difficult to assess the impact of the so-called electronic church — and especially its commercialization of religious symbols — on *political* consciousness. In Latin America, radio, as Hugo Assman has suggested, may be more pervasive, and persuasive, than television. *Latinamerica Press* 30 April 1987.

References

Beeson, Trevor, and Jenny Pearce
1978   *A Vision of Hope.* London: Collins.

Cleary, Edward L.
1985   *Crisis and Change.* Maryknoll, N.Y.: Orbis Books.

CONEP (National Evangelical Concilium)
1987   *Report: Lima, Peru.*

Cuenca Communique
1986   Consultation of Latin American Bishops and Pastors. Cuenca, Equador.

DSB (Department of State Bulletin)
1969   "Quality of Life in the Americas—Report of a Presidential Mission for the Western Hemisphere." Washington.

Kirkpatrick, Jean
1985   *The Reagan Doctrine and U.S. Foreign Policy.* Washington: Heritage Foundation.

Klaiber, Jeffrey
1976   *Religion and Revolution in Peru 1824–1976.* Notre Dame, Ind.: University of Notre Dame Press.

LP (Latinamerica Press)
1986   to date. Lima, Peru.

Latourette, Kenneth Scott
1943   *A History of the Expansion of Christianity V.:* New York and London: Harper.

Lermoux, Penny
1980   *Cry of the People.* New York: Doubleday.

Newsweek Magazine

RA (Report on the Americas)
1966   to date. Washington: NACLA.

Reichley, A. James
1985   *Religion in American Public Life.* Washington: Brookings Institution.

SDA (Security and Development Assistance)
1985   *Hearings before the Committee on Foreign Relations.* Washington: U.S. Senate Publications.

SFD (Santa Fe Document)
1980   "Committee of Santa Fe — A New Inter-American Policy for the Eighties": Washington.

Wall Street Journal.

5

Liberation Theology:
Its Implications for Latin American Politics and American Catholicism

Juan Carlos Navarro

The aim of this paper is to assess the impact of liberation theology on contemporary society and politics. The focus is upon the social and political impacts of liberation theology rather than purely doctrinal or theoretical developments within Catholic theology, from the perspective of social science instead of theology. After a brief review of the main characteristics of liberation theology as a social and political phenomenon, I will examine recent sociopolitical changes in Latin America that have been associated with liberation theology. In the third and last section, I look at the implications of liberation theology for American Catholicism.Throughout, the attempt is to develop a systematic but preliminary framework for the analysis of religion and world order.

Liberation Theology as an Intellectual and Social Movement

Let's define liberation theology, to begin with, using the words of Gustavo Gutierrez, recognized as one of most outstanding proponents and for many the founder of liberation theology, as "critical reflection on Christian praxis in the light of the Word." Published in 1970, this brief definition captures the majority of the essential elements included in the liberationist approach to theology, and certainly it is fully compatible with any major development of it ever since. Because our goal here is not theological accuracy but rather operational expedience, I will not try to formulate a more elaborate formal definition accounting for recent doctrinal developments. Instead, I will provide a brief review of some elements, concerning both theory and institutional practices related to it, that have been associated with liberation theology since its original appearance and that, taken as an integrated whole, provide a generally accurate picture of liberation theology as a complex social phenomenon.

The key element, because it provides an organizing core for the rest, is the "preferential option for the poor" or, simply, "option for the poor." One of the most characteristic traits of liberation theology is its insistence on the priority that the Christian religion has to put on the poor, a claim that receives a strong support from the kind of scriptural-based theological reflection typical of the writings and praxis of liberation theologians; as such, the option for the poor has received wide support as a clear and legitimate Christian option not only among Latin American Catholics in general but also from the Vatican and a significant group of major theologians all around the world.

From the option for the poor some additional elements associated with liberation theology can be directly derived: first, the fact that the poor are situated in a privileged position to interpret and understand their personal and social situation, so the task of theology has to be understood as a critical reflection by the poor and with the poor rather than an exclusively theoretical process in which, at best, some thought is given to their situation; this tenet of liberation theology is normally referred to as the hermeneutic privilege of the poor. Such privilege, nevertheless, does not eliminate the need for mediation in the analysis of social and political situations—a point stressed by all liberation theologians—and the mediating role has to be played by the social sciences.

The hermeneutic privilege, in turn, leads to the active promotion of communal forms of organization in which such theological reflection and Christian practice finds its adequate place; self-determination becomes a salient feature of the new Christian communities favored by liberation theology as a model, a model usually well popularized in its Brazilian version, the Basic Ecclesial Communities (BEC), and strikingly contrasting with the traditional church-directed organizations among the lower classes.

The scriptural-based concern for the poor includes also an emphasis on distributive justice that can also find firm roots in the Bible, specially in the Gospels and in the prophetic literature. Such emphasis can be found in almost any work of liberation theology, and it also plays an important role in official documents influenced by it, like those produced by the Latin American bishops in Medellin and Puebla. In a continent where poverty is the rule rather than the exception for vast majorities of people who have been plagued with authoritarian regimes, such commitment to redistribution of material wealth had been accompanied with an emphasis on the defense of human rights and strong criticism of the National Security State. Understandably, in general, liberation theology is less hesitant in discussing political and social conflict as a part of the context in which Christians have to live than previous trends of Christian theology.

Even if they have not been universally welcomed or adequately understood — in fact, sometimes they have been even decidedly opposed — by all Latin American Catholics and members of the institutional church, the combination of the preceding elements led many of them to shift loyalties and develop new and unprecedented commitments in society and politics, sometimes with significant consequences not only in the internal life and organization of the church but also in more inclusive social contexts. Such consequences have varied among individual countries according to particular societal contexts and specific historical legacies received and developed in different regions with respect to the internal life and organization of the church. A detailed comparative analysis of such variations is beyond the scope of this paper, and I refer to some recent and excellent literature available on the subject [Adriance, 1988; Crahan, 1988; Levine, 1981; Maduro, 1982].

There is, however, a different level of analysis in which some general social and political consequences of liberation theology can be found; those consequences, to some extent, can be considered uniform all over the continent and, in turn, are very likely to be the source of any impact that liberation theology might have in other places.

The Implications of Liberation Theology for
Latin American Society and Politics

The more general and influential impact of liberation theology in Latin America has been the profound change that it has produced in the role of the church as an agency of legitimation of the social order. The Catholic church in Latin America played, since the early European conquest, a key role in providing a complete and coherent justification of the social and political order. Culture and society themselves were understood as a Christendom, organically contained in and filled with religious meaning. After the revolutionary wars at the beginning of the nineteenth century, the new independent republics maintained a strained relationship with the institutional church that many times was the source of political conflicts — violent in occasions — but, with a few exceptions, the secular state was not successful in fully replacing the church as an important and in many instances the primary source of legitimation.

By the middle of this century, the Catholic church was still customarily considered an extremely conservative social influence in Latin America, and both popular opinion and expert analysis were used to think about the church as a tacit but natural ally of every military strongman or dictator. Beyond politics, cultural and social conservatism was also the rule almost without exception. Wherever social and political activism could be found in the church, it was with a dominant element of defensive strategies faced with disruptive secular influences or, sometimes, challenging Protestant competitors. Social and political institutions, their relationships with the church, and the role played by religion in society were rarely if ever analyzed or judged, except from the viewpoint of whether they represented a direct threat to the existence of the traditional institutional church. Not surprisingly, a natural affinity prevailed with the dominant classes, except with those groups advancing clear anticlerical agendas, and a vertical and detached attitude was the rule in the relationships with the lower classes.

The last twenty-five years, however, have transformed this picture radically. The links between the Catholic church and the privileged strata have been broken, at least to a significant degree. The church and Catholicism are no longer counted among the ranks of conservative forces, and, on the contrary, they are more often accused of excesses of radicalism than of any other fault. A remarkable feature of this development is that such a drastic shift in loyalties has been made with no loss of moral authority or legitimacy. As David Martin has said, ''Where once the old-style military could rely on the Church, the new-style bureaucratic soldiery of the 'National Security State' often find in the Church the one institution able to maintain and develop a critical independence'' [Martin, 1988, p. 14].

Liberation theology has to be credited with the central role in producing the theoretical framework and the institutional dynamism that has made possible such changes: its relentless insistence on the point that God has to be found among the poor, its emphasis on the mediating role of modern social sciences in analyzing the social environment in which the Church exists, the priority given to the necessity of combining personal conversion and social activism and on building communities where such combination can be adequately developed, its commitment to distributive justice and the defense of human rights, all of these characteristics of liberation theology as an intellectual and social movement are primarily responsible for the kind of transformation just described.[1]

Perhaps the best way of looking at the nature and importance of the changes that are being described is to briefly compare the social and political role of the church face to revolutionary movements in Latin America. An excellent point of comparison can be found in the extremely different attitudes that the institutional church and Catholicism as ideology have played in the Cuban and the Nicaraguan revolutions.

The Cuban Revolution was the occasion of a direct confrontation between the revolutionary government and the church, which had an active and vocal participation in the antirevolutionary movement from the start after a period of silence during the corrupt and repressive dictatorship that preceded the revolution. The church was instrumental in organizing the antirevolutionary sentiment of the middle class, and, more significantly, once the middle and upper classes had left the country, it followed them, leaving Cuba almost without any ecclesiastic organization to take care of the rest of Cubans, who had not enjoyed a well-developed network of church organizations or representatives before the revolution.

More than twenty years later, the Nicaraguan case shows a strikingly different development in spite of the similarities between the ideological and political characteristics of both revolutionary movements and, eventually, governments.[2] People explicitly identified as Catholics played a significant role in the revolution — including four priests in the original cabinet of the revolutionary government — and influenced it in many ways. The bishops participated actively in the opposition to the Somoza regime, even legitimizing the rebellion against it from a Christian viewpoint and insisting on the importance of a democratic commitment from the new government. The church has not left following significant amounts of emigrants.

The most fundamental fact, however, is that the nature itself of the problem faced by the church in the middle of a revolutionary movement has changed. The problem is no longer the inability to develop any significant understanding of the revolutionary process as a consequence of a narrow social identity, but instead the church faces the double challenge of participating in and contributing to a process of change without losing control of its own symbols and legitimacy, without becoming a simple instrument in the game of reactionary or radical forces, and retaining its capacity for criticism and its voice in the defense of human and Christian values. The current divisions in the Nicaraguan church are the living proof of the difficulties found in maintaining such balance but also of the richness of the new approach of the church to a revolutionary process.

The case of a revolution, however, is an extreme one. It has been used in the context of this paper to illustrate the dimension of change in the Latin American Catholic church, and not to suggest that Nicaragua or the particular evolution of the Catholic church in that country should mechanically be taken as a model for the rest of Latin America. The Sandinista Revolution exhibits a typical mix of nationalistic and class-related elements that are usually associated with revolutionary processes in the context of relatively traditional societies with low levels of economic differentiation and political development; it represents one of the possible outcomes of social and political conflict in a country were the path to economic growth and development has yet to be defined and the struggle against a specific dictator becomes identified with the idea and the possibility of the nation. In this connection, the Nicaraguan case shares many essential characteristics with other Central American countries, but it is sharply contrasting with the majority of the rest of Latin American societies.

In such countries, even in those in which sociopolitical or class conflict is divisive and often violent, the societal context is different in some basic aspects: generally speaking, they are societies with more diversified economies, important industrial sectors, relatively more complex social hierarchies and a more structured set of political institutions, so the existence of the nation itself is not really at stake in any particular conflict. In general, they have acquired the basic set social and economic institutions typical of capitalist economies. Experience has shown that socialist governments are not impossible, at least for limited periods of time, but when they occur, they do not usually seize power through a social revolution similar to the Cuban or Nicaraguan movements.

In fact, the most significant change in recent Latin American politics has been the decline of extreme right National Security regimes and their replacement by democratically elected administrations, generally reformist with a popular orientation. Paradoxically, I think that this development—the existence of more or less stable and politically open political regimes in the continent—is the one that represents the next and probably extremely complex challenge to liberation theology.

At the moment of the initial appearance of liberation theology, closed political systems, in which there were few if any opportunities for open criticism of the status quo or for legal, social and political organization of the poor, were prevalent in many Latin American countries, and, even more importantly, the prevailing view of the source and causes of poverty and underdevelopment in the continent were thought to be the joint outcome of the capitalist economic organization and the exploitative relationship between developed countries—especially the United States—and Latin America.

Such view was in part the result of the widespread influence of dependency theory as the dominant theoretical framework in Latin American social sciences at the time, and given the insistence of liberation theologians on the importance of the mediating role of social sciences, dependency theory influenced strongly the first social analyses undertaken by them. At least in some of its well-known versions, dependency theory concluded that any process of real economic development was impossible in Third World countries—and Latin American countries in particular—within a capitalist system, and, therefore, the actual socio-political options were reduced to revolutionary change in the direction of a socialist society or barbaric forms of exploitative capitalism made possible in combination with extremely repressive military regimes. In the political environment in which the early liberation theology developed, such conclusions had credibility, at least as far as the organic relationship between exploitative capitalism and repressive military dictatorships was concerned. The early liberationist, sharing the burden of extreme poverty and political persecution with the lower classes, and the disappointment with respect to capitalism produced by the failure of some Latin American countries in achieving economic and social development in spite of all the expectations that existed during the fifties and early sixties, developed a sympathy—and in some cases explicit adherence—to socialist ideologies and political proposals.

The fact is, however, that socialist revolutions never occurred—except in Nicaragua, of course—and repressive regimes were replaced by relatively open democratic governments across the region, none of which has challenged capitalism as the dominant form of social and economic organization in each country. Economic growth and development seem to be as remote as usual, but orthodox socialist solutions seem to have suffered a significant loss of attraction for a part of Latin American intellectual and political elites. At the same time, the intrinsic desirability of open and democratic political institutions, even in a capitalist system, have come to be appreciated. Dependency theory, in turn, if not completely discredited, has been strongly criticized, and current systematic analyses of underdevelopment tend to emphasize the internal unexploited opportunities for development rather than the negative consequences of international economic subordination.

The consequences of these developments for liberation theology could be, I think, extremely important both at the doctrinal and the practical level. Paul E. Sigmund (1986) has recently suggested that a sort of deradicalization of liberation theology is already taking place, noting that recent publications by leading liberationists seem to be emphasizing solidarity with the poor and community organization rather than class struggle and the idea of revolution as the more likely and desirable outcome of the sociopolitical process in Latin America. If that suggestion proves to be true, both a process of internal maturation in liberation theology as a trend of theological thinking and the just-mentioned changes in the societal environment in which such thinking takes place should be considered responsible for the changing emphasis.

On the practical side, there are good reasons to believe that the availability of open channels of political participation and organization are bound to have an impact in the BEC. In a closed political environment they were, during the long period of military rule, both religious communities and centers of political activism. It remains to be seen how the role of BEC is going to be redefined in a context in which social and political activism is increasingly developed in conventional labor and party organizations and religious communities are no longer the exclusive alternative.[3]

All these developments are recent enough as to inhibit precise predictions concerning their future. One thing is certain: any return to the kind of relationship between church and politics and society typical of the period before liberation theology is not possible; traditional loyalties have been broken, and new ones have been created that will not be easily or rapidly modified. The preceding remarks, however, are intended to convey the general impression that, beyond this crucial but general conclusion, the social and political implications of liberation theology have to be analyzed as a dynamic process both because of the inner evolution of liberation theology and because of the changing environment in which it exists.

Liberation Theology and American Catholicism

In recent years, liberation theology has received increasing attention outside Latin America. Rome has issued at least two official documents exclusively devoted to it, and recent papal statements have either mentioned it or even incorporated some of its characteristic themes. Professional journals of theology in Europe usually contain articles dealing with liberation theology in one way or the other, and Catholic groups in Africa and Asia have generally welcomed liberation theology as compatible with many of their own characteristic concerns.

The United States has not been an exception. Many Latin American Catholics know of and appreciate the efforts of Maryknolls, Jesuits, and others to give publicity to recent liberationist theology in the United States, and the work of many American Catholics in Latin America has produced a better and direct channel of communication that has, no doubt, had an impact in the inner dynamic of the American Catholic church.

It remains to be seen what the real form and dimension of such impact will be. A recent authoritative review of the current situation of American Catholicism was in fact written without even mentioning liberation theology [Coleman, 1988]. On the other hand, even the most superficial reader of "Economic Justice for All," the recent pastoral letter on Catholic social teaching and the United States economy issued by the American Bishops, would have noticed certain similarity between some of the points emphasized by the bishops and well-known themes of liberation theology. In this last section of the paper, I will focus on the content of such letter because, being a very important document by its very nature, it provides at the same time a complex but suggestive picture of the potential and eventual limits of the impact of liberation theology in American Catholicism and society. Given the fact that the letter represents the official opinion of the bishops and it was the result of an extraordinarily wide and open process of consultation, there are good reasons to believe that it is at least partially representative of the dominant views of the American Catholic church.

I think that the influence of liberation theology is specially clear in the priority given by the bishops to the welfare of the poor. They even mention the option for the poor as a basic building block of their discourse, a particularly interesting emphasis in a letter directed to members of the most affluent society in the world. Topics like distributive justice and the moral responsibility of rich nations face to underdeveloped countries play also a salient role in the letter. Direct biblical sources are repeatedly used as starting point in theological reflection.

All these themes are not exclusive of liberation theology: many secular sources can be found in which some of these themes are forcefully articulated, and modern theological thinking—and even official Catholic social teaching — has generally evolved along lines that are consistent with the just-mentioned issues and methods. Other, more practical influences, like the increasing relative importance of Latin American immigrants living in poverty could also be responsible for the new emphases in the letter. It is difficult, however, to avoid the impression that liberation theology can be credited with at least a significant share of the inspiration behind important aspects of the letter.

In fact, as Anthony Tambasco has pointed out, the adoption of some characteristic liberationist viewpoints seems to be combined with some reluctance to accept the whole perspective implied in liberation theology [Tambasco, 1986]. Especially worth noting is the translation of the somewhat conflictual and class-focused approach that is found in liberation theology to a language of rights. The point of whether this is due to insufficient understanding of the Latin American viewpoint, a transitory or essential inability to do full justice to it, or an intentional attempt to develop an argument adapted to the American context is another point that I am not in position to develop fully here; the issue should receive additional attention because its clarification would surely provide fundamental insights in the potential and limits of liberation theology in the American context.

An illustration of the point that has just been made can be found in a brief review of some criticism that the letter has received concerning aspects like preference for the poor, emphasis on distributive justice, and

related concerns [Douglass, 1986; Gannon, 1987]. Some critics have rejected the bishops' message as an unacceptable endorsement of the so-
called liberal agenda in American politics or as dangerous to American
capitalist economy. Even many observers that have been sympathetic
with the intention and the content of the letter have found some of the
points in which an influence of liberation theology is more evident at least
distracting if not irrelevant to the authentic problems of American Catholicism and to the challenge posed by an advanced industrial society to
Catholic social teaching. To such critics, the emphasis on the poor seems
to be at least misplaced in an affluent middle-class society; the priority
given to distributive justice seems unilateral to say the least, and the interventionist state envisaged by the bishops as an important part of their
policy proposals sounds rather old-fashioned even for contemporary specialists that by no means can be considered conservatives in matters of
social or economic policy [Douglass, 1986].

I think that criticisms like these cannot be disregarded without
careful consideration, given the drastic differences between the economic and political environments of South and North America and their
Catholic traditions. It is not automatically clear what the contribution of
liberation theology could be to the revitalized American Catholicism described recently by some commentators, to the "Catholic Moment" in
American culture and society, which they say is about to start [Coleman,
1988]. Many key issues on the American Catholic agenda are simply non-
issues from a liberationist viewpoint — married priests, for instance —
and vice versa. The demographically dynamic, upwardly mobile middle-
class mainstream of American Catholicism seems to be already predominantly tolerant, open and liberal enough in the American social and political context as to accept and probably even be sympathetic to the social
and economic teaching of the bishops, but whether the conditions for a
wider and more profound reception of liberation theology in American
Catholicism are present remains to be seen, as well as the convenience
itself of that reception. One could easily imagine a future Catholic leadership alienating the respect and identity of its followers as a result of the
lack of relevance of their social teaching and, subsequently, losing the
contribution that American Catholicism could make to American society
and the world given its characteristics as a tolerant, relatively open, and
participative version of Catholicism.

As for liberation theology, the alternative to full reception does not
necessarily have to be outright rejection. A probably more fruitful outcome would be, as it has already been, an increased awareness of Latin
American problems in the United States coupled with a process of mutual
enrichment of diverse Catholic traditions. Perhaps the American bishops

have already started to move in such direction if, as some have pointed out [Tambasco, 1986], they have retained the basic insight of the option for the poor, but, well aware of the kind of society to which they are addressing their teaching, they prefer to draw a lesson of self-criticism and self-denial that is different from the Latin American interpretation of the option for the poor, but fully consistent with it.

Closing Remarks

I need not repeat the many partial and provisional points that I have developed in this paper. I would limit myself to insist on what I think are the main points in each section. Concerning the Latin American situation, I have tried to emphasize that liberation theology is an evolving phenomenon, which is and will continue to be changing as a result of both internal development and contextual modifications, and that the recent process of democratization in many Latin American countries, a development to which liberation theology has made an invaluable contribution, probably represents the most important challenge ahead.

In the case of the influence of liberation theology on American Catholicism, the main point is the need to define the relevance of liberation theology to the American context in order to develop adequate expectations concerning any possible adoption of the liberationist perspective by American Catholics, accounting for the drastic difference between sociopolitical contexts and religious traditions of Latin America and the United States.

Notes

1. I have intentionally omitted the role of Christian Democratic political parties in the process under review in order to avoid distractions. I think that such simplification does not introduce a severe bias in the analysis presented in this paper.

2. Again, considerable simplification has been introduced in this part of the argument in order to emphasize the contrast between the Cuban and Nicaraguan revolutions. A complete analysis should pay attention to significant historic differences in the Catholic traditions of both countries, as well as to the extraordinary changes introduced in Catholicism by events like Vatican II, which have no doubt had an influence that is at least partially independent of the changes produced by liberation theology. A recent and much more detailed comparison of the role of the church in both revolutionary processes can be found in Crahan, Margaret, 1988. "Cuba and Nicaragua: Rebellion and Revolution."

3. In a recent paper, I have suggested that the case of the Venezuelan church could have some general interest, given that its recent development, even if profoundly affected by exceptional historic circumstances, has taken place in the most stable, open and nonconflictual political environment in Latin America during the last three decades. See Navarro, Juan Carlos, 1988. "Liberation Theology: The Venezuelan Case."

References

Adriance, Madeleine
1988   "Brazil and Chile: Seeds of Change in the Latin American Church." In *World Catholicism in Transition,* ed. Thomas M. Gannon, S.J. New York: Macmillan.

Coleman, John
1988   "American Catholicism." In *World Catholicism in Transition,* ed. Thomas M. Gannon, S.J. New York: Macmillan.

Crahan, Margaret
1988   "Cuba and Nicaragua: Religion and Revolution." In *World Catholicism in Transition,* ed. Thomas M. Gannon, S.J. New York: Macmillan.

Douglass, R. Bruce, ed.
1986   *The Deeper Meaning of Economic Life: Critical Essays on the U.S. Catholic Bishops' Pastoral Letter on the Economy.* Washington, D.C.: Georgetown University Press.

Douglass, R. Bruce
1986   "First Things First: The Letter and the Common Good Tradition." In *The Deeper Meaning of Economic Life: Critical Essays on the U.S. Catholic Bishops' Pastoral Letter on the Economy,* ed. Bruce R. Douglass. Washington, D.C.: Georgetown University Press.

Gannon, Thomas M., ed.
1987   *The Catholic Challenge to the American Economy: Reflections on the U.S. Bishops' Pastoral Letter on Catholic Social Teaching and the U.S. Economy.* New York: Macmillan.

Gutiérrez, Gustavo
1973   *A Theology of Liberation: History, Politics and Salvation.* Maryknoll, N.Y.: Orbis Books.

1983   *The Power of the Poor in History.* Maryknoll, N.Y.: Orbis Books.

Levine, Daniel H.
1981   *Religion and Politics in Latin America.* New Jersey: Princeton University Press.

Maduro, Otto
1982 "La Specificité Politique du Catholicisme Venezuelien." Mexique: Xth. Congres Mondial de Sociologie. Typescript.

Martin, David
1988 "Catholicism in Transition." In *World Catholicism in Transition*, ed. Thomas M. Gannon, S.J. New York: Macmillan.

Navarro, Juan Carlos
1988 "Liberation Theology: the Venezuelan Case." Atlanta: Association for the Sociology of Religion. Annual Meeting. Typescript.

Second General Conference of Latin American Bishops (Medellin, 1968)
1973 *The Church in the Present-Day Transformation of Latin America in the Light of the Council: Conclusions.* Washington, D.C.: United States Catholic Conference.

Sigmund, Paul E.
1986 "Liberation Theology: An Historical Evaluation." Washington D.C.: The Wilson Center. Working Papers. Typescript.

Tambasco, Anthony
1986 "Option for the Poor." In *The Deeper Meaning of Economic Life: Critical Essays on the U.S. Catholic Bishops' Pastoral Letter on the Economy*, ed. Bruce R. Douglass. Washington, D.C.: Georgetown University Press.

Third General Conference of Latin American Bishops (Puebla, 1979)
1979 "Evangelization in Latin America's Present and Future, Final Document." In *Puebla and Beyond*, ed. Eagleson, J. and P. Scharper. Maryknoll, N.Y.: Orbis Books.

United States Catholic Conference
1987 "Economic Justice for All: Catholic Social Teaching and the U.S. Economy." In *The Catholic Challenge to the American Economy*, ed. Thomas M. Gannon. New York: Macmillan.

6

Martin Luther King, Jr., and the Third World

James H. Cone

When Martin Luther King, Jr., achieved international fame as the leader of the Montgomery bus boycott in 1955–1956, no African country below the Sahara had achieved political independence from the colonial regimes of Europe. When he was assassinated twelve years later (1968) in Memphis, Tennessee, the great majority of African countries had gained their independence. Since 1968, black Africans have continued their "stride toward freedom," overcoming the political domination of Europeans in every country except South Africa. Today black South Africans and their supporters, under the leadership of Archbishop Desmond Tutu, Alan Boesak, Nelson and Winnie Mandela, and a host of others in the African National Congress and similar organizations, are currently engaged in a protracted, life-and-death struggle against apartheid.

As with Africa, similar struggles for freedom happened in Asia and Latin America. The struggles of the poor in all societies remind us that the fires of freedom are burning, and nothing short of justice for all will establish peace and tranquility in the world.

As we reflect upon the significance of the life and thought of Martin Luther King, Jr., for the people of America, it is important to remember that the meaning of his life is not bound by race, nationality, or creed. Speaking of the international significance of his son, Daddy King was correct when he said: "He did not belong to us, he belonged to the world" (King, C. 1969:294). I would add that Martin Luther King, Jr., belonged particularly to the Third World, the world of the poor and the disinherited. It is, therefore, important to ask about his significance for the peoples of Africa, Asia, and Latin America and of their significance for him. What impact did the liberation movements in the Third World (particularly in Africa) have upon the actions and ideas of Martin Luther King, Jr.? What influence did Martin King's life and thought have upon Third World people struggling for freedom?

To answer the first question, I will examine King's writings (published and unpublished) and actions regarding liberation movements in Africa, Asia, and Latin America. Regarding the second question, I will use personal interviews with leaders and workers among grass-roots people (mostly members of the Ecumenical Association of Third World Theologians (EATWOT)[1] showing their impressions of Martin King's influence in their communities. My assessment also will include interviews with Third World university and seminary students residing in the United States and in their respective countries. Lastly, my interpretation will refer to comments about King in the writings and speeches of Third World people, especially among theologians, political leaders, and other informed persons. Hopefully I will be able to give a meaningful interpretation of an image of King that is emerging in the Third World.[2]

The Impact of the Third World upon Martin Luther King, Jr.

Martin King's thinking on this and other questions falls into two periods.[3] The first begins with the Montgomery bus boycott in December 1955 and ends with the enactment of the Voting Rights Bill in August 1965. The second period commences in the fall of 1965 as King begins to analyze more deeply the interrelationship of racism, poverty, and militarism in the policies of the United States government. In both periods his ideas are defined by his faith in the God of justice, love, and hope. The difference between the two periods is the shifting emphases among these attributes as he seeks to develop a nonviolent philosophy of social change that will eliminate racial and economic exploitation and establish peace in America and the world.

During the first period, King's thinking is defined by an *optimistic* belief that justice can be achieved through love, which he identified with nonviolence. The place of the Third World liberation movements in his thinking was to reinforce his liberal optimism regarding the certainty of the rise of a new world order of freedom and equality. In the early months of the Montgomery bus boycott, Martin King began to interpret the black struggle for justice in America as "a part of [an] overall movement in the world in which oppressed people are revolting against . . . imperialism and colonialism . . . '' (King 1956a). He believed that black people's fight against segregation in America was identical with the spirit that led Africans, Asians, and Latin Americans to revolt against their European colonizers. Both revolts (blacks in the American and the poor in the Third World), according to King, signify "the birth of a new age." Using that phrase for the title of an address to the Alpha Phi Alpha Fraternity (August 1956), he said: third World people have "lived for years and centuries under the yoke of foreign power, and they were dominated politically, exploited economically, segregated and humiliated" (King 1956b:86). Because King saw little difference between colonialism in Africa and segregation in America, he employed the same language to describe both experiences. Speaking about the impatience of black and Third World peoples with oppression, King often said:

> There comes a time when people grow tired, when the throbbing desires of freedom begin to break forth. There comes a time when people get tired of being trampled over by the iron feet of the tramper. There comes a time when people get tired of being plunged across the abyss of exploitation, where they have experienced the bleakness and madness of despair. There comes a time when people get tired of being pushed out of the glittering sunlight of life's July and left standing in the pitying state of an Alpine November. (King 1956b:86)

With this and many statements like it, King's point was to emphasize that black and Third World people became fed up with segregation and colonialism. "In the midst of their tiredness," something happened to them. They began to reevaluate themselves, and as a result, they "decided to rise up in protest against injustice" (King 1957a:26). The protests of the oppressed throughout the world, King believed, were nothing but a signal that "the time for freedom has come" (1961). No resistance from the oppressors can abort freedom's birth because, as King often said (quoting Victor Hugo), "there is no greater power on earth than an idea whose time has come" (1961:25).

Martin King's travels to the independence celebration of Ghana (1957), the rapid achievement of the independence of other Third World nations, and his study-tour of India (1959) deepened his optimism that freedom would soon be achieved.[4] Analyzing the motivations of students in the sit-in movements (which also reflected his own views), King wrote:

> Many of the students, when pressed to express their inner feelings, identify themselves with students in Africa, Asia and South America. The liberation struggle in Africa has been the greatest single international influence on American Negro students. Frequently I

hear them say that if their African brothers [and sisters] can break
the bonds of colonialism, surely the American Negro can break Jim
Crow. (1961:118)

King's optimism regarding the prospect of freedom's achievement
is derived partly from the success of the civil rights movement in America
and liberation movements in the Third World. The Montgomery bus boycott, sit-ins and freedom rides, Birmingham, March on Washington,
Selma March, and other less-publicized civil rights victories throughout
the South—all were linked with the success of anticolonialist movements
in the Third World. King believed that freedom's time had come because
oppressed peoples all over the world were demonstrating that they would
no longer accept passively their exclusion from the material riches of
God's creation.

In Martin King's view, segregation in America and colonialism in
the Third World are nothing but the denial of the dignity and worth of human beings. Both the segregator and the colonialist are saying by their
actions that blacks and other colored people are inferior beings, incapable
of governing themselves or living in a relationship of equality with white
Americans and Europeans. As long as there was insufficient resistance
from black and Third World peoples, the old order of segregation and colonialism remained unchanged. The new age of freedom began to break
forth when a "new Negro" was born in America and a "new human
being" began to rise up from among the ragged and hungry masses of the
world. Armed with a new sense of dignity and self-respect, both started
to march together toward the promised land of freedom.

Martin King's optimism about the new world order is portrayed
with passion and excitement in his early speeches.

Those of us who live in the Twentieth Century are privileged to live
in one of the most momentous periods of human history. It is an ex-
citing age filled with hope. It is an age in which a new social order is
being born. We stand today between two worlds—the dying old and
the emerging new. (1957a:25)

King was aware that not everyone shared his euphoria about the
coming new age, especially the guardians of the vanishing old order.

I am aware of the fact that there are those who would argue that we
live in the most ghastly period of human history. They would argue
that ... the deep rumblings of the discontent from Asia, the uprisings in Africa ... and the racial tensions of America are all indica-

tive of the deep and tragic midnight which encompasses our civilization. They would argue that we are retrogressing instead of progressing. (1957a:25)

To answer the critics of Third World liberation and civil rights movements, King employs the liberal theological perspective dominant in the social gospel movement in the late nineteenth and early twentieth centuries.

Far from representing retrogression or tragic meaninglessness, the present tension represents the necessary pains that accompany the birth of anything new. Long ago the Greek philosopher, Heraclitus argued that justice emerges from the strife of opposites, and Hegel, in modern philosophy, preached a doctrine of growth through struggle. It is historically and biologically true that there can be no birth and growth without birth and growing pains. Whenever there is the emergence of the new we confront the recalcitrance of the old. So the tensions which we witness in the world today are indicative of the fact that a new world order is being born and an old order is passing away. (1957a:25)

Of course, Martin King was aware that oppressors do not voluntarily grant freedom to the oppressed. He was also aware that white segregationists and European colonists had much more military power than their victims. Yet he contended that the coming of new world order of freedom was inevitable. How could he be so sure? The answer is found in his faith in the biblical God of justice, love, and hope. No idea or strategy that King advocated can be understood correctly apart from his deep faith in the Christian God as defined by the black Baptist and liberal Protestant traditions. The new age is coming and cannot be stopped because God, who is just and loving, wills that the oppressed be liberated. That is why King can say:

Oppressed people cannot remain oppressed forever. The urge for freedom will eventually come. This is what happened to the American Negro. Something within has reminded him of his birthright of freedom; something without has reminded him that he can gain it. Consciously and unconsciously, he has been swept in by what the Germans call the *Zeitgeist,* and with his black brothers of Africa, and his brown and yellow brothers of Asia, South America, and the Caribbean, he is moving with a sense of cosmic urgency toward the promised land of racial justice. (1963:8)

The German word, *Zeitgeist,* was employed often by King to refer to his belief that "the universe is under the control of a loving purpose, and that in the struggle for righteousness [we have] cosmic companionship" (1981a:154). This is what he had in mind when he said that Rosa Parks "had been tracked down by the *Zeitgeist*—the spirt of the times" (1958:44). He made a similar statement in relation to himself when he offered his resignation to Dexter Avenue Baptist Church in Montgomery: "I can't stop now. History has thrust something upon me which I cannot turn away . . . " (King, C. 1969:183). King was referring to a historical movement of freedom that was rooted in ultimate reality and thus was not exclusively dependent on human decisions.

The role of God in King's idea of the coming new age is reflected also in his use of the striking image of the "dream." Although he spoke often of the "American Dream," referring to the idea of equality in the Declaration of Independence, the Constitution, and the Jewish-Christian scriptures, King's dream, however, was not limited to racial equality in the United States but was defined chiefly by its universality and eternality. To say that the dream is universal means that it is for all—blacks and whites, men and women, the peoples of Africa, Asia, Latin America, the United States, and Europe. To say that it is eternal means that equality is not a right conferred by the state; it is derived from God, the creator of all life.

When Martin King urges people to "make the dream a reality" or to "face the challenge of a new age," he almost always tells them to "develop a world perspective." "All life is inter-related" because God is the creator of all. "No individual . . . [or] nation can live alone" because we are made for each other. No people can be who they ought to be until others are who they ought to be. "This is the way the world is made" (1968) (a).

When Martin King received the Nobel Peace Prize in 1964, it deepened his commitment to global justice and peace and reinforced his belief that God willed it. "I have the audacity to believe," he said in his acceptance speech, "that people everywhere can have three meals a day for their bodies, education and culture for their minds, and dignity, equality, and freedom for their spirits" (1968b:21). For King, the Nobel Prize was an "unutterable fulfillment," given in recognition of those fighting for freedom all over the world. His dream of a coming new age of freedom is eloquently expressed in his "Nobel Lecture."

What we are seeing now is a freedom explosion. . . . The deep rumbling of discontent that we hear today is the thunder of disinherited masses, rising from dungeons of oppression to the bright hills of freedom. . . . All over the world, like a fever, the freedom movement is spreading in the widest liberation in history. The great masses of people are determined to end the exploitation of their races and land. They are awake and moving toward their goal like a tidal wave. You can hear them rumbling in every village, street, on the docks, in the houses, among the students, in the churches and at political meetings. (1964:5)

Because God is involved in the freedom struggles, King believed that it cannot be halted. Victory is inevitable. Success in the civil rights and Third World liberation movements combined with his deep faith in God's loving justice gave King an optimistic hope that freedom was not too far away.

Many persons have misunderstood Martin King's commitment to nonviolence because they have separated it from his faith in God. While he encouraged persons without his faith to endorse nonviolence for the practical reason that neither black nor Third World peoples have the military technology to wage a violent fight for freedom, King's *own* commitment to nonviolence was derived from his faith in a loving and just God who created us for each other and for eternity. He did not believe that one could participate with God in the creation of the beloved community and at the same time use violent methods. Violence is derived from hate, and hate contradicts God. People who use violence have lost faith in the God of love and, thus, have lost hope that a beloved community can be created.

Nothing is more central to King's philosophy than the idea that oppressed people must use moral means to achieve just ends. Whether he spoke of the civil rights struggle in the United States or of Third World liberation struggles, he was certain that nonviolence was the "only road to freedom." (1966a). He was pleased that Ghana and other African nations had achieved their independence with little or no violence. Gandhi's success in India had an even greater impact upon King. "I left India," he said, "more convinced than ever before that nonviolent resistance is the most potent weapon available to oppressed people in their struggle for freedom" (1959:86).

Much more important than the success of nonviolence in India or Ghana or even the civil rights movement was Martin King's faith in a God of justice and love. King's faith and theology enabled him to reject violence absolutely while, at the same time, granting him the conviction that a new order of justice is coming into being. His affirmation of nonviolence is derived from his deep conviction that there is a personal, creative, divine power at work in the world establishing freedom in and through the nonviolent actions of the weak and helpless.

Turning to the second period of King's thought, 1965–1968, I want to emphasize that certain bedrock ideas did *not* change. He did not change his mind regarding the basic principles of his faith or regarding the goal of freedom in the civil rights movement. In fact, his convictions regarding God's will to inaugurate a new age of freedom were deepened in the last years as he gave himself totally to the struggles for justice and peace in America and the world. His faith in nonviolence remained completely unshakeable. What, then, was new or newly emphasized in the later period?

1. One thing was his great disappointment regarding the failure of the majority of white moderates in the North and South (in government, labor, church, business, and even the civil rights movement) to support the goal of genuine equality for blacks and other poor people. For several years he thought that he could win the support of the decent, "white majority" in America through a moral appeal to religion and the democratic traditions, which they claimed to live by. As early as his *Playboy* interview (January 1965), however, he acknowledged his great letdown regarding government officials and white moderates:

> I have been dismayed at the degree to which abysmal ignorance seems to prevail among many state, city and even Federal officials on the whole question of racial justice and injustice. . . . But this white failure to comprehend the depth and dimension of the Negro problem is far from being peculiar to Government officials. . . . It seems to be a malady even among those whites who like to regard themselves as "enlightened." . . . I wonder at [persons] who dare to feel that they have some paternalistic right to set the timetable for another [person's] liberation. Over the past several years, I must say, I have been gravely disappointed with such white "moderates." I am inclined to think that they are more of a stumbling block to the Negro's progress than the White Citizens' Counciler or the Ku Klux Klanner. (1965)

When summer riots became a regular occurrence during the second half of the 1960s, King became impatient with whites who withdrew their support for the civil rights movement and began to say that "law and order" ought to be the highest priority of government. "I say to you," proclaimed King, " . . . the riots are caused by nice gentle, timid white moderates who are more concerned about order than justice . . . " (1967a:9).

Martin King's disappointment with moderate whites reached its peak during his preparations for the Poor People's campaign only a few weeks before his death. According to King, racism was a disease, a cancer in the body politic, but many whites seemed unconcerned about it as he deepened his analysis of the "sickness of America" (1968c). White indifference to racism puzzled him:

> The thing wrong with America is white racism. White folks are not right. Now they've been making a lot of studies about the Negro, about the ghetto, about slums. It's time for America to have an intensified study on what's wrong with white folks. . . . Anybody that will go around bombing houses and churches, it's something wrong with him. (1968d:3-4)

2. Another disappointment for Martin King was his failure to win the support of the majority of blacks to nonviolent direct action as the primary method for gaining their freedom. The Watts riot (August 1965) and others, which followed in the urban centers (along with Black Power), revealed the great gap between King's optimism about nonviolence and the despair found in the random acts of violence in the ghettos of American cities.

During the first ten years, Martin King and others in the southern-based civil rights movement had assumed that blacks of the North would benefit in a derivative fashion from the victories gained in the South. The Watts riot and the subsequent rise of Black Power during the Meredith March (June 1966) showed that King badly miscalculated the self-esteem that northern blacks would receive from "straightened up backs" of southern blacks. When he went to Watts, he was surprised that many blacks there had never heard of him, and even more astonished when he heard a group of young blacks boasting, "We won." "How can you say you won," King asked, "when thirty-four Negroes are dead, your community is destroyed, and whites are using the riots as an excuse for inaction?" "We won because we made them pay attention to us," they responded to him (1968e:112). When King reflected on that response and the hostile reactions his message of nonviolence received from Chicago street gangs and young Black Power advocates during the Meredith March, he began to realize that the Civil Rights Act (1964) and the Voting Rights Bill (1965) did not affect significantly the problems of racism and poverty, especially among northern blacks.

To Martin King's further dismay, some black preachers and theologians began to support openly the rise of Black Power by interpreting positively the Christian Gospel in its light.[5] No longer willing to endorse King's absolute commitment to nonviolence, they began to move toward the black nationalism of Malcolm X and even to talk about the revolutionary writings of Franz Fanon, especially *The Wretched of the Earth,* in an affirmative manner.

3. Martin King experienced a third disappointment. He expected the success of American blacks with nonviolence to help persuade the majority of the oppressed of Africa, Asia, and Latin America to adopt a similar method in their struggles for freedom. Instead of adopting the creative method of nonviolence, however, many Third World people were openly advocating armed revolution. King was aware that even some theologians in Latin America were joining revolutionary groups in their efforts to overthrow oppressive governments.

All of this caused him to reevaluate *not* the efficacy of nonviolence but the depth of the problem of injustice in a global manner. When King began to analyze seriously global injustice, he concluded that the three evils of racism, poverty, and militarism were interrelated and deeply rooted, both in the sociopolitical life of America and in the international economic order. King's focus on the global implications of racism in relation to poverty and war led him to the conclusion that the slums in American cities are a "system of internal colonialism" (1966b:3)[6] not unlike the exploitation in the Third World by European nations.

> I am appalled that some people feel that the civil rights struggle is over because we have a 1964 civil rights bill with ten titles and a voting rights bill. Over and over again people ask, What else do you want? They feel that everything is all right. Well, let them look around at our big cities. (in Oates 1982:390)

King's global vision helped him to see that the sociopolitical freedom of blacks was closely tied to the liberation of their sisters and brothers in Africa, Asia, and Latin America. Token integration (that is, a few professionals moving into the existing mainstream of American society) was not true freedom. "Let us," King wrote in *Where Do We Go From Here?*, "not think of our movement as one that seeks to integrate the Negro into all the existing values of American society" (1968e:133).

The economic exploitation of the Third World nations and the deepening poverty of the poor in the United States led King to the conclusion that there is something desperately wrong with America (1968e:133).

> Why are there forty million poor people in a nation overflowing with such unbelievable affluence? Why has our nation placed itself in the position of being God's military agent on earth, and intervened recklessly in Vietnam and the Dominican Republic? Why have we substituted the arrogant undertaking of policing the whole world for the high task of putting our own house in order?

These questions suggested to King the "need for a radical restructuring of the architecture of American society" (1968e:133), so that it can serve the needs of humanity throughout the world. That was why he said:

> However deeply American Negroes are caught in the struggle to be at last at home in our homeland of the United States, we cannot ignore the large world house in which we are also dwellers. Equality with whites will not solve the problems of either whites or Negroes if it means equality in a world society stricken by poverty and in a universe doomed to extinction by war. (1968e:167)

4. The later years of Martin King's theology are also defined by a shift in emphasis and meaning regarding the themes of love, justice, and hope. Except for his great Holt Street address (December 5, 1955), with its powerful focus on justice, the first period of King's spiritual and intellectual development is centered on love, with justice and hope being interpreted in its light.[7] As a result of the bleak reflections just described, hope becomes the center of Martin King's thinking, with love and justice being interpreted in *its* light. The main difference between his early and later years regarding the idea of hope is this: In the early period, King's hope was similar to a naive optimism because it was partly based on the progress of the freedom movement in America and the Third World and the support it received from both the oppressed (by their active commitment to nonviolence) and the majority in the dominant classes (by their apparent commitment to formal equality). In contrast, King's hope, in the later years, was not based upon the backing he received from blacks and whites in the United States or from the international community. Rather, his hope was grounded almost exclusively upon his faith in the God of the biblical and black traditions who told him, during the early months of the Montgomery bus boycott: "Stand up for righteousness. Stand up for justice. Stand up for truth. And lo, I will be with you, even until the end of the world" (1967b:14).[8]

Instead of trusting human allies to produce a victory over the forces of organized evil, King's hope was now a transcendent one, focusing on the biblical God of the oppressed who "put down the mighty from their thrones, and exalted those of low degree" (Luke 1:52 RSV). This comes out in his critique of Vietnam, which he knew would alienate his former allies.

5. Nothing pained Martin King more than America's military involvement in Vietnam and the criticisms he received from his white and black friends (in government, media, and the civil rights movement) for opposing it. America's escalation of the war in Vietnam, along with a de-escalation of the war on poverty and its indifference toward massive pov-

erty in the Third World, motivated King to become one of the most severe
critics of the domestic and foreign policies of his government during the
second half of the 1960s. He begins to speak like a prophet, standing before the day of judgment, proclaiming God's wrath and indignation upon
a rich and powerful nation that was blind to justice at home and indifferent
to world peace. Instead of speaking of the American dream as he had
done so eloquently in the first half of the 1960s, he began to speak, over
and over again, of an American nightmare, especially in Vietnam.[9]

Martin King did not enjoy criticizing his government. He loved
America deeply, particularly its democratic and religious traditions of
equality and justice as articulated in the Declaration of Independence,
the Constitution, and the Jewish-Christian scriptures, but he could not
overlook the great contradictions of racism, poverty, and militarism. For
King there was no greater inconsistency between creed and deed than
America's military adventures in Vietnam. He frequently referred to
Vietnam as a small nation of people that quoted our Declaration of Independence in its own document of freedom when the people declared their
independence from the French in 1945. "Yet," King said, "our government refused to recognize them. President Truman said they were not
ready for independence. So we fell victim as a nation at that time of the
same deadly arrogance that has poisoned the international situation for
all these years" (1967c:8).

The arrogance that King was referring to was racism. "I don't believe," he wrote in a *Playboy* essay:

> We can have world peace until America has an "integrated" foreign
> policy. Our disastrous experiments in Vietnam and the Dominican
> Republic have been . . . a result of racist decision making. Men of
> the white West . . . have grown up in a racist culture, and their think-
> ing is colored by that fact. . . . They don't respect anyone who is not
> white. (1969:4)

King also felt that the vehement criticisms that he received from the
white community regarding his opposition to the Vietnam war were motivated by racism. He spoke against his white allies in government and the
media who supported his stand on nonviolence during the sit-ins and
freedom rides and in Birmingham and Selma and then rejected his position on Vietnam (1967c:6).

> They applauded us in the sit-in movement when we nonviolently de-
> cided to sit in at lunch counters. They applauded us on the freedom
> rides when we accepted blows without retaliation. They praised us

in . . . Birmingham and Selma, Alabama. Oh, the press was so noble
in its applause and . . . praise when I would say "Be nonviolent
toward Bull Connor," . . . "Be nonviolent toward Jim Clark." There
is something strangely inconsistent about a nation and a press that
would praise you when you say, "Be nonviolent toward Jim Clark,"
but will curse and damn you when you say," Be nonviolent toward
little brown Vietnamese children!"

Many blacks in the civil rights movement joined the chorus of criticisms against King's views on Vietnam. There were even sharp disagreements about Vietnam within the Southern Christian Leadership Conference (SCLC). King often found himself alone and isolated. In one of the
most agonizing periods of his life, he turned to the God of the prophets
and Jesus as he took his stand for humanity. "It is just as evil," he proclaimed in a sermon at Ebenezer, "to kill Vietnamese as it is to kill Americans, because they are all God's children" (1966c:9).

Martin King refused to accept the idea that being an American citizen obligated him to support his country in an unjust war. He refused to
equate "dissent with disloyalty," as many of his critics did. On the contrary, he contended that he was the true patriot because in his opposition
to the war, he was in reality defending America's tradition of freedom and
democracy, which was being violated in Vietnam. Furthermore, as a Nobel Laureate, King believed that he was obligated to transcend nationalism, and thereby to take a stand for world peace. Much more important
than his obligation as an American citizen or of the world was his vocation as a minister of God, the creator of universe. When people queried
him about the wisdom of mixing peace and civil rights, King responded:

Before I was a civil rights leader, I answered a call, and when God
speaks, who can but prophesy? I answered a call which left the
spirit of the Lord upon me and anointed me to preach the gospel. . . .
I decided then that I was going to tell the truth as God revealed it to
me. No matter how many people disagreed with me, I decided that
I was going to tell the truth. (1967c:3,4)

For Martin King, telling the truth meant proclaiming God's judgment upon America for its failure to use its technological resources for
the good of humanity. "Here we spend thirty-five billion dollars a year to
fight this terrible war in Vietnam and just the other day the Congress refused to vote forty-four million to get rid of rats in the slums and the ghet-
toes of our country" (1967d:7–8). "The judgment of God is on America
now" (1967d:6), he said. He compared America to the rich man, Dives,

who passed by the poor man, Lazarus, and never saw him. Like Dives, who went to hell because he refused to use his wealth to bridge the gulf that separated him from Lazarus, "America," King said, "is going to hell too, if she fails to bridge the gulf" (1968f:13) that separates blacks from whites, the United States and Europe from the Third World.

Martin King believed that America's war in Vietnam violated its own democratic values and the moral principles of the universe; he could not keep silent. There comes a time "when silence is betrayal" (1982:1). A nation that spends $500,000 to kill an enemy soldier in Vietnam and only $50 to get one of its citizens out of poverty is a nation that will be destroyed by its own moral contradictions.[10] "If something doesn't happen soon," King said, "I'm convinced that the curtain of doom is coming down on the U.S." (1968g:7). The more the American government and its citizens tried to ignore King, the more forcefully he proclaimed his message:

> America, I don't plan to let you rest until that day comes into being when all God's children will be respected, and every [person] will respect the dignity and worth of human personality. America, I don't plan to allow you to rest until from every city hall in this country, justice will roll down like waters and righteousness like a mighty stream. America, I don't plan to let you rest until from every state house . . . , men will sit humbly before their God. America, I don't plan to let you rest until you live it out that "all . . . are created equal and endowed by their creator with certain inalienable right." America, I don't plan to let you rest until you believe what you have read in your Bible that out of one blood God made all [people] to dwell upon the face of the earth. (1967e:15)

Although King was often depressed about his government's refusal to stop the war in Vietnam and to eliminate poverty at home and in the Third World, he did not lose hope. In "A Christmas Sermon on Peace," he proclaimed that despite the nightmare of racism, poverty and war, "I still have a dream, because . . . you can't give up on life. If you lose hope, . . . you lose that courage to be, that quality that helps you to go on in spite of all" (1967f:76).

Martin King's hope sustained him in the midst of controversy, enabling him to make solidarity with the victims of the world, even though he failed to achieve the justice for which he gave his life. King's hope was grounded in the saving power of the cross of Jesus Christ, and it enabled him to see the certainty of victory in the context of an apparent defeat.

When you stand up for justice, you never fail. The forces that have the power to make concession to the forces of justice and truth . . . but refuse to do it . . . are the forces that fail. . . . If there is no response from the federal government, from the Congress, that's the failure, not those who are struggling for justice. (1968h:11)

The Impact of Martin Luther King, Jr., in the Third World

No black American or American church official and few Americans of any profession have made an international impact in the area of justice and peace comparable to that of Martin Luther King, Jr. This is particularly true in Africa, Asia, and Latin America, where the vast majority of the people are colored and poor. Martin King's influence may be described at two levels: symbolic and substantive.

The symbolic influence of Martin King in the Third World can be seen in four areas: (1) as a symbol of the black struggle for justice in the United States; (2) as a symbol of the Third World peoples' struggles for justice against colonialism and neocolonialism; (3) as a symbol of the best in the American democratic and Christian traditions; and (4) as a symbol of the struggle for world peace through nonviolence.

1. The name, Martin Luther King, Jr., is widely known in Africa, Asia, and Latin America as the symbol of the United States civil rights movement during the 1950s and 1960s. He is thought of as the leader of black people's successful struggle for constitutional rights, emphasizing that Americans of all races must learn to live together in a beloved community, defined by justice and love, or they will perish together as fools.

Martin King's international prominence began with the Montgomery bus boycott. People admired his commitment to justice and his courage to stand up to white bigots of the American South with intelligence, dignity, and Christian love. Many Third World people wrote to King informing him of the inspiration they received from his leadership. "What you are doing," wrote a person from Singapore, "is a real inspiration to us here in the part of the world where the struggle between democracy and communism is raging" (1958:81).

In addition to the Montgomery bus boycott, King is also known for his success in gaining constitutional rights for blacks, his solidarity with the black poor, even to the point of giving his life, and his elevation to a national symbol of America with his birthday as a federal holiday.

During the 1950s and 1960s and, to a large degree, through much of the 1970s and 1980s, most Third World persons thought of King almost exclusively as a symbol of black people's struggle for equality in the

United States. Now that King has been made a national symbol, some leading Third World theologians and scholars say that many persons in their countries mistakenly conclude that full freedom has been granted to black Americans. As evidence that blacks have been integrated success-fully into American society, they not only point to Martin King's name as a national symbol of the country, but they also refer to the electoral suc-cess of many well-known disciples of King, such as Jesse Jackson and Andrew Young, to support their claim. Other highly visible black person-alities in politics, business, media, movies, sports, and music are often mentioned to demonstrate that racism is a thing of the past in the United States.

The assumption that African-Americans have achieved equality in American society has led to an alienation between African-Americans and Third World persons struggling for freedom. Consequently, when the United States is criticized for its military excesses or for stifling demo-cratic change in the Third World (as is often the case), many do not make distinctions between white and black Americans.

2. While some Third World peoples' image of Martin King defines him primarily as a black leader of the civil rights movement, others view him as transcending race, nation, and religion. For these persons, King is a symbol of poor people on all continents who are fighting against racism, poverty, and political oppression. Four things served to make Martin King's name an important symbol of the poor fighting for justice in the Third World: (a) his association with the black freedom songs of the civil rights movement, especially its theme song, "We Shall Overcome"; (b) his devotion to the life and teachings of Gandhi, a prominent figure in the Third World; (c) King's interpretation of the Nobel Peace Prize as placing him in solidarity with "two-thirds of the people who go to bed hungry at night" (1964:13); and (d) his passionate opposition to the war in Vietnam, defending the right of self-determination of a small colored nation.

The theme song of the civil rights movement, "We Shall Over-come," is widely used by oppressed groups in Africa, Asia, and Latin America. I have heard it sung by the masses in many countries on all con-tinents. I will never forget when I first heard it in South Korea. It was in May 1975, in the context of the infamous "Presidential Emergency Mea-sure No. 9" of the Park regime. I had been invited to lecture on a black theology of liberation. The situation was filled with tension as the Korean CIA (KCIA) agents carefully proctored the occasion. I was fearful that I might say something that would cause some of my Korean friends to be arrested. I spoke about the black struggle for justice in the United States, hoping that my frequent use of the black spirituals of slavery would cam-ouflage (for the KCIA) the political implications of my talk for the current struggle for democracy in Korea. I was greatly moved when the Korean audience responded by singing enthusiastically "We Shall Overcome."

Third World nations have paid tribute to Martin King's memory in many ways. The most popular has been to recognize his birthday with special programs, recalling his words and deeds on behalf of the poor. Governments also frequently recognize King with the issuance of commemorative postage stamps. Still another way is to have his name attached to streets, libraries, parks, and other public properties.[11]

A special session of the United Nations' Special Committee against Apartheid was held in Atlanta (January 1979)—"International Tribute to Martin Luther King, Jr." Most of the participants were representatives of Nations of Africa, Asia, and Latin America. They used the occasion to define King as "one of the most courageous freedom fighters of our times" who "fought for the liberation of the oppressed all over the world" (Collins in United Nations 1979:46).

Because King is viewed as "an inspiring example to the liberation struggle the world over" (Vomani in United Nations 1979:23), some Third World people resent the use of his name as a symbol of the nation that they regard as the major enemy of Third World initiatives toward freedom. Tissa Balasuriya, director of the Centre for Society and Religion (Columbo, Sri Lanka) and Asian coordinator of the Ecumenical Association of Third World Theologians, puts it sharply: "America kills him, and then makes a hero of him in order to neutralize his true meaning. To attack the leaders for justice during their lifetime and then, after killing them, to incorporate them into the value system is to perform a contradiction far greater than the ones that King spoke out vehemently against" (1986).[12]

3. As one who appealed to the moral conscience of America, King became known as a person who represented the best in the Christian and the democratic traditions of freedom in the United States. By his frequent references to the Declaration of Independence, the Constitution, and the Bible in his sermons and addresses, King presented a compelling perspective on American culture and its people that Third World people rarely know much about.

The peoples of the Third World are mainly poor, colored, and devotees of other faiths than Christianity. The people of the United States are chiefly affluent, white, and adherents of the Christian faith. King was a Christian black and identified with the poor everywhere; he helped many Third World people to make a distinction between the American government's foreign policy and the will of its people. This has especially been true in regard to the peoples of Southeast Asia, Southern Africa, and Central America. With the Bible in one hand and the Declaration of

Independence in the other, King challenged the American government to use its great technological resources for good and not evil. In the *La Nueva Biblia Latinoamericana* (1972), King's photo is appropriately placed among the prophets of the Old Testament, opposite of the one of Don Helder Camara, with the comment that he was a pastor and freedom fighter who was assassinated like other prophets.

4. Nothing established King as a symbol of peace in the Third World more than his devotion to nonviolence and his heroic opposition to the war in Vietnam. He is a dominant personality in many peace organizations in Africa, Asia, and Latin America. In some instances, the King image is more widely used among non-Christian groups than among Christians in the Third World. This is especially true in Asia, where Gandhi and King often appear together as symbols of achieving peace through nonviolence.

The Christian identity of Martin King has made it possible for a few Christians to work for world peace in societies that are predominately non-Christian and in which Christian churches seem essentially white, Western, and indifferent to peace. Ironically, King is often not as influential among Christian groups as he is among student, peace, and left-oriented intellectuals interested in developing a methodology of social change.

Martin King's Substantive Impact in the Third World

The substantive impact of Martin King refers to those instances in which Third World people have studied seriously his ideas and actions for the purpose of assessing their usefulness in their struggles for freedom. King's life and writings have been examined primarily in the context of a small number of Third World Christians who are interested in the role of the church in societies defined by poverty, racism, and political oppression. Like King, they have asked: What methods of social change are ethically appropriate and inappropriate for Christians who are fighting for justice in society? In regard to their debate about Martin King, the issue, as most would expect, has focused on his absolute commitment to nonviolence, with some Third World Christians agreeing with King and others seriously questioning the applicability of his perspective for their situation.

It is, perhaps, accurate to say that most Third World theologians (who are actively engaged in the struggle against poverty, racism, and political repression) disagree with Martin King's absolute commitment to nonviolence. During the 1950s and early 1960s, Third World activist Christians and theologians shared King's optimism about the coming new age, a time when colonialism and imperialism will be no more. African and Asian nations were rapidly gaining political independence from their European colonizers, and the United States and Latin American nations were making an "alliance for progress." By the middle of the 1960s, however, it had become clear to many of the Third World analysts that what the United Nations had called the "decade for development" (1950s) was in fact a decade of dependence. The economic gap between the rich nations of Europe and North America and the poor nations of Africa, Asia, and Latin America was growing wider instead of narrowing. When Third World activists, Christians, and theologians began to study history and the social sciences, they discovered that their economic deprivation was a logical development of their dependent relation with rich nations. Their analysis of the political situation of their countries and of the international economic order convinced many that poverty in the Third World is created by unfavorable trade relations between rich and poor nations and unjust economic relations between haves and have-nots within nations. Because oppressors do not give up their privileges through an appeal to morality, it is questionable whether nonviolence is *always the most appropriate method for dislodging priviledged classes. This perspective on ethics naturally placed these activist Christians into sharp debate with King's philosophy of nonviolence.*

The first major international discussion of the relevance of King's views on nonviolence for the Third World happened at the World Council of Churches' (WCC) well-known World Conference on Church and Society in Geneva, Switzerland, July 1966. There were 420 participants from eighty nations and 164 churches, with almost half from Africa, Asia, and Latin America. According to the official report, "the Conference was charged with advising the churches and the WCC on their ministry in a world undergoing revolutionary change" (1967:6). Martin King was invited to address the conference but could not attend in person because of riots in Chicago. However, he "was seen by millions of viewers on the European television network, and his voice was heard in the service in the Cathedral of St. Pierre in Geneva, since a film of his sermon had been flown to Switzerland . . . " (World Conference 1967:41). King's sermon, "A Knock at Midnight," reflected his mood and that of others at the conference.

It is . . . midnight in our world, and the darkness is so deep that we can hardly see which way to turn. . . . On the international horizon nations are engaged in a colossal and bitter contest for supremacy. Two world wars have been fought within a generation, and the clouds of another war are dangerously low. . . . In the terrible mid-

night of war, [people] have knocked on the door of the church to ask
for the bread of peace, but the Church often disappointed them. . . .
Those who have gone to the Church to seek the bread of economic
justice have been left in the frustrating midnight of economic deprivation. . . . The Church today is challenged to proclaim God's
son, Jesus Christ, to be the hope of [people] in all of their complex
personal and social problems. (1981b)[13]

Although many Third World participants were deeply impressed by
Martin King's solidarity with the poor and his commitment to establish
justice on their behalf, they openly challenged the usefulness of his philosophy of nonviolence in liberating their countries from the "remaining
vestiges of old western colonialism, which keeps one people subject to
another, and of neocolonialism, which keeps peoples from the right to determine their own political and economic life" (Thomas 1967:111). In a
preparatory essay, entitled "Awakened Peoples, Developing Nations and
the Dynamics of World Politics," M. M. Thomas of India, chairman of
the Church and Society Conference, referred to a "kind of conversion
from nonviolence to violence [that] is taking place every day" in South
Africa, Rhodesia, Angola, and other Portuguese territories of that period
(1967:113).[14] In some situations, Thomas contended, the liberation of the
oppressed can only be achieved through violence. Thomas also supported his point by quoting from the report of the consultation (spon-
sored by the WCC and the South African Institute of Race Relations) on
race relations in South Africa, which was held in Mindolo, Zambia
(1964).

The urgency of the situation in South Africa is further increased by
the conviction of leading Africans that, as all peaceful measures
tried by African political organizations over a period of many years
to bring about an ordered change have proved abortive, only one avenue remains open — that of violence. . . . For many Christians involved in the struggle for a just solution, the question of possible
violence as the only remaining alternative has become an urgent and
ever-pressing one. (1967:114)

Much of Thomas's essay analyzed the question of whether King's
philosophy of nonviolence was appropriate for the developing societies in
Africa and Asia. Many European and white North American participants
strongly promoted King's philosophy of nonviolence as the *only* option
for Third World Christians engaged in political activity. Thomas and
other Third World Christians agreed that King's nonviolent direct action

was most appropriate for a racial minority seeking constitutional rights in a nation founded on democratic values like the United States; they denied that it is applicable in all situations, especially in many countries in the Third World. In a sharp critique of liberal humanism, and with King's philosophy in mind, Thomas said:

> There still seem to be some theologians who have not learned the necessity of dealing with the relativities of politics and society. There is no evidence that the forces of liberal humanism, Christian humanism, or even nonviolent militancy have fully understood the working of the political, economic and social powers that are seeking to consolidate white extremist elements, especially in Africa. [People] are thus left struggling for their rights, with the path of violence their only choice. (1967:114)

The Geneva Conference represented a major turning point in Protestant thinking as articulated in "Christians in the Technical and Social Revolutions of our Time" (World Conference 1967:6). For the first time, Third World Protestants began to search for a radical commitment to social change in their societies that did not depend upon the approval of the dominant theologians of Europe and North America. A similar turning point occurred in Catholic thinking at Vatican II during the same period. Following Vatican II, the famous Second General Conference of Latin American Bishops was held in Medellin, Colombia (1968). It gave support to an emerging Latin American liberation theology.[15] Both Catholic and Protestant Christians of the Third World began to develop a perspective on the church and society that did not exclude violence as a method for achieving justice. While Martin King's life and writings continued to influence their thinking in Christian ethics, they contended that the sociopolitical situation of the Third World required a different option of them than the one chosen by King. C. S. Banana, the president of Zimbabwe and an ordained Methodist minister, made this distinction in a Martin Luther King Lecture at Wesley Theological Seminary in 1981.

> In pursuing our goals we might have differed from him [Martin King] as we had to use tactics adopted to the realities of our country and to the nature of the colonial situation. We fully agreed with him in the goals and motivations. The goals were exactly the same—the freedom and fulfillment of the people. The motivation could only be one: the great love that Jesus showed us when he chose "to lay down his life for his friends" (John 15:13). To a great extent the methods and tactics to follow in any revolutionary process are de-

termined by the historical context. By analyzing the circumstances in which the Civil Rights Movement developed and the circumstances which press for armed solutions in the Third World countries, one may be able to prove that there are not "prefabricated" answers which may be applied to any existing situations. Answers have to be found in the process of liberation by the very people involved in it. (1981:1–2)

Despite the many of Third World Christians who reject Martin King's commitment to nonviolence as being inapplicable to their situation, there are others who strongly endorse it. The two most prominent Third World representatives of the nonviolent approach to social change are Allan Boesak and Desmond Tutu of South Africa. Like King, both view the Gospel as a demand for justice and refuse to separate the salvation of the soul from the health of the body. Like King, Boesak and Tutu are black leaders in a society sharply defined by white racism. Both define, as King did, the problem of racism as a moral issue. Unlike King, who could appeal to the moral demands of democracy and Christianity as found in American history and culture, Boesak and Tutu are struggling against a South African white government that is openly defiant of any demand for the sociopolitical equality of blacks and whites. The idea of a beloved community is anathema to most whites in the government and the churches.

Although there are differences between Boesak and Tutu of South Africa and King of America, they are minor when compared with their similarities. In taking their stand against racism, all three have based their resistance to it upon moral values derived from the Christian Gospel. According to this Gospel, all people were created by God for each other. Any government, therefore, that gives privileges to a few at the expense of the necessities of the many must be passionately and nonviolently resisted.

Allan Boesak, who has devoted a great deal of study to the life and thought of Martin King, has adopted fully his views on nonviolence. For Boesak, as for king, it is not a matter of what is practical but rather what is Christian. He contends that the Gospel, as defined by the cross of Jesus Christ, demands a love that is both powerful and nonviolent.

Boesak's perspective on nonviolence has evolved over a period of years, beginning with his studies in graudate school on King and Malcolm X, continuing with the publication of his first book on black theology, and now being refined in the struggle against apartheid in South Africa. In his first book, seeking to express the insights from both King and Malcolm X, Boesak reluctantly acknowledged that the retaliatory violence of the oppressed is sometimes unavoidable (1977:70).

Whereas we do not deny that a situation may arise where retaliatory violence is forced upon the oppressed and no other avenue is left open to them, we do so with a clear hesitancy, knowing full well that it will probably prove a poor "solution" and that violence can never be "justified." Furthermore, the questions of King ... haunt us still. Behind these questions lies the deeply disturbing theological question for any Christian, namely this: Is it not the essence of discipleship that the Christian is required to react on a completely different level in order to create and keep open the possibilities for reconciliation, redemption, and community?

When Allan Boesak discussed the issue of violence and nonviolence in 1985 with a group of theologians from both the United States and South Africa, there was no hesitation as he advanced an absolute commitment to nonviolence, explicitly indentifying his view with Martin King's perspective.

Unlike Alan Boesak, Desmond Tutu's commitment to nonviolence is not absolute.

People are making a big mistake. I am not in the same league as he [King]. He was quite outstanding, and I am not trying to be falsely modest. When you think of him as an orator, I don't even get anywhere near that. He was more than anything else a pacifist. I am not a pacifist; I am a peace-lover. He believed firmly and absolutely in non-violence and never going to war. There may be situations where war is justifiable, like when you are fighting Nazism; that is to say there is such an evil existing that you have to use a lesser evil to overthrow it. (1986a:11A)

While Tutu believes that "apartheid is as evil and as vicious as Nazism" (1984:158), he has been careful not to condone violence in South Africa. Rather, he has endorsed a deep *practical* commitment to nonviolence with the hope that the white people of South Africa will see the wisdom of his view. As the white South African government continues to turn a deaf hear to him, however, Tutu is finding it more difficult to continue to advocate nonviolence. According to the *Daily News* (June 2, 1986) of Toronto, Canada, Tutu told a rally of ten thousand that "if economic and diplomatic sanctions failed to persuade Pretoria to abandon apartheid, 'the church would have no alternative but to say it would be justifiable for Christians to use violence and force to overthrow an unjust regime.'"

Although Desmond Tutu differs slightly from Martin King regarding the nature of his commitment to nonviolence, the spirituality that undergirds his struggle for justice is very similar to King's. Like King, his deep love for his people and country shows in everything he does and says. Like King, he initially expressed much optimism in dismantling apartheid by appealing to the moral conscience of whites in government and the churches. He too, like King, was greatly disappointed with the failure of whites to experience enough moral outrage to cause them to join with blacks in the struggle against apartheid.[16]

Like King, Tutu became bitterly angry when Western governments (especially the United States, Britain, and West Germany) refused to support his nonviolent initiative by instituting tough economic sanctions against South Africa. In response to President Reagan's speech on South Africa (and the support he received from Prime Minister Margaret Thatcher of Great Britain and Chancellor Helmut Kohl of West Germany), Tutu (sounding like King during the Vietnam war and the deepening crisis in America's cities) angrily expressed his frustrations with white Western governments that apparently place little value upon the lives of black people. He referred to the president's speech as "utterly racist and totally disgusting" because "we are completely dispensable and can forget about help from them." "The West," he said, "as far as I am concerned can go to hell" (1986c:1).

In the midst of the daily killing of black children, women, and men by the white government, Tutu, again in the spirit of King, refuses to lose hope. Despite the evil that people do, Tutu still believes that God, not white South Africans, is in charge of the world.

As a human being, I just say, "Look at these guys. Do they have any sense at all?" And as a human being, I feel hopeless sometimes. But as a Christian I hold on to the belief that this is God's world and He is in charge. It may not always seem so. One also believes in the resurrection of Our Lord Jesus Christ, and I end up being a prisoner of hope. Sometimes I hold on to that by the skin of my teeth. (1986b:114)

Insights From Martin King and the Third World

There are several insights about humanity that we can derive from the life and thought of Martin King and from the fighters for freedom in the Third World.

1. "There is nothing in all the world greater than freedom" (1957a:34). Martin King gave his life for it. South African blacks, endowed with the same liberating spirit, are facing death daily because they

do not believe that whites have the right to determine the nature and the date of their freedom. Poor people throughout the world are demonstrating with their bodies that one cannot begin to live until one is ready to die for freedom. Freedom is that quality of existence in which a people recognize their dignity and worth by fighting against the sociopolitical conditions that limit their recognition in society.

2. Martin King's foremost contribution as a moral thinker was his penetrating insight into the meaning of justice during his time. No one understood justice with more depth or communicated it with greater clarity in the area of race relations in the United States and the world than Martin Luther King, Jr. Because of King, the world is not only more aware of the problem of racial injustice but equally aware of its interrelatedness with poverty and war. "Injustice anywhere is a threat to justice everywhere" (in Watters 1971:366).

3. The "anemic democracy" to which King pointed is still present in America and around the world. The dream is still unfulfilled. Whether we speak of the relations between nations or of the relations between persons within nations, the rich few are still getting richer and the poor who are many are getting poorer. To incorporate the true meaning of Martin Luther King, Jr., into America's national consciousness would mean using our technological resources to bridge the huge economic gap that separates the rich and poor nations.

4. Martin King's greatest contribution was his ability to communicate a vision of hope in extreme situations of oppression. No matter how difficult the struggle for justice became, no matter how powerful were the opponents of justice, no matter how many persons turned against him, King refused absolutely to lose hope because he believed that ultimately right will triumph over wrong. He communicated this hope to the masses throughout the world, enabling them to keep on struggling for freedom and justice even though the odds were against them. "I am not going to stop singing 'We Shall Overcome,' " he often said,

because I know that "truth crushed to the earth shall rise again." I am not going to stop singing "We Shall Overcome," because I know the Bible is right, "you shall reap what you sow." I am not going to stop singing, "We Shall Overcome," because I know that one day the God of the universe will say to those who won't listen to him, "I'm not a playboy. Don't play with me. For I will rise up and break the backbone of your power." I'm not going to stop singing, "We Shall Overcome," because "mine eyes have seen the glory of the coming of the Lord. He's trampling out the vintage where the grapes of wrath are stored. Glory hallelujah, his truth is marching on." (1968f:21)

Notes

1. The ecumenical Association of Third World Theologians is an organization of Asian, African, Latin American, Caribbean, and United States minority Christian scholars and activists. It was founded in Dar es Salaam, Tanzania, in 1976 for the purpose of encouraging persons in each region to work together in order to deepen their analysis of the sociopolitical and religio-cultural structures in their countries and because of the need to develop a theology that is accountable to the poor masses. International conferences have been held in Accra, Ghana (1977), Wennappuwa, Sri Lanka (1979), Sao Paulo, Brazil (1980), New Delhi, India (1981), and Geneva, Switzerland (1983). For an interpretation of EATWOT, see Cone (1985) and Cone (1983). See also Witvliet (1985). An account of each international conference has been published by Orbis Books.

2. The impact of Martin King's life and thought in the Third World is obviously more difficult to evaluate. Scholars have just begun the painstaking task of assessing King's impact upon American life and culture. Of course, much more time will be needed before an adequate assessment can be made regarding his significance for the Third World.

3. For the purposes of this essay, I will limit my analysis chiefly to two periods in King's thinking. However, it is important to note that I have found three periods in the development of his life and thought from the time of the Montgomery bus boycott (December 5, 1955) to his assassination (April 4, 1968). The first period is quite brief (early weeks of the boycott) and is defined by his primary focus on justice. The second period (early 1956 to his assassination in 1968) focuses primarily on hope, with love and justice being interpreted in its light. The distinctions are not rigid but rather a matter of emphases in his thinking. In all periods the concern for justice, love, and hope are always present and intertwined. For an interpretation of the development of King's thinking in terms of the three periods, see Cone (1986).

4. For King's interpretation of the impact of the independence celebration of Ghana upon himself, see especially King (1957b). See also Jack (1957). For King's interpretation of his trip to India, see King (1959).

5. For an account of the origin of this theological movement, widely known as black theology, see Cone (1984).

6. James Bevel, one of King's aids, spoke often of the Chicago slums as a "system of internal colonialism." King also adopted the same description for his addresses.

7. See note 3.

8. This sermon includes King's account of his deep crisis of fear during the Montgomery bus boycott, which led to his appropriation of the faith of his early childhood. I think this is the most critical turning point in King's life. Although I

have always maintained that King's faith, as defined by the black church, was indispensable for understanding his life and thought, David Garrow was the first person to identify the "kitchen experience" (as it might be called) as the decisive experience in defining his faith. See especially Garrow (1986). My interpretation of the experience is found in Cone (1986:26f).

9. For an account of the development of King's position on Vietnam, see Fairclough (1984).

10. This was a point that King repeatedly made.

11. For an account of the international celebrations of King's legacy, see Green (1986).

12. In addition to Balasuriya, other interviews with EATWOT members regarding King's impact in the Third World included Jose Miguez Bonino (Argentina), Carmen Lora (Peru), Virginia Fabella (Philippines), and Engelbert Mveng (Cameroon). I also interviewed a young Chinese university student (Zhang Lei), our interpreter during EATWOT's visit to China, and Theresa Chu (our guide) of the Canada China Programme. I also have had many conversations with graduate students from the Third World in my class ("Martin Luther King, Jr. and Malcolm X") at Union Seminary. My interpretation of King's impact in the Third World is greatly influenced by these conversations.

13. See Oates (1982:410) for a discussion of King's invitation to speak at the WCC meeting.

14. See also Thomas (1978). This collection (which includes the preparatory essay quoted here) is quite useful for analyzing the development of radical thinking in the international church meetings among Protestants. Thomas is perhaps the most influential Asian (and possibly Third World) Protestant theologian in the second half of the twentieth century. He has shown a special interest in King. See also Thomas (1969) and (1970).

15. The classic text on liberation theology in Latin America is by Gutierrez (1973). An excellent introduction to this theology is Bonino (1975). In response to my question regarding King's impact in Latin America during the 1960s and 1970s, Bonino said: "Although Martin King was widely known as the most prominent leader of the black freedom struggle in the 1960s, his impact on Latin America was not significantly felt during the 1960s because of the powerful presence and enormous influence of Che Guevara and his advocacy of radical change through violent revolution. It was not until the 1970s that Martin King's voice was heard by many Latin Americans. He was best known for his advocacy of radical change through nonviolence, and Don Helder Camara was his most articulate and influential supporter." Bonino gave two major reasons for the turn toward Martin King: (1) "the failure of the guerrilla movements in many Latin American countries (Bolivia, Uruguay, Argentina, etc.), due both to the strength of the military and the lack of support of the masses of the people"; and (2) "the takeover by

military regimes in country after country. . . . This forced the people to think of an alternative form to resist persecution and repression. Thus both the idea of nonviolent resistance and the methods of the Civil Rights Movement in the U.S. were adopted by many groups in Latin America'' (Beijing, China, May 1986).

16. Commenting on white South Africans who failed to express moral outrage regarding the oppression of blacks (1986b:113), Tutu said: "I don't think they get appalled. Shouldn't they have been appalled by 69 people being killed at Sharpeville? Shouldn't they be appalled that many hundreds have been killed? Children are being put in jail. Where is the moral outrage?''

References

Balasuriya, Tissa
1986   Interview with James H. Cone. Beijing, China: May.

Banana, C. S.
1981   "In Search of Human Justice." Martin Luther King Lecture delivered at Wesley Theological Seminary, Oct. 22.

Boesak, Allan
1977   *Farewell to Innocence: A Socio-Ethical Study on Black Theology and Black Power.* Maryknoll, N.Y.: Orbis Books.

Bonino, Jose M.
1975   *Doing Theology in a Revolutionary Situation.* Philadelphia: Fortress.

Collins, The Rev. Canon L. John
1979   "International Tribute to Martin Luther King, Jr." Speech presented at United Nations.

Cone, James H.
1983   "Black Theology and Third World Theologies." In *My Soul Looks Back.* Maryknoll, N.Y.: Orbis Books.
1984   *For My People.* Maryknoll, N.Y.: Orbis Books.
1985   "Ecumenical Association of Third World Theologians." *Ecumenical Trends* 14(8):119–122.
1986   "The Theology of Martin Luther King, Jr." *Union Seminary Quarterly Review* 40(4):21–39.

Daily News
1986   Article reprinted in *Christian Worker* Second Quarter, Colombo, Sri Lanka:34.

Fairclough, Adam
1984   "Martin Luther King, Jr. and the War in Vietnam." *Phylon* 45(1).

Garrow, David
1986   *Bearing the Cross: Martin Luther King, Jr. and the Southern Christian Leadership Conference, 1955–1968*. New York: William Morrow.

Green, Carroll
1986   "A Man for All Nations." *American Visions* 1(1):36–37.

Gutierrez, Gustavo
1973   *A Theology of Liberation*, trans. Caridad Inda and John Eagleson. Maryknoll, N.Y.: Orbis Books.

Jack, Homer
1957   "Conversation in Ghana." *Christian Century* April 10:446–448.

King, Coretta Scott
1969   *My Life With Martin Luther King, Jr.* New York: Holt, Rinehart and Winston.

King, Martin Luther
1956a   "The Legitimacy of the Struggle in Montgomery," a one-page statement, May 4. Atlanta, Ga.: King Center Archives.
1956b   "The Birth of a New Age," August 7–11. Atlanta, Ga.: King Center Archives.
1957a   "Facing the Challenge of a New Age." *Phylon* April.
1957b   "Birth of a New Nation." Address delivered at Dexter Avenue Baptist Church, April.
1958   *Stride Toward Freedom*. New York: Harper.
1959   "My Trip to the Land of Ghandi." *Ebony* July.
1961   "The Time For Freedom Has Come." *The New York Times Magazine* September 10.
1963   "Letter from Birmingham City Jail." *The New Leader* June 24.
1964   "The Quest for Peace and Justice," Nobel Lecture, Dec. 11, Oslo, Norway. Atlanta, Ga.: King Center Archives.
1965   "Playboy Interview: Martin Luther King." *Playboy* January.
1966a   "Nonviolence: The Only Road to Freedom." *Ebony* October.
1966b   "The Chicago Plan." Statement delivered Jan. 7. Atlanta, Ga.: King Center Archives.
1966c   "Who Are We?" Feb. 5. Atlanta, Ga.: King Center Archives.
1967a   "Transforming a Neighborhood into a Brotherhood." An address for the National Association of Real Estate Brokers, San Francisco, Aug. 10. Atlanta, Ga.: King Center Archives.
1967b   "Thou Fool." Sermon preached at Mt. Pisgah Baptist Church, Chicago, Aug. 27. Atlanta, Ga.: King Center Archives.
1967c   "Why I am Opposed to the War in Vietnam," sermon preached at Ebenezer Baptist Church, April 30. Atlanta, Ga.: King Center Archives.
1967d   "Standing By the Best in an Evil Time." Sermon preached at Ebenezer Baptist Church, Aug. 6. Atlanta, Ga.: King Center Archives.

1967e "Which Way Shall We Go?" Voter Registration Rally, Louisville, Ky., Aug. 2. Atlanta, Ga.: King Center Archives.

1967f "A Christmas Sermon on Peace." Sermon on file at King Center Archives.

1968a "The American Dream." Commencement address at Lincoln University, June 6, 1961. *Negro History Bulletin* May: 10–15.

1968b "The Acceptance Speech of Martin Luther King, Jr. of the Nobel Peace Prize on Dec. 10, 1964." *Negro History Bulletin,* May.

1968c "The Sickness of America." Address delivered in Los Angeles, March 16. Atlanta, Ga.: King Center Archives.

1968d "Rally Speech," Laurel, Mis., March 19. Atlanta, Ga.: King Center Archives.

1968e *Where Do We Go From Here: Chaos or Community?* Boston: Beacon Press.

1968f "To Minister to the Valley." An address at the Ministers' Leadership Training Program, Miami, Fla., Feb. 23. Atlanta, Ga.: King Center Archives.

1968g An address at a rally of the "Pre-Washington Campaign." Albany, Ga., March 22. Atlanta, Ga.: King Center Archives.

1968h "The Other America." Address at Local 1199, Hunter College, March 10. Atlanta, Ga.: King Center Archives.

1969 "A Testament of Hope." *Playboy,* January.

1981a "Pilgrimage to Nonviolence." *Strength to Love.* Philadelphia: Fortress.

1981b "A Knock at Midnight." *Strength to Love.* Philadelphia: Fortress.

1982 "Martin Luther King, Jr.: Beyond Vietnam." Pamphlet of Clergy and Laity Concerned, April 4, 1967, Riverside Church.

Oates, Stephen B.
1982 Let the Trumpet Sound: The Life of Martin Luther King, Jr. New York: Harper.

Thomas, M. M.
1967 "Awakened Peoples, Developing Nations and the Dynamics of World Politics." In *The Church Amid Revolution,* edited by Harvey Cox. New York: Association Press.

1978 *Towards a Theology of Contemporary Ecumenism: A Collection of Addresses to Ecumenical Gatherings (1947–1975).* Madras: Christian Literature Society.

1969 "Basic Approaches to Power — Gandhiji, Andrews and King." *Religion and Society,* September:15–25.

1970 "Significance of the Critique of Gandhian Presuppositions by Martin Luther King for the Development of a Non-violent Strategy of the Revolution." In *Humane Geselleschaft Beitrage zu Ihrer Sozialen Gestaltung,* edited by Arthur Rich, 319–332. Zurich: Verlag furchef Zwingle.

Tutu, Desmond
1984   *Hope and Suffering*. Grand Rapids, Mich.: Eerdmans.
1986a   "King Was a Pacifist; I'm Just a Peace-lover." *USA Today,* January.
1986b   "Penthouse Interview: Bishop Desmond Tutu." *Penthouse,* June.
1986c   *Pine Bluff Commercial,* July 23.

Vomani, Paul
1979   "International Tribute to Martin Luther King, Jr." Speech presented at United Nations.

Watters, Pat
1971   *Down To Now: Reflections on the Southern Civil Rights Movement.* New York: Pantheon Books.

Witvliet, Theo
1985   *A Place in the Sun: An Introduction to Liberation Theology in the Third World.* Maryknoll, N.Y.: Orbis Books.

World Conference on Church and Society
1967   *Official Report,* with a description of the conference by M. M. Thomas and Paul Abrecht. Geneva: World Council of Churches.

Part III

Mission and Ideology

7

World Christianity, the Missionary Movement and the Ugly American

A. F. Walls

The history of the great religions of the world displays different types of expansion. In India religious expansion has been unifocal, absorbing and reformulating influences from many quarters but maintaining one geographical focus for its great creative religious activity. Iranian religion has been catalytic, profoundly influencing other religious traditions but leaving only small communities to embody its own. Islamic expansion has been progressive, steadily spreading out from its original center (which retains a cosmic significance), claiming the allegiance of the whole world and, with few exceptions, maintaining the gains it has made. By contrast, Christian expansion has been serial. It has not maintained a single cultural or geographical center; it has always retained a substantial separate identity; it recedes as well as advances, declines or dies out in the areas of its greatest strength and reappears, often transformed, in totally different areas of quite distinct culture. Christian history is a series of cross-cultural movements, which result in a succession of different Christian "heartlands" as the geographical and cultural center of christianity has changed. Changing patterns of world order are thus integrally linked to religious history.

The destinies of empires and nation-states have often had greater consequence than religious activity itself. Peripheral religious activity is not to be discounted. The New Testament itself shows that the work of Paul was peripheral to the early church;[1] yet only the Gentile mission made possible the survival of Christianity as anything other than a Jewish fringe movement after the fall of Jerusalem in A.D. 70. The spread of Christianity among peoples beyond the imperial frontiers, such as the Eastern Goths or the Irish, was a marginal activity in terms of the busy

hive of fourth-century Christianity in the Roman Empire, but its significance proved momentous when the frontiers of that empire wavered or
collapsed. The missionary movement was, often to its own despair, almost always a marginal activity of Western Christianity, and for centuries
it did little to alter the demography of Christianity. At the beginning of the
twentieth century there were signs that the Christian center of gravity had
begun to shift across the Atlantic, though the heartland was still Western
and Caucasian in culture and race. Now, towards the end of the century,
Christianity is more widely diffused, and culturally more diverse,
than ever before, and its heartlands are increasingly in the southern
continents.

Cultural diversity is inbuilt in Christianity; its different forms are
affected by historic contingency, by the application of its norms and the
accommodation of its institutions to the differing priorities of different
cultures. It has no absolute unconditioned determinant, no equivalent of
the Qur'an. Its central symbol, Christ, and its foundation documents, the
scriptures, are in principle "translatable"; they get applied to, and become clothed in, local forms of thought.

Three specially important changes in the Christian center of gravity
have produced, or are producing, such cultural transformation. The first
occurred within the first century, when Christians, originally an entirely
Jewish community, became overwhelmingly Hellenistic-Roman in
expression, character, priorities, agenda, and organization. The second
came over a much longer period as Christianity was transformed from the
religion of the urban literary and technological civilization of the Medi-
terranean to the faith of peasant cultivators of the north and west. This
development, with the social transformation it assisted, produced the
idea of Christendom, of the corpus of Christian countries, of a Christian
part of the globe, of Christianity as territorially expressed, which under-
lies the missionary movement.

The third critical process of change began in the sixteenth century
and reached its sudden climax in the twentieth century. It is marked by a
massive recession from Christianity in the West and a massive adhesion
to Christianity in the southern continents. In 1900 83 percent of professed
Christians lived in Europe and North America; the best figures available
for the late 1980s suggest that some 56 percent of the world's Christians
now live in Africa, Asia, Latin America, and the Pacific, and that proportion continues to rise.[2] In 1900 there were perhaps ten million Christians
in the African continent (Barrett, 1982: Global table 2). Today's figure is
more like 224 million, and that figure is rising, too.[3] The Christian heartlands are changing again.

This most recent transformation has some relationship to the general impact of Western culture and hegemony on the southern world, just

as the last accompanied both the absorption by the Northern and Western peoples of a good deal of classical Roman culture mediated by the Latin language and new degrees of political centralization, but the relationship is not a straightforward one. The simple concept of the extension of territorial Christendom, known to early modern Europe after apparent initial success, proved intractable. Metropolitan states discovered that they could not maintain unchanged in their colonies the religious settlement of the homelands (Walls, 1990b). The powers of Christendom rarely displayed more than moderate interest, and not always that, in that extension of the Christendom idea, the missionary movement. The period of the Western colonial empires is quite as important for making possible the revival of Hinduism, and in enabling an immense expansion of Islam, as for anything it did for Christianity.

The United States and the "Great Century of Missions"

The most recent shift in the Christian center of gravity has a peculiar feature that arises from an earlier shift in that center of gravity within the West itself. If the nineteenth century was, in K. S. Latourette's phrase, "the great century of missions,"[4] the century's greatest missionary achievement was the Christianization of the United States. A nation with only a modest degree of active church participation at the time of independence saw (except during the Civil War period) steadily advancing church membership throughout the nineteenth century (Latourette, 1961: 81). By the century's end no other Western country could match the scale of church activity reflected in the United States. This occurred despite a huge increase in population, despite repeated uprootings of families with the threat to religious ties, despite the scattering of population over vast areas, with the accompanying strain on ecclesiastical organization, and despite the emergence of new industrial and urban complexes, the very types of society that proved so unfriendly to sustained church life in Europe.

American Christianity cannot be explained simply as an extension of European religion. Nor is it an expansion of old Christendom by emigration in the way that Latin America at first seemed to be an extension of old Christendom by conquest and settlement. For as North America developed into the new Christian heartland, old Christendom was moving into recession.

Australia and New Zealand were, like North America, repeopled by emigration from Europe, but those countries saw nothing like the American religious phenomenon. They imported Christianity in recession, and its recession continued there. The new cities and industrial conurbations of Europe, unlike those of the United States, saw no substantial movement towards participation in the churches, and few significant new versions of Christianity to mark its penetration of a transformed society. Despite a century of church effort and the adoption of various special forms of home missions, the industrial masses of Britain, for instance, largely stayed away from the churches they had never effectively belonged to. In some European countries, anticlerical movements became institutionalized in the structures of the state, calling into question the very assumptions on which Christendom was based. Despite the durability of the concept of the Christian nation, by the end of the century the champions of missions sensed that they were operating in a hostile intellectual and political climate (Walls, 1983). In the New York of 1900, however, with all the American insistence on the separation of church and state, a missionary conference could claim for its platform the president of the United States, a former president and a future president.[5]

It is not surprising if American Christians came to believe in a "Manifest Missionary Destiny" for their nation (G. H. Anderson, 1988). In 1886, an Andover professor wrote that Americans should see the United States as:

> ... first and foremost the chosen seat of enterprise for the world's conversion. Forecasting the future of Christianity as statesmen forecast the destiny of nations, we must believe that it will be what the future of this country is to be. (Phelps, 1891)

Austin Phelps wrote at the beginning of a shift in the Christian center of gravity from old Christendom to a new heartland across the Atlantic. It was also the beginning of a process by which North America became the leading contributor to the missionary movement, the main instrument by which the great southward movement of Christianity took place.

In one sense the Protestant missionary movement was born in North America, the place of the first sustained encounter of Protestant Christians with a non-Christian people. The American influences on Carey and the early British missionary movement are important, and American overseas missions have an existence of their own from at least 1810, but for the first half of the nineteenth century, overseas missionaries from America were few. Most missionaries were British or from German-speaking countries, many of the latter group serving under British auspices. After the transformation of America by expansion and the remaking of American religion that went along with that expansion, the United States became a major "sending" country. In one sense the transformed America was itself the product of the missionary movement, or at least of the religious inspiration that lay behind it. In the later part of the nineteenth century, the United States not only produced large numbers of missionaries, but it produced a series of initiatives that galvanized a flagging European movement, enlarged the concept of a missionary, and provided missions with an international structure and organization. At the center of the first key initiative, the Mount Hermon Conference of 1886, was the emblematic figure of Dwight L. Moody, the personification of the mass Christianizing of America.

By 1911, despite the late appearance of American missionaries in large numbers, a third of the world's Protestant missionaries were from North America. By 1925 the proportion was a half (G. H. Anderson, 1988: 105; Hogg, 1977). In the late 1980s, the figure is probably over 80 percent;[6] for the future, despite the increasing number of missionaries from certain new sending countries, notably Korea, it is likely that a Protestant missionary will be assumed to be American unless otherwise stated.

In its origins the missionary movement was a natural expression of that territorially based conception of Christianity — Christendom — which had developed from the nature of Christianization of northern and central Europe. It implied "Christian lands" from which evangelisers "went out" to "heathen lands." Today, Christianity is no longer Christendom. Its territorial basis in Europe is broken and cannot be replicated in the new Christian heartlands with their plural societies and secular nation-states. Christianity in the southern continents has survived the Western colonial empires almost without noticing their passing. In the West, especially in the states that maintained those empires, Christianity has receded; in the southern continents its expansion is most noticeable now. The original motor of that expansion was the missionary movement from the West, but the dynamics of the Christianity of Africa, Asia, and Latin America are coming into situations as new to Christian experience as were the dynamics of the Hellenistic world brought to the earliest Jewish Christians. The demographic and economic basis of the European missionary movement has eroded, and many African and Asian churches already have histories in which the missionary period is an episode concluded.

Yet there are now more Western missionaries serving overseas than ever before; this is due largely to American Protestantism. More than four-fifths of the recent calculation of 67,200 (Wilson and Siewert, 1986: 572 — see note 6). Protestant missionaries are North American. Looking more closely at the composition of this group, it is clear that well under a tenth of it comes from the historic traditions of American Protestantism.[7] The characteristically American expression of conservative evangelical religion is reflected in missions affiliated to the Interdenominational Foreign Mission Association (IFMA, founded in 1917) and the Evangelical Foreign Missions Association (EFMA, founded in 1945). These have maintained the traditional missions emphasis (much dampened in the historic Protestant churches) and to a considerable extent the traditional mission structures and missionary roles, but for the past twenty years the number of missionaries connected with the EFMA and IFMA has remained almost static (Coote, 1986: 39f). The great majority of American missionaries are from source that have achieved dominance only in the last two or three decades: from churches and missions affiliated neither to the National Council of Churches of Christ or to the regular conservative evangelical groupings. These unaffiliated missions are mainly Pentecostal in character, thus representing another tradition profoundly shaped by peculiarly American conditions.

The United States is the base for many organizations that call or work for total Christian evangelization. Christians probably now constitute a slightly smaller proportion of the world's population than a century ago. Such organizations point not only to the huge non-Christian cultures but to ''unreached peoples'' unaffected by the new churches of the Southern continents and to ''hidden peoples,'' many of them coherent groups living in the midst of, but apart from, well-churched societies. In the nature of things, only a tiny proportion of the missionary force is likely to be engaged in primary evangelism, in the first-time presentation of the Christian faith. A high proportion of the new American missionaries are stationed where churches already exist in multitudes; in Latin America, for instance, and less predictably, Papua New Guinea (a result of that country's open-door visa policy).

The impact of American religion in the southern continents is not, of course, restricted to its missionaries. The influence is conveyed in a host of ways, both direct (literature, cassette and other electronic means, campaigns by visiting evangelists) and indirect (the effects of theological education and training, shaped by the varying concerns of historic Protestantism and regular conservative evangelicalism as well as the newer types of fundamentalism and Pentecostalism). The impact is mediated through the capacity of American agencies to find or to withhold funding, and through the structures of international organizations formed under American auspices.

The position of the United States in the world Christian situation is thus peculiar; it represents the West — indeed the West writ large — and the West will matter progressively less in Christianity as the South comes to mean more. America bears the marks of the Christian recession, which has come upon the West, but, because modern America is itself a mission product, the recession started later and has proceeded more slowly than in Europe. (It is no accident that the "older" areas know the recession most; New England is religiously more like old England than are lands to the west.) Over vast areas of the United States it is still possible to conceive of Christianity in territorial terms. North American Christianity still has immense human, financial, and technological resources, the capability, and the ethos for an energetic, forceful missionary movement. The society to which it belongs is not, like those of Europe, retreating from a world role, or seeking a purely regional one. Contemporary American missions are the last flourish of Christendom.

Reading the Signs of the Times

Contemporary American missions, however, arise out of a peculiarly American missionary tradition. In another place (Walls, 1980a) I have tried, as an uninformed outsider looking in, to delineate some of the specifically American dimensions of the missionary movement, finding them evident as far back as the first major commentator on American missions, Rufus Anderson writing in the 1830s.

The missionary movement was the product of a particular period of Western economic, political religious development. This is recognized by Anderson in a sermon of 1837, entitled "The Time for the World's Conversion Come" (R. Anderson, 1837), in which he seeks to read the signs of the times. A similar note of crisis, of call to seize the occasion, runs right through American mission literature. Anderson's European evangelical contemporaries when trying to read the signs of the times were more likely to move into the apocalyptic realm — the conversion of the Jews, the prediction in scripture of current events of the "Eastern question." Anderson eschews the transcendent for the pragmatic. His providential view of history (a history in which the emergence of America holds a significant place) demands specific and immediate human activity. In this Anderson adumbrates the practical, activity-directed style of argument of later American proponents of mission — of A. T. Pierson, John R. Mott, Robert E. Speer, Donald A. McGavran, and Ralph Winter. Anderson's signs of the times are intellectual, political, economic, and ecclesiological. World evangelization has become possible, he urges, only in the present century by the expansion of the frontiers of knowledge, by the development of technology, and by the growth of world trade.

How came the reckless, indomitable *avarice* of the world not to break forth over all the earth, as it has done in our age even in advance of the gospel? It did not only because it could not. Its pro-

gress was barred, in respect to the greater portion of the world, as
it now is in respect to the kingdom of Japan . . . (R. Anderson (ed.),
1967: 62)

Political developments — civil and religious liberty in stable societies,
backed by widespread habits of reading and widely dispersed knowledge,
are equally propitious, and are

> the result of that intelligence and large intercommunity of thought,
> and feeling and freedom of action, which belong to the age of print-
> ing, and distinguish the Protestant world of modern times. So far as
> the apostolical and later ancient churches were able to act together
> for the propagating of the gospel, it was by platoons and companies,
> while the evangelical churches of our day act by division and armies,
> with the momentum of great masses. (R. Anderson (ed.), 1967: 63)

Above all, the signs indicating that the time for the world's conversion is
come are theological and ecclesiological. Anderson asserts, but does not
dwell upon, the process of reformation and purification of the church so
dear to Protestant writers in Europe. He is more concerned with questions of organization:

> It was not until the present century that the evangelical churches of
> Christendom were ever really organized with a view to the conver-
> sion of the world. (R. Anderson (ed.), 1967: 64)

The ecclesiological development that made world evangelization
possible was the voluntary society:

> The Protestant form of association-free, open, responsible, em-
> bracing all classes, both sexes, all ages, the masses of the people —
> is peculiar to modern times, and almost to our age. Like our own
> form of government, working with perfect freedom over a broad
> continent, it is among the great results of the progress of Christian
> civilization in this "fullness of the time" for the world's conversion.
> (R. Anderson (ed.), 1967: 65)

Anderson was clearly correct in positing a connexion between the
voluntary society and prevailing political conditions, but there is more to
it than his diagnosis that voluntary societies cannot flourish under des-
potic governments. They also require a social system in which people neither desire nor are required to act always in conformity or in concert with

their neighbors. Voluntary societies imply a highly developed sense of the individual and of individual autonomy, and a relatively complex form of social organization in which several layers of social activity are possible. Such associations to operate at a distance, as missionary societies must do, under certain implied economic conditions. Missionary societies could not have emerged where substantial cash surpluses were not available or where application of such surpluses was subject to outside control. Anderson rightly recognized that America provided the conditions for the voluntary association to operate to an extent previously unparalleled anywhere. He is equally correct in his assessment of the ecclesiological importance of the voluntary society. The early missionary movement in Britain had demonstrated that none of the existing church structures, representing all the classical forms of church government (Episcopal, Presbyterian and independent), was logistically capable of initiating and sustaining overseas missions. In both England and Scotland, it was the voluntary society that first performed these functions. Religious voluntary societies imply a certain conception of the nature of the church, which allows for initiatives by individuals outside the formal structures. The agonizing of many earnestly evangelical Anglicans over the compatibility of a missionary society with proper church order (Hennell, 1958) illustrates just how foreign to the main European Protestant traditions was the voluntary concept. Indeed, their agonizing was justifiable because the voluntary society came to subvert and bypass all the established structures of Western Protestantism (Walls, 1988).

For the voluntary society to be a principal organ of Christian activity requires, in fact, an atomized church, decentralized and dispersed. Again, nineteenth-century American provided just such conditions. Even in the 1830s Anderson speaks not, as an Evangelical clergyman of the Church of England might have done, of "the Church of Jesus Christ," but of "the evangelical *churches* of Christendom." He identifies the line of opportunity not simply in terms of the spiritual preparedness of the churches but in terms of the logistical potential of the way they are organized.

In Europe the distinction between church and voluntary society was fundamental, and the relationship was often pregnant with theological, and even political, content. Fundamental questions of identity could be at stake, especially where a society became in effect a church within the church. For many the thought of "leaving the church" was inconceivable, or painful beyond words. Voluntary societies of a religious character in Europe developed *in spite of* the churches, as a means of supplementing church life and activity or of undertaking what would not or could not be attempted through church structures. In America the line between church and voluntary association was much more blurred, until church membership itself became almost like that of a voluntary association. A congregation, a whole denomination, could be thought of as a voluntary society, open to an individual to join or not. In times of strain or dissent, it could be no great matter to leave and join — or even start — another.

Anderson readily links the voluntary association with American ways of government, seeing both as the fruit of the Protestant Gospel. The voluntary association is "free, open, responsible, embracing all ages, the masses of the people." Such language, hinting at "democracy," would hardly be to the taste of contemporary English evangelical clergy, anxious to make clear that "the distinguishing doctrines of the Gospel" (and a church missionary society committed to them) did not threaten but rather maintained both ecclesiastical and social order. Anderson, however, goes on to connect the principle of free association with "our own form of government" and especially with the operation of that form of government "over a broad continent" as one of the outstanding signs of Christian progress. Here already in the 1830s is the enunciation of the providential preparation of America for its missionary destiny, which Austin Phelps was declaring half a century later. At least they had this justification: all the factors — political, intellectual, economic, social, and religious — that made the Protestant missionary movement possible in its European beginnings were present in far greater abundance in America. In missions as in so much else, America proved to be the West writ large.

Frontier Missions and Foreign Missions

I have already argued that the greatest success of the nineteenth-century missions was the Christianization of the United States. There was a reflex result of this. The American overseas missionary movement itself was a continuation and extended application of the evangelical process at home. The American missionary movement even today is deeply marked by the frontier experience and the movements that brought religion so spectacularly to the cities.

Even in the 1830s Anderson thought of Christian civilization working "over a broad continent." The sense of space is a fundamental of American experience. American thinking is conditioned to expansion. Anderson's European contemporaries, if they thought of space at all, were most likely to think of "empty" lands as a possible destination for surplus population or unwanted elements within it; that is, of off-loading a problem, which could thereafter be forgotten.

This conditioning has its effect in the religious sphere. European Christians, even those who dissented from their state churches, thought of Christianity in essentially territorial terms, of "the parish," of maintaining the church's activity in a particular locality. By the middle of the nineteenth century they were aware of a religious crisis, especially in the large cities and the industrial towns, but they thought of it as a pastoral crisis. Reports abounded on church attendance or the lack of it. The remedies were to serve the churchless poor: more churches, larger churches, better-sited churches, more free seats in proportion to rented pews, special churches where decent clothes were not required, more or better ministers, or more systematic parish visitation. Another churchly preoccupation was education, and the proper place of the church in its provision. Anti-Christian (or at least anticlerical) sentiments in society or in government led others to rally the faithful to defend the church as the basis and moral guarantee of a healthy society—the Christendom principle in fact. Evangelicals shared this essentially backward-looking thinking with other types of churchmen. Europeans saw the religious crisis of the nineteenth century as a decline from an accepted standard, of departure from norms established long before.

By contrast, America was a mission field. The moving frontier received primary evangelism, the delivery of the elements of the Christian gospel. Frontier religion called for individual commitment yet socialized the individual and strengthened the family unit. It gave emotional release, supplied support for endurance of difficulties, and provided elements of a popular culture. Its leading representatives visibly shared the life and conditions of the communities they served. While its presence was a link with a lost and irrecoverable past, it was unencumbered by old institutions or distant power centers.

The apparently limitless space of America, the rolling movement of population, inhibited both the European parish principle and ponderous, centralized strategies controlled by remote hierarchies. Even the accumulated experience of the well-established East Coast churches was little use on the frontier. American Christianity could keep up with the population movement only by being entrepreneurial. There was scope for the inspired individual, for the eccentric, even for the charlatan. It was the triumph of the voluntary principle.

The development of the American cities simply extended the principle of frontier evangelism, with its flexibility, adaptation, and innovation. As early as 1835 it was possible to set up in New York a seminary that was adapted to city concerns, directed to social service as well as the pastorate, and specifically detached from denominational structures (Handy, 1987)—an institution that would have been inconceivable in Britain in the period. New methods of evangelism emerged, designed for the city, such as the evangelistic campaign. New modes of Christian thinking —adventism, apocalypticism, the holiness movement, and Pentecostal-

ism—developed in the new setting, laying claims to the discovery or rediscovery of a lost Christian substance. Europe, on the whole, was not
much impressed by the American experience and generally did not expect to learn much from it. Nevertheless, Christianity expanded in the
cities of America rather than in those of Europe.

In the United States, as in Europe, effective overseas missions had
begun not within the official church structures but in voluntary societies.
By the Civil War period most of the major denominations had set up a
board of missions, and the societies were thereby coopted into the
churches (Rabe, 1978); the most important society, the American Board,
was left to the congregationalists by default. Even here the voluntary
principle took over. Far from missions being absorbed into ecclesiastical
structures, a wave of new mission societies emerged in the later nineteenth century, transferring to overseas missions values, activities, and
attitudes, which had made possible the evangelization of the frontier and
the cities.

Making Friends by the Mammon of Unrighteousness

The Christianization of America reached its climax as American industrial enterprise and capacity took on a world significance. This combined with the frontier antecedents to give American missions a distinctive style only partly modified by the immense theological divergences,
which American missions display. The style is innovative, entrepreneurial, and problem-solving. It is marked by a stress on organization and efficient business methods, including a readiness to invest in what might
crudely be called product development and market research. The academic study of missions began in Scotland (Myklebust, 1951) but, despite
a sizable British Mission involvement, found no permanent home in Britain. In the Netherlands and Germany it became a specialized branch of
systematic theology. In the United States its characteristic development
has been a plethora of surveys, analyses, atlases, and statistical reviews.
In its attitude to money the American missionary movement has been uninhibited.

Much of this may be due to the circumstances surrounding America's rise to be the premier industrial nation in the same period as its emergence as a major (and ultimately the major) source of Christian missionaries. In America the relationship between entrepreneurial effort and
efficiency and financial reward was more direct and less ambiguous than
in Europe; in America industrial transformation was accompanied by
Christian expansion, whereas in Europe industrialization usually coincided with Christian decline. At any rate, American missions seem to

have accepted unquestioningly the norms of entrepreneurial activity, efficient organization, and full financing exalted by American business.[8] The voluntary principle made American religious organization societal rather than ecclesiastical. While this loose structure might be, as Anderson said, "free, open, responsible, embracing all classes, both sexes, all ages, the masses of the people," it was peculiarly open to wealthy businessmen, and to the influence of their ideas and methods. John R. Mott believed that part of the greatness of D. L. Moody as an evangelist was his mobilization of Christian businessmen to maintain missions at home and abroad. Mott himself emulated Moody in this respect, freely soliciting funds from wealthy patrons to finance international student organization and relying for funding of many of his special projects on a few very rich people.

European missions also benefited from the wealthy supporter, especially for special projects, as the story of "Arthington's million" shows (Fullerton, 1929). There was, however, often an uneasy conscience about wealth, an anxiety not to overstress money, a suspicion of organization lest it supplant reliance on the Holy Spirit, and sometimes a conviction that the solicitation of funds for God's work was actually to be avoided. This was specifically so in the faith missions, especially the China Inland Mission, which profoundly influenced the spirituality of the British missionary movement. The extension of organization and a "worldly" attitude to money were things that the new spirituality deplored in the older missions.

Church and State

The self-evident excellence of "our own form of government" remained axiomatic amongst American friends of missions. It was an easy step from this to the universal applicability of "our own form of government," despite the fact that it manifestly does not flourish over a great part of the globe. Nothing more marked the departure of American and European governmental models than the separation of the church and state, a formal (though far from an actual) abandonment of the Christendom principle.

The effects have been paradoxical. The separation of church and state has not only become a constitutional axiom; it has become a sort of theological virtue, almost an article of faith of American Christianity. It has been carried by American missions into many complex situations overseas. The combination of this dogma with faith in the superiority of the American Constitution (to which many American institutions not constitutional in character have been unconsciously assimilated) has sometimes led to simplistic political attitudes on the part of American missionaries: It is as though a belief that the church and state should be separate somehow miraculously separates the spheres of religion and politics so that they cannot be confused. American missions have frequently underestimated the political implications of their work and even of their presence. A recent study shows how American missionaries in Vietnam sincerely believed themselves to be maintaining the principle while using United States Army facilities and identifying openly with American troops and aims; the agonizing of other American missionaries with a historic "peace tradition" as the political implications of relief work began to dawn (James, 1989).

Premillenarian beliefs, strong in certain areas of American Christianity, have tended to sharpen the distinction between a spiritual and a secular sphere, and to interpret the main Christian responsibility in the former as the convincing enunciation of verbal statements. Puzzlement has followed when others have seen such activity as having political implications.[9] An older, but not necessarily much more politically sophisticated, American missionary tradition has openly applied itself to social change abroad. This was exemplified in the identification with the early twentieth-century Chinese revolution and the efforts to assist the Kuomintang in the modernization of China (Rabe, 1978; Thomson, 1969). The tradition has been maintained more recently by the older American churches' support for sizable development programs. It is rooted in another well-established American concept: the church separate from the state but actively mobilizing the community for good purposes. In the United States the Christendom idea was transmuted, not destroyed.

In the imperial era American missions were sometimes, with varying degrees of justification, seen as undermining colonial government authority. Apocalyptic preaching, more characteristic of American than of other missions, was not usually welcome; an insecure administration was unlikely to relish the confident predictions of a cataclysmic end to the existing order. The adventist Joseph Booth was the inspiration for John Chilembwe, shot by the British for the Nyasaland Rising of 1915 (Shepperson and Price, 1958). In India during the later phases of the British *raj* more conventional American missionaries could be under suspicion as supporters of the national movement (Keitahn, 1973; Thomas, 1979). If nowadays an American presence is denounced as imperialist, at an earlier stage it was a reminder of the first colonial independence movement, a beacon of inspiration to the first generation of nationalist leaders in both India and Africa.

A number of scholars have pointed to the influence of Scottish common-sense philosophy on America, and its rigorous application to the theology (Noll, 1985). One result was the development of theology as though it were an exact science, with biblical data deployed as statements of unconditioned fact. This method is not uniquely American, but it has been particularly influential there. Within the mainline churches it helped to shape old Princeton theology.[10] A very different manifestation of a similar method appears in the dispensational schemes of C. I. Schofield and others (Sandeen, 1970: 222–224), and it is worth remembering that one intended use of the Schofield Bible was as a ready reference for busy missionaries.

Frontier conditions may have caused the development of a specially American form of Protestantism — indeed arguably a new tradition of Christianity to be distinguished from historic Reformational Protestantism. The success of frontier evangelism, the vigor of new Christian communities in the new lands or the new cities, must constantly have brought the sense of bringing the church to birth or rebirth, of starting Christian history again. The application of common sense to the biblical data in such an atmosphere made natural a development that might be called "patternism." Statements in the scriptures were used as a basis of deduction of an absolute "New Testament pattern" to which church life should conform, irrespective of society, history, or culture. Church history is largely irrelevant to patternism, except insofar as it illustrates approximation to a declension from the deduced pattern. Adventist, Pentecostal, holiness, and other movements, which announced a new start in the rediscovery of some particular New Testament phenomenon, had an obvious interest in patternism, but its influence was much wider. A. B. Simpson, a major figure in one line of American mission development, discerned a New Testament pattern for the church in which elements from his Reformed background mingled with elements of standard American evangelicalism, holiness teaching, and spiritual healing. Despite a strong emphasis on the congregational unit, the crucial nature of the pattern was reflected in the establishment of a central Bible college; the model has been repeated overseas in the Christian and Missionary Alliance, which derives from Simpson's work.

Methodological common sense applied to the Bible, with the foreshortened historical perspective, the supremacy of the voluntary principle, and the fragility of the church principle combined with a pragmatic, activist problem-solving orientation, produced the characteristically American phenomenon of fundamentalism. This tradition is to be distinguished from Protestant evangelicalism and pietism and conservative and confessional forms of Protestantism, though all these contributed to the making of fundamentalism and many of their concerns and beliefs overlap with it. The contrast is seen in two related features of the American phenomenon, both of which have had an impact in the international sphere.

The first of these is the growth of what are in effect new creeds: catalogues of belief set out as statements of unconditioned fact. The Christian faith becomes progressively defined on topics as various as the fixity of biological species, the exact order of events in the last days of Jesus, and even the scriptural mode of financing missionary support. There are plenty of examples in earlier Christian history of consideration and speculation on such topics, but creedal statements about them are most characteristic of modern America. It is a problem-solving instinct at work again. The order is: identify the problem which is disturbing people; apply the tools to hand and solve the problem; then pass on to the next problem. Fundamentalism is problem-solving theology.

The second particularly American development is the use of such extended creeds as tests of fellowship or cooperation. This principle of separation is perhaps the converse of the principle of free association, which was so potent in the making of American religion. Where the church concept is virtually absorbed into the voluntary society concept, fellowship is virtually identified with association; it is an atomized vision of the church.

European evangelicalism of the last two centuries can produce examples of patternism. Some of the most dramatic (Irvingism, for example) proved peripheral and temporary. The most significant patternist movement, the brethren movement, has had a complex history (Rowdon, 1967) and been influential within European evangelicalism but has ever remained small. (Many of its ideas have found a new home in American patternist traditions — Schofield is thoroughly Darbyite.) On the whole, however, European movements that have arisen from the evangelical revival have looked back to the ancient creeds and the Reformation confessions in defining their beliefs, being eager to demonstrate their continuity with the main Christian tradition of the West. For the most part European evangelicals have been in no hurry to separate from their historic churches, nor have they developed extended creeds.

America and the Twentieth-Century Development of Christianity

Much of American Christianity and much of the American mission presence, past and present, irrespective of its theological color, reflects the same energetic expansionism, resourcefulness, adoption of contemporary technology and business methods, and uninhibited use of money; the same comparatively short-range historical consciousness; the same mental separation of the spiritual and civil realms combined with a conviction of the superlative excellence, if not the universal relevance, of the

United States Constitution and American values; and the same approach to theology, church life, and mission activity in terms of addressing problems and finding solutions.

The frontier pioneer ideal, backed by an entrepreneurial, problem-solving, business-oriented approach, was characteristic of American missions across the theological spectrum. William R. Hutchison has recently explained the background and demonstrated the dynamics of a major phase of the American movement, quoting a description from one of his informants of "Peace Corps types before the Peace Corps" (Hutchison, 1987). This movement could, for instance, deploy substantial human resources to the modernization of China's educational, medical, agricultural, and eventually political processes in the years when China faced west. People within it could see service with the Chinese government as an extension of the missionary vocation; and John R. Mott himself nearly became the United States ambassador to China. The same ideals and methods, *mutatis mutandis*, lay behind successive efforts for the mobilization (a favorite word, replacing the metaphors of military occupation and conquest that once came naturally to British lips) of verbal evangelism on the part of those for whom such secular concerns seemed trivial or distracting because when the Gospel had been preached to all lands the return of Christ would bring healing to all earth's ills.

This American impact on the missionary movement at the end of the last century came at a crucial time, just as the Christian center of gravity began to shift to North America. The missionary movement helped to bring distinctive, homegrown features of American Christianity into the mainstream of Christian life, organization, and transmission in the twentieth century. America did not invent the missionary conference; there was a large-scale meeting in Liverpool as early as 1860, and the idea goes back as far as William Carey. America did develop the "targeted" conference, which was not only a forum for consultation but a springboard for activity and a megaphone to announce it. In 1886, the year when the already elderly Austin Phelps was declaring America's manifest destiny to be the great missionary nation, D. L. Moody convened the Mount Hermon Conference, which was directed at college students. At the conference, 100 students dedicated themselves to be "foreign missionaries"; within two years, three thousand had made a similar declaration (G. H. Anderson, 1988: 99). Though most of the early student volunteers served within regular mission organizations of the churches or other established societies, the organization of the movement on a student basis bypassed all the existing church structures. It was far more effective than the recruiting mechanisms of any or all of those existing organizations. Its *bona fides* were guaranteed by the support of national figures — Moody, Pierson, and Gordon — but the visible leadership was of the student or recently ex-student generation. It combined the principle of active local cells with an articulate central policy and propaganda and an energetic traveling staff, as well as the unashamedly American mobilization of Mammon for the sake of mission. Because of its flexible, adaptive character, and ability to appeal to a common constituency, that of Christian students in various countries, it could assume an international and transconfessional character that would have produced formidable barriers for any movement beginning within the church structures. The American-originated student missionary movement produced an informal ecumenical movement well ahead of effective initiatives from within the churches.

The conciliar character of twentieth-century Christianity is one of its most marked features. Despite the greatly increased cultural pluriformity, there has never been so much effort put into international Christian consultation. In the case of the World Council of Churches, which now represents many orthodox as well as Protestant bodies, the connection with the movement we have been considering is direct (Hopkins, 1979: chapters 11 – 12; Rouse and Neill, 1986). The World Missionary Conference, Edinburgh 1910, is the council's lineal ancestor, and the International Missionary Council, which arose from that conference, was long ago absorbed into the council; the Edinburgh conference undoubtedly owed much to the activities associated with the volunteer movement. Within the Roman Catholic church this conciliar character has entered, too, by means of the Synod of Bishops since the Second Vatican Council; though there are apparently current centralist pressures to curtail its powers, the institution has shifted the balance of representation in the church. A third conciliar force, itself of American origin, has arisen in the Lausanne Committee for World Evangelization (Douglas, 1975), thought of almost as an alternative World Council of Churches in some quarters. Creedally creative American evangelical Christianity could not reconcile itself to a world council more concerned with accommodation and exchange than with definition and separation. The priority of verbal evangelism and the detachment from ultimate theological concern for social change engendered by premillennialism and the insistence on church-state separation could not be reconciled with the council's increasing concern for social justice as a Christian preoccupation. What some participants saw as primarily an instrument for more effective evangelism, others saw as an ecumenical movement among evangelicals. As the Lausanne movement has developed, however, participants from the southern continents, whose churches originate from the American evangelical tradition, have brought to it new emphases on social justice and renewal. This cooperation is perhaps a natural fruit of the combination of global communications, worldwide differing Christianity, and national consciousness of identity, but its development has much to do with American missionary movements.

The line from the student volunteer movement to the Edinburgh conference and the International Missionary Council is carried by the figure of John R. Mott, who embodies the application of business methods to religious societies. He provided an infrastructure for an international missionary movement. There was no conceivable basis for this in any of the structures that had emerged from the century of European missionary endeavor.

The application of business methods produced an application to research and development. It was the large-scale American entry to the missionary movement that produced massive, if crude, works of research like J. S. Dennis's *Christian Missions and Social Progress* (Dennis 1897– 1899: 13). Mott developed the business habit of targets. The appeal of the student watchword, "the evangelization of the world in this generation," to British volunteers was essentially rhetorical — a rallying cry to a tired movement and a self-regarding church. To Mott it was a business proposition, with a careful definition and a figure attached — he calculated it would need fifty thousand missionaries (Robert, 1986). He was capable of building long-term research into mission planning. Using the Young Men's Christian Association (YMCA) as a front organization, he had scholars like J. N. Farquhar and K. J. Saunders work on Hindu and Buddhist literature. When circumstances seemed to require it, he even secured funding for Farquhar to divide his year between India and Oxford (Sharpe, 1953).

These features have remained a mark of the American missionary movement and notably of its principal, the evangelical, arm. The Missions Advanced Research and Communications Center holds vast data banks on the world missionary situation. The Foreign Mission Board of the Southern Baptist Convention is the source of some of the most thoroughgoing attempts at statistical assessment of Christianity and its environment. It might be thought that some features of American Christianity would make cultural factors in Christian transmission irrelevant. It was, however, in evangelical circles that the Institute of Church Growth and the Fuller School of World Mission took foot, allying cultural research to a theory of evangelism, so that "culture" sometimes sounds almost like an evangelistic method. A new category has been identified, "unreached peoples," as a prime target for evangelism. Unreached peoples can range from ethnolinguistic units (the Tuareg) to social or occupational groups (bus girls in Seoul). An analysis of unreached peoples is produced regularly. The U.S. Center for World Mission and the frontier missions movement, associated especially with the work of Ralph Winter, maintain a conscious link with the nineteenth-century student movement, with a target of "a church for every people by the year 2000" and precise personnel and logistical targets for attaining this goal. One estimate is for a North American Protestant mission force of 135,000 (Coote, 1988: 68f).

The American Missionary Movement

The American missionary movement that entered into its prime in the 1880s registered some remarkable achievements. It reinvigorated European missions, gave new goals and, by means of the student volunteer movement, attracted not only crowds of new missionary recruits, but a new type of well-educated missionary recruit. It was responsible for the effective organization of missions both on a national and an international basis, which enabled missions to develop largely untrammeled by the home church structures of Europe and America, and in some respects to influence those churches, and it, more than any other single factor, set on foot the movement towards cooperation, which is perhaps the most outstanding new feature of twentieth-century Christianity with its newfound global density.

All this came from the mainstream of the American movement, and this is far from the whole story. This paper has not considered the black American missionary movement at all. Its full significance needs still to be explored, but apart from all else it affected Ethiopianism in Africa and helped to produce independent forms of African Christianity (Johnson, 1977; Natsoulas, 1981). More recently, American black theology was critical for the emergence of an important theological current in South Africa (Moore, 1974).

Even some more peripheral movements in American Christianity, which seem particularly tied to the specificities of an American situation, have proven catalytic in the Christianity of the southern continents. Adventism (and its Russellite by-form) had potent effects in Central Africa (Greschat, 1967) and Melanesia (Oosterwal, 1973; Forman, 1982: 52–54) and influenced as significant a West African figure as the Prophet Harris (Shank, 1980). J. A. Dowie's Zion City is now something of a historical curiosity (Wacker, 1985), but it was an important ingredient in the rise of Southern African Zionism, now the spiritual home of millions (Sundkler, 1961 and 1976). In each case the American influence was significant but transitory. The movement once initiated had a dynamic of its own, which took it far beyond the American original. Pentecostalism, long on the fringe of American Protestantism, has developed as the Protestant orthodoxy of some Latin American countries; but its very success there may be linked by its adoption into a logic and a worldview that belong more to traditional local worldview than to Azuza Street (Westmeier, 1986).

All of which helps in the consideration of the significance of contemporary American missions and the other exported forms of American religion. The most important factor is neither the number of American missionaries nor their specific orientation but that southward movement of the Christian center of gravity with which we began. This means that the concerns and priorities of African, Asian, Latin American, and Pacific Christians are likely to shape the next phase of Christianity. The histories of the World Council of Churches and the Lausanne movement illustrate how even within conciliar organizations the original Western agenda can be modified or bypassed. In Lausanne circles, for instance, to judge from the trend of literature, evangelicals of the southern continents seem to evince more interest in questions of culture and indigenity and social justice than in the inerrancy debate or in eschatological specifics. On the other hand, the catalytic effects of American Christianity may continue. In Nigeria and Ghana the most rapidly growing Christian sector is probably no longer the independent prophet-healing churches, whose links with African tradition are so obvious but the new life movements, which have some resemblances to American Pentecostalism but a quite distinct form of leadership and ethos (Ojo, 1988; Hackett, 1989). Some Nigerian urban Christians have similarly caught on to elements of dispensational teaching, but it is the context that determines the significance. In a country where the numbers of Muslims and Christians are approximately in balance, where each community fears domination by the other, where a rumor or a religious procession may spark a riot, a car sticker declaring the approach of the Rapture or announcing "Jesus is coming!" has a force different from that of a similar emblem in Texas.

Notes

1. The crucial decision, whether gentile believers in Jesus must be treated as proselytes to Judaism, has to be made by the Jerusalem church (Acts 15). Even at a later stage, with the gentile mission well established, the Jerusalem church, which set the Christian norms, is represented as seeing the seal on its work as the conversion of zealous observant Jews (Acts 21:20).

2. The proportions here are extrapolated from the data in Barrett 1982, Global table 2.

3. Barrett, 1989: 20–21. These figures represent a downward revision of the figures he projected in 1982 but are still huge, and the direction of the trend continues the same.

4. "The Great Century" is the title of the three volumes of his *History of the Expansion of Christianity* relating to the period 1800–1914 (New York, 1941–47).

5. The president was William McKinley; the ex-president, Benjamin Harrison; the future president, Theodore Roosevelt. See *Ecumenical Missionary Conference New York 1900 Report*.

6. Wilson and Siewert (1986: 572) give the proportion as 60–65 percent; but their total world figure for Protestant missionaries is 80,000–85,000, and their figure for United States Protestant missionaries is 67,200 (as at 1985). The proportion is thus, on their own figures, far too low. Coote (1986) gives figures to show that many Western countries (above all, Ireland) produce more missionaries per head of population than does the United States; the overwhelming majority of these missionaries are Roman Catholic.

7. Coote (1986: 38) dates the "precipitous" decline of NCC-related mission agencies from about 1967. He shows that the figure of 1:9 of NCC-related missionaries to the total American Protestant force is distorted by two special cases, the Seventh Day Adventists and the Mennonite Central Committee, neither typical of the American historic Protestant churches. Without these, the ratio goes down to 1:14.

8. Well illustrated in both the title and the book by C. H. Patton, an officer of the American Board, *The Business of Missions*.

9. A recent press item reveals some interesting perceptions: "At Neak Luong [Cambodia] . . . the boatman shows his shoulder which was shattered when the first of seven US bombs which killed 300 people . . . fell on the market and the hospital at dawn during January 1973. . . . 'But the Americans built us a kitchen,' says a hospital worker, pointing out a prefabricated building built by the Mennonite Central Committee." *Guardian*, 27 December 1986.

10. The first paragraph heading of Charles Hodge's *Systematic Theology* (Vol. 1, New York 1872, 10) is "Theology a science."

References

Anderson, Gerald H.
1988   "American Protestants in Pursuit of Mission: 1886–1986." *International Bulletin of Missionary Research* 12:98–118.

Anderson, Rufus
1837   "The Time for the World's Conversion Come." *Religious Magazine* (Bos-

ton); as reprinted in R. Pierce Beaver (ed.), *To Advance the Gospel. Selections from the Writings of Rufus Anderson*. Grand Rapids: Eerdmans.

Barrett, David (ed.)
1982   *World Christian Encyclopedia*. Nairobi: Oxford University Press.

Barrett, David
1989   "Annual Statistical Table on Global Mission." *International Bulletin of Missionary Research* 13(1): 20–21.

Coote, Robert T.
1986   Samuel Wilson and J. Siewert (eds.) *Mission Handbook: North American Protestant Ministries Overseas*, 13th edition 36–76. Monrovia, California: MARC.

Douglas, James D.
1977   "Let the Earth Hear His Voice." *International Congress on World Evangelization Official Reference Volume*. Minneapolis: Lausanne Committee on World Evangelization.

Forman, Charles W.
1982   *The Island Churches of the South Pacific*. Maryknoll, N.Y.: Orbis Books.

Fullerton, W. Y.
1929   *Arthington and After. The Man and the Missions*. London: Carey Press.

Greschat, Hans-Jürgen
1967   *Kitawala, Ursprung, Ausbreitung und Religion der Watch Tower—Bewegung in Zentralafrika*. Marburg: Elwert.

Hackett, Rosalind I. J.
1988   *Religion in Calabar. The Religious Life and History of a Nigerian Town*. Berlin: Mouton de Gruyter.

Handy, Robert T.
1987   *A History of Union Theological Seminary in New York*. New York: Columbia University Press.

Hennell, Michael M.
1958   *John Venn and the Clapham Sect*. London: Lutterworth.

Hopkins, C. Howard
1979   *John R. Mott 1865–1955. A Biography*. Geneva: World Council of Churches, and Grand Rapids: Eerdmans.

Hogg, W. Richey
1977   "The role of American Protestantism in World Mission." In R. Pierce Beaver (ed.) *American Missions in Bicentennial Perspective*. South Pasadena: William Carey Library, 354–402.

Hutchison, William R.
1987 *Errand to the World: American Protestant Thought on Foreign Missions.* Chicago: University of Chicago Press.

James, B. Violet
1989 *American Protestant Missionaries and the Vietnam War.* Ph.D. dissertation, University of Aberdeen.

Johnson, W. N.
1977 *Worship and Freedom: A Black American Church in Zambia.* New York: Africana Publishing.

Keitahn, Ralph R.
1973 *Pilgrimage in India.* Madras: Christian Literature Society.

Latourette, Kenneth Scott
1961 *Christianity in a Revolutionary Age.* Vol. III. London: Eyre and Spottiswoode.

Moore, Basil
1974 *Black Theology: The South African Voice.* London: Hurst.

Mott, John R.
1900 *The Evangelization of the World in this Generation.* New York: Student Volunteer Missions Union.
1910 *The Decisive Hour of Christian Missions.* New York: Student Volunteer Missionary Union
1944 *The Larger Evangelism.* New York: Abingdon Cokesbury.

Myklebust, Olav Guttorm
1955 *The Study of Missions in Theological Education. An Historical Enquiry into the Place of World Evangelization in Western Protestant Ministerial Training with Particular Reference to Alexander Duff's Chair of Evangelistic Theology.* Oslo: Forlaget Land of Kirke.

Natsoulas, T.
1981 "Patriarch McGuire and the Spread of the African Orthodox Church to Africa." *Journal of Religion in Africa* 12(2): 81–104.

Noll, Mark A.
1985 "Common sense traditions and American evangelical thought." *American Quarterly* 37(2): 216:238.

Ojo, Matthew A.
1988 "Deeper Christian Life Ministry: A Case Study." *Journal of Religion in Africa* 18(2): 141–162.

Oosterwal, Gottfried
1973 *Modern Messianic Movements as a Theological and Missionary Challenge.* Elkhart, Ind.: Institute of Mennonite Studies.

Patton, C. H.
1924   *The Business of Missions*. New York: Macmillan.

Phelps, Austin
1891   *Introduction to Josiah Strong, Our Country*.

Rabe, V. H.
1978   *The Home Base of American China Missions, 1880 – 1920*. Cambridge, Mass: Harvard University Press for Council on Asian Studies.

Robert, Dana L.
1986   "The Origin of the Student Volunteer Watchword." *International Bulletin of Missionary Research*, 10(4): 146–149.

Rouse, Ruth, and Stephen Charles Neill
1986   *A History of the Ecumenical Movement 1517–1948*, 3rd edition. Geneva: World Council of Churches.

Sandeen, Ernest R.
1970   *The Roots of Fundamentalism: British and American Millenarianism 1800 –1930*. Chicago: University of Chicago Press.

Shank, David A.
1980   *A Prophet of Modern Times: The Thought of William Loade Harris, West African Precursor of the Reign of Christ*. Ph.D. dissertation, University of Aberdeen.

Sharpe, Eric J.
1953   *John Nicol Farquhar. A Memoir*. Calcutta: Association Press.

Shepperson, George, and Thomas Price
1958   *Independent African: John Chilembwe and the Origins, Setting and Significance of the Nyasaland Native Rising of 1915*. Edinburgh: Edinburgh University Press.

Sundkler, Bengt
1961   *Bantu Prophets in South Africa*, 2nd edition. London: Oxford University Press for International African Institute.
1976   *Zulu Zion and Some Swazi Zionists*. Lund: Gleerup.

Thomas, George
1979   *Christian Indians and Indian Nationalism 1885 – 1950*. Frankfurt: Peter Lang.

Thomson, James C., Jr.
1969   *While China Faced West: American Reformers in Nationalist China, 1928 –1937*. Cambridge, Mass.: Harvard University Press.

Walls, Andrew F.
1975   "Towards Understanding Africa's Place in Christian History." In J. S. Po-

bee (ed.) *Religion in a Pluralistic Society: Essays Presented to C. G. Baëta* 180–189. Leiden: Brill.
1983 "Such Boastings as the Gentiles Use: Thoughts on Imperialist Religion." In R. C. Bridges (ed.) *An African Miscellany for John Hargreaves* 109–116. Aberdeen: University of Aberdeen African Studies Group.
1984 "Christian Expansion Reconsidered." In Monica Hill (ed). *How to Plant Churches* 34–43. London: MARC Europe.
1988 "Missionary Societies and the Fortunate Subversion of the Church." *Evangelical Quarterly*, 88(2): 141–155.
1990a "The American Dimension in the History of the Missionary Movement." In Joel Carpenter and Wilbert R. Shenk (eds.) *Earthen Vessels: Evangelicals, Culture and the American Missionary Enterprise*. Grand Rapids: Eerdmans.
1990b "Kolonialismus." In *Theologische Realenzyklopädie*. Göttingen: Vandenhoek und Ruprecht.

Westmeier, Karl-Wilhelm
1986 *Reconciling Heaven and Earth. The Transcendental Enthusiasm and Growth of an Urban Protestant Community, Bogota, Colombia.* Frankfurt: Peter Lang.

Wilson, Samuel, and J. Siewert
1986 *Mission Handbook: North American Protestant Ministries Overseas*, 13th edition. Monrovia, California: MARC.

Winter, Ralph D.
1970 *Twenty-five Unbelievable Years, 1945 to 1969.* Pasadena: William Carey Library.

8

The Yogi and the Commissar: Christian Missions and the New World Order in Africa

Lamin Sanneh

It is a firm and widespread view that Christian missions everywhere introduced forces of disruption and antagonism, that, with forethought, they interfered with mechanisms of control, and thus masterminded the capitulation of indigenous societies under Western hegemony. There is, of course, some evidence for this, yet, without qualifying the charge, it overlooks the mixed legacy of mission in Africa and makes missionaries partners in the Western subjugation of Africa.

As it happens, missionaries themselves wrote substantially about their reasons and motives of service, which for some included bringing Africans into the "light of civilization," and thus into continuity with the Western experience. On this basis, it has been easy to portray missionaries as overseas agents of their countries. Consequently, Christian missions have been depicted as a vehicle for Western political and cultural dominance, cutting a wide and accessible path through indigenous societies and securing the spiritual surrender of the people before formal suzerainty was imposed. In this view, the Supreme Being of missionary preaching was practically synonymous with the dominant worldview of the colonial overlords, so that colonialism itself was moralized into a religious system. It follows from this that African converts were political surrogates, finding in Western hegemony subservience to the God of the West. The school and the church became twin engines that thrust upon Africa the Western machinery of exploitation and accelerated Africa's disinheritance. Thus, through educated converts the West came within striking range of societies now stripped of the capacity to resist. The missionary and the colonialist were, therefore, the yogi and the commissar who complemented each other: the one supplied pacified natives for the other's aggressive strategy.

This conspirational interpretation of the religious history of the West has assumed great significance in Africa in the light of Western economic dominance there. The popularity of the theory has been its great asset, although its tacit premise, that the mission was pseudopolitical ideology, raises more questions than answers. One major difficulty is the element of paradox and prophetic self-scrutiny in religion, something that generates both the theme and its counterthrust, as I shall describe in this paper. At any rate, those scholars who view the mission in this way have placed Africa within the worldwide system of Western economic hegemony and its disruptive effects.

This is the great theme that has galvanized more than one generation of scholars and has animated a good deal of the field. Its intellectual legacy was extended by two main channels: first, by finding in missionaries an abundant source of the paradoxical villain of history, and, second, by seeing native converts as classic symbols of Western oppression. In the general post-World War mood of irony, writers flocked to the subject of missionaries to confirm how history belied religious motives and good intentions, and to conversion as primal reaction to superior Western power.

I attempt here a three-part exposition that revises standard approaches to the history of missions. Whatever the worldwide system into which missions brought, or are alleged to have brought Africans, it was not at the price of profound indigenous self-understanding. In the first part I shall raise briefly the question of how the study, or lack of study, of missions has affected the self-image of the West. In the second, I shall discuss some of the negative criticisms that have been made of missions, and point out gaps in the material. In the third and final part, I shall offer an alternative evaluation of the evidence. I shall for the most part limit the field to South Africa, although similar instances will be signaled for other parts of Africa.

Mission and the Western Image: Part I

Seldom does history deliver so severe and unanimous a verdict as that concerning the faults of mission, one that has hardened into an ideological sentence, making the missionaries guilty whatever the facts: if they failed to make converts, or make good ones, that proved the naiveté of their religious credentials, and if they made any, then they are guilty of political or economic manipulation. African societies are similarly stigmatized: if they show evidence of unfruitful Christian contact, that is put as a charge to their primitive state, and if they adopt the new religion, they are dismissed as naive imitators. In either case, evidence of Christianity in Africa is regarded as evidence also of the superior claims of Europe over Africa, claims that enlightened opinion must reject. Given the presumed connection between missions and Western hegemonic interests, it was natural for scholars to prosecute the whole enterprise on a premise of presumed guilt, with their own labors as suitable restitution.

Missionaries themselves encouraged, or were seen to encourage, through confessions and admissions, such hand-wringing tendencies, which the habit of recordkeeping preserved in copious detail. Consequently, a number of scholars were unable to avoid the methodological trap of substituting solid, face-value documentation for rigorous analysis, content with the superficial impression of how religious agents confirmed, or appeared to confirm, Western mischief-making. Presumption acquired the force of verdict, with opinions differing perhaps on the severity of the judgment. Even missionary protagonists had a tendency towards special pleading, something that merely hardened the mood and unwittingly pushed the subject to the margins of European and American critical self-understanding. Anyone surveying the scene today will be struck by how the subject of Christian missions has been comprehensively banished from nearly all respectable academic syllabi and from mainstream religious scholarship. The few admirable exceptions we have are of historians and other professional academics who are not necessarily disposed to take seriously the religious factor in mission. Thus, the great imbalance between academic interest and the religious standard acts to insulate the unfavorable image of the West from corrective scrutiny in the light of missionary experience.

Motives and Intentions

The decision of scholars to pursue the subject with the themes of resistance and capitulation, therefore, encourages the conspirational view. A certain guilt-ridden circularity is built into the process, a repetitive mode in which allegation is joined to final judgment by a chain of predisposed evidence, procedure, and inference. The result is that religious evidence is stripped of religious content, and religious motives of any shred of credibility. "Motives" and "intentions" are in fact erected into covert pillars of domination and paternalism, and as such as reasons for discounting the enterprise. When scholars have taken account of projects of Western domination in the Third World, they have found in the issue of motive and intention the necessary evidence for missionary culpability.

While accepting a good deal in those charges, I would like to suggest that we build the case for or against Christian missions on a different foundation if we are to make sense of what missions accomplished, or failed to accomplish, in Africa and elsewhere. My proposal, henceforth, is in two stages: first, to shift the center of interest from missionary motives, or what are alleged to be missionary motives, to missionary practices and effects on the ground, and, second, to pursue the implications of vernacular context for existing categories of interpretation. In that second stage I shall return to the question of motives in the context of missionary self-scrutiny. My approach will reaffirm many of the old formulations and, relating them all to the Christian religious standard on the ground, draw a radically different conclusion. I shall, therefore, reiterate in part the important connection between religion and politics, mission and colonialism, salvation and economics, conversion and culture, foreign agency and indigenous leadership, motive and consequence, Christianity and civilization, social cohesion and individualism, and so on, before attempting an overhaul of the interpretive apparatus. One of the major questions we shall try to answer is what part, if any, Christian missions played in the emergence of the new world order in Africa, and how that may or may not have impinged on the colonial strategy as such.

Conversion and the Assault on the Old Order: Part II

We should examine in this part an important argument that persists through the history of Christian missions, and this is the serious charge that mission suppressed indigenous creativity and thus hindered social advancement and cultural progress.

In a forceful and influential article published some thirty years ago, Bertram Hutchinson (1957) examined the harmful legacy of Christian missionary activity in South Africa, calling attention to the disruptive impact of Christian teaching on African social life and institutions. He takes up the question of the premeditated assault missionaries launched, or are charged with having launched, upon the fabric of African life and custom. The chief fault of the missionary, Hutchinson argues, was that the change he wished to introduce in Bantu society "was premeditated. Knowing the social changes he wished for, the missionary worked deliberately to achieve them" (1957:175), although, even if we agreed with the proposition of Allmacht der Gedanken,[1] missionary wishes often lagged far behind reality. Here is a description in Natal in 1894–95 of the extreme social dislocation that conversion was said to have created for Africans.

The Natives are averse to the mission stations, as enticing first their daughters, then their sons, and so severing their families . . . Some become in that way so severed from their parents as to be homeless, and wander to towns or elsewhere and come to grief; but if they remained at home under entire control of their parents, out of school hours . . . whatever little schooling or industry they learnt would be made good use of. Much misery and trouble is brought on parents by the interference and enticing away of their children, and this has become a general grievance, and to such an extent that in several instances owners of kraals have, in a body, objected most strongly to have a school or teacher located in their vicinity. (Cited in Hutchinson, 1957:174)

The thrust of Hutchinson's message is that missionaries were intolerant of African customs, instituted measures to discourage or punish converts who observed traditional sanctions, and created widespread confusion of values among the people. Yet reading between the lines, this frontal attack on the mission has to be qualified by factors of missionary inadequacy, ineffectiveness, ignorance, self-criticism, resource limitation, logistics of range and supply, and manpower shortage, all of which taken together paints a picture of fundamental powerlessness by the missionary as an agent of wholesale social change. However, it would be wrong to exclude entirely the missionary role in the dramatic changes that entered African society from the nineteenth century, and in this Hutchinson's article makes several useful points. It would be appropriate, therefore, to deal with the issues he raises before turning to the final stage in our exposition.

On the question of mission as a colonialist fifth column, Hutchinson offers the example of Dr. Philip of the London Missionary Society who made the link in 1828 between missionary pioneering and the penetration of European power into Africa, saying, "Missionary stations are the most efficient agents which can be employed to promote the internal strength of our colonies, and the cheapest and best military posts a government can employ" (See Philip, 1828:227). This created a useful collaboration between missions and the British government, although on the ground local chiefs sought missionary aid for the opposite reason: as a bulwark against the encroachments of European settlers, a difference in perception highly relevant to the case I shall advance about the repercussions of the vernacular principle in missionary work. In the context of changes afoot in South Africa, missionaries acted as brokers between the Africans and Europeans. The missionaries, Hutchinson writes, "gave invaluable aid to the Bantu people in negotiations with Europeans on land questions, on cattle-raiding, frontier incidents, and other matters which exacerbated relations between black and white. The missionary was therefore rarely molested. Even among tribes which had never seen a missionary his reputation preceded him and preserved him from attack" (1957:161). At this stage of things, Africans perceived missionaries as friends rather than as foes. As a consequence, missionaries found themselves being wooed and competed for by Bantu chiefs who sought to attract missions to their areas as a buffer and a prestige symbol. There was, of course, an enormous risk in this enterprise, both from the disruptive potential of missions within chiefdoms and from losing their footing in interchiefly disputes and wrangles. Nevertheless missions had not yet acquired a bad reputation among Africans, although clearly they had aroused unrealistic hopes.

A similar problem pertains to the charge of missions as "enclaves," whereby converts are removed from society and placed in mission stations under missionary tutelage. Enclaving did occur, and was pursued by many missions as a basic policy in the conversion process.[2] In addition, enclaving did introduce disruptive change by encouraging atomistic individualism and parasitic dependence at the same time. The adoption by African converts of European names and clothing, the consumption of European goods, the use of new tools and implements, enrollment in European schools, taking up of European habits and tastes, all these and more ruptured tribal bonds of solidarity and reciprocity and induced dependence on foreign customs. Furthermore, enclaving did allow the missions to exercise considerable leverage with potential converts, offering economic rewards as inducement for belonging to the society of the mission station, particularly at a time when missions were being given generous land concessions by the government (Hutchinson, 1957).

However, enclaving can be argued to have had serious limitations, and those relatively few Africans who did avail themselves of it soon became disenchanted with it, a situation which just as soon convinced the missionaries, too, of the obstacles it did create for their goals. One missionary wrote ruefully in 1840 about how the whole scheme had backfired.

> We discovered that many of the Fingos who had come to us, did so in the idea that we could procure for them rich pastures for the grazing of their cattle: being disappointed in this hope, their good will was exchanged for bitter enmity; they refused to attend our worship, and spoke loudly against the doctrine of God's Word. (Cited in Hutchinson, 1957:165)

In time opposition to missions as enclaves was raised to the highest levels of traditional authority, with the chiefs pointing out the deleterious effects of enclaving in contrast to the other aspects of missionary practice. As the Bantu chiefs saw it, enclaving was, perhaps not unwittingly, promoting missionaries into the role of rival chiefs, encouraging scof-flaws to seek asylum from constituted authority there, a position from which mission stations could only have emerged as inferior in relation to the system of justice dispensed in the kraal. One representative chief summed up the situation in these words, taking care to challenge missionaries on their own ground:

> I like very much to live with the teachers (i.e., missionaries) if they would not take my people, and give them to the Government; for they are my people. Let these school people pray for me. How is it that the Government takes them to spill blood? How is it that you teachers take them away? Whenever one believes, he goes away from me. Why is it that you call them all to live in one place? Is it God who tells you to do so? I do not like your method of breaking up the kraal. Let the believing Kaffir look to his own countrymen, and not go away, but teach others. (Cited in Hutchinson, 1957:169)

Thus, what started out as an advantageous position for missions turned out to be a liability, and converts who should have capitulated un-questioningly to missionary tutelage were raising awkward questions in defiance. Instead of producing commissars to pattern, the mission stations were turning away misadjusted refuseniks. The unenviable missionaries, who were stranded square in the cross fire of European intentions and African aspirations with little to show for their troubles, deserved sympathy.

They got little of that from senior colonial administrators who, aware of the opposition missionary methods had incurred among the Africans, despaired of rekindling earlier optimism and began questioning the usefulness of Christian missions altogether. The governors of Cape Colony in 1847 and 1848, for example, spoke of having seen neither substantial conversions in the missions nor an increase in demand for European merchandise among the Africans thus affected (Hutchinson, 1957:169), wondering in effect to what purpose the whole enterprise, and its ancillary political attachments, was being undertaken. In 1853 the governor spoke derisively of missions having only stimulated the appetite for ardent spirits, muskets, and gunpowder, hinting thereby at the setback of the spiritual goals missionaries had set and which, for slightly different reasons, colonial officials had encouraged.

From other parts of Africa we have instances of similar resistance to the presence of missionaries. For example, when European missionaries first arrived in Ashanti, Ghana (former Gold Coast), the Asantehene, the king, responded to the call to send children to school by saying that no sensible person could countenance a project that required children to be released from productive labor on farms and have them sit all day idly learning "hoy, hoy, hoy!" (Sanneh, 1983). The repository of her people's customs and traditions, an old Ewe grandmother counseled a royal conclave of her area against sending their children to Western schools then appearing in the country. "I myself," she remonstrated in one case, "do not approve of Foli learning from books; for the son of a king does not wear shoes nor carry an umbrella before he is a king. If he now goes to school and learns to read, he will adopt the white man's custom, he will wear shoes and carry an umbrella, and in doing these things he will break the sacred laws of our family" (Westermann, 1949:45). While it is true that European education, and in particular the dominant segment of it that Christian missions controlled, changed Africa in real and enduring ways, it is difficult to claim it as the source of social and cultural breakdown in Africa.

A major fault of missionaries, according to the prevalent view, was their fundamental antipathy to the African social and religious values, and to the traditional family institution that embodies them. The African family, therefore, was the logical place for missionaries to strike in order to bring the changes they saw as a prerequisite for Christian conversion. For this reason the missionaries among the Bantu targeted lobola, the marriage dowry, polygamy, and circumcision for concerted action. Lobola was the custom whereby a young man preparing to marry offers cattle as payment to the bride's family. That and the other customs were vehemently opposed by missionaries. Lobola, for example, was erroneously described as wife purchase, and therefore illegal. As for polygamy, it was proof to the missionaries of the proverbial lust of the African, while circumcision provided a cover for barbaric indulgence.

For the missionaries, lobola, like much else, proved a prickly pear to grasp. As an integral part of the marriage system, it safeguarded against abuses in the marriage system, was a protection for the woman against an irresponsible husband, and, in cases where highly valued cattle constitute the lobola, it was tangible evidence of the worth of the woman, a means of reciprocity between the families-in-law, and a warrant giving access to the woman to seek divorce as a remedy (Westermann, 1949). Furthermore, as missionaries soon discovered to their chagrin, lobola acted to encourage fidelity, and by suppressing it they removed a venerable restraint even for Christian converts. So, whether it concerns the stability of marriage or, in divorce, the stability of the kin structure, lobola was at the center of the social organism. An attack there would be felt through the entire society, as appears to have happened.

Measures were adopted to replace the lobola with church weddings in which no payments were made, although European dress which was required involved the parties in relatively high expenditure. Such expenditure was in fact counterproductive, as missionary observers saw. It became evident to them that "a greater evil has arisen in connection with these Christian marriages in which a young man spends on his marriage feast quite as much as would be considered sufficient for an ikazi (i.e., lobola) ... No one is benefited by this waste, which if it has not taken place, the proceeds might have been handed over to the girl's relations, and which in case of need would give her or her children a claim on those who received the ikazi. But upon the whole, in regard to these marriages in which no cattle have been paid, there are quite as many if not more separations than in the case of purely native marriages in which cattle have been paid" (Hutchinson, 1957:172).

As these and other comments make clear, the measures against lobola failed, or else produced highly unsatisfactory results. Marital infidelity among Christian converts became a widely noted occurrence, forcing missionaries to resort to the unwieldy strategem of two forms of marriage: a lower form performed in the schoolroom or the missionary's study, and a higher form conducted in the church (Hutchinson, 1957:172 – 3), a split-level distinction that undercut the supposedly single foundation of marriage. One official reported that the Africans who had contracted a "church" marriage incurred a double jeopardy: they had removed themselves from the check of the old customs and were out of range of the sanctions of the missionary. "The result," he concluded, "is more widespread immorality and a generally lowering effect on the Native. Both men and women are constantly coming to me with complaints of matrimonial difficulties resulting from these 'church' marriages" (Hutchinson, 1957:173). A father of two married daughters who had received no lobola voiced apprehensions about the possible outcome of the marriages, for if something went wrong and the women were returned to him, he should have nothing for their upkeep (Hutchinson, 1957:172).

What is equally serious, the attack on lobola deterred conversions, or at any rate deterred converts from seeking the fellowship of the church. To take the slightly different matter of polygamous families, one missionary was told by an African elder who stopped short of receiving baptism in spite of long exposure to Christianity that he "observed that many who had done so had driven away their wives and children, like so many things of no value; that although he might live with only one wife, yet he liked the others, and he could not think for a moment of driving away his children. Such is the feeling of most of the natives" (Hutchinson, 1957:171).

The reference to polygamy opens a notoriously intractable problem in the annals of mission. For nineteenth-century missionaries, their moral landscape primed by a short-fused Victorian sensibility, polygamy triggered all the virulent stereotypes of the lustful African. Yet polygamy, an ancient and widespread institution, was scarcely amenable to the simple solutions offered by missionaries, and the African response was to ignore the rule of monogamy required of them by Europeans, or else, as so often happens with hard laws, to show outward conformity hand in hand with inward denial. As missionaries gained a better understanding of the custom, they modified their opposition, as happened with the Anglican Bishop John Colenso, who wrote a short treatise defending the institution against his astounded missionary colleagues. Colenso's line of defense follows a consistent religious rule: he asked how his missionary colleagues could justify asking polygamists to commit the sin of divorce to remedy the offense of polygamy. Few were willing to grasp that nettle, though many continued to blame him for the confusion of values that was said to result from public disagreement among missionaries before Africans on such a thorny issue. In fact it was claimed that the decline in conversions at this time was due to Colenso's ill-advised pronouncements on polygamy (Hutchinson, 1957:170), though it is hard to understand how, if opposition to polygamy failed to bring converts, its advocacy should also fail to win souls. At any rate in this matter, too, the missionaries' engagement with the issue rapidly exposed their inadequacy.

The issue of male circumcision in like fashion brought missionaries into acute tension with Africans. Africans considered circumcision as a *rite de passage* making for manhood. Those who were uncircumcized, whatever their age, were regarded not fully mature, and therefore unfit for responsibility or leadership, including marriage and all that it implied. Girls declined to marry uncircumcized men for fear of attracting the stigma that went with it. Boys who resided in missionary stations were secretly abducted and initiated into the rite. When they possessed the vernacular Bible, Africans could justify the practice from the example of Jesus and his leading disciples. It could not have helped missionaries to continue to press ahead when by so doing they would set back their own goals.

Assessing the Negative Criticism

There is a general thesis that can be discerned in all the negative criticisms of missions thus far considered, and that may be simply stated thus: many people, including missionaries, are said to have assumed that the greatest opportunities for planting Christianity would occur when society was being broken up and culture in a state of disarray, so that conversion in the religious sphere would find its counterpart in collaboration in the political. In other words political capitulation by Africans, critics assert, was sought by missionaries for the assumed benefits it held for Christianity. Therefore, creating the requisite social disruption of capitulation would be perceived by missionaries as auspicious for the Gospel, and although it would be too extreme to say that missionaries in general perpetrated acts of sabotage to upset the equilibrium, some at least sought comfort from the thought. For example, in 1859 Robert Moffat, the father-in-law and protegé of Dr. David Livingstone, and himself a missionary in South Africa, gave vent to his feelings on this point in the following words:

> It is where the social organization is most perfect, and the social system still in its aboriginal vigour, that the missionary has the least success in making an impression. Where things have undergone a change and the old feudal usages have lost their power, where there is a measure of disorganization, the new ideas which the gospel brings with it do not come into collision with any powerful political prejudice. The habits and modes of thinking have been broken up, and there is a preparation for the seed of the word. (Cited in Wallis, 1945:70–71)

All this heady theorizing, however, and the wider negative criticisms against missionaries, had little factual substantiation, not at least in the terms of the sensational rhetoric. Political upheavals might make Christianity comparatively more attractive, but, on the other hand, they might do the reverse. It is this ambiguity which the confident assertions of critics fail to recognize. Moffat himself was less gullible than his words might indicate. In practice, he said, the reality may be very different. "I am not," he confessed, "sanguine on this point in regard to the Matabele" (Wallis, 1945:71).

Constructive Reappraisal: Part III

When all this evidence is taken together and separately, it points inexorably in one direction. Missionary encounters with African culture, however superficial or sustained, made the indigenous factor indispensable for the religious enterprise to which they were committed. The capitulation of Africans to Western political control, many missionaries found, did in fact conflict with the task of Christianizing the people, or at any rate complicated it. The fact that missionaries failed, even where they did try, to impose Western cultural norms on Africans demonstrates the fundamental limitations of Western forms for the appropriation of the

Gospel, and to this fact numerous missionaries were alert. Even those who persisted in spite of the evidence helped to define the issues: missionary criticism produced, if it did not provoke others to produce, abundant field evidence on times and issues that might otherwise have dropped out of the historical record. When they condemned customs and practices as heathen, missionaries set about collecting whatever information they could find in order to make the strongest possible case for themselves. The logic of the situation demanded that they did not underestimate the strength of the opposition or ignore powerful interlocutors in the community. When we add to this consideration the fact that by their ordination and subsequent commissioning for service, missionaries were de facto under oath, then we have an environment that can support the building up of excellent field data. This may explain why there seems a litigious thoroughness to much of their testimonies and deliberations. In any case what they offered in evidence was often not simply in their own defense but in mitigation of the African. Consequently much of missionary criticism, however hostile, has enlarged the scope of African history and deepened understanding of customs and practices.

Another factor of immense significance for African history is clear. In much of the evidence missionaries were self-critical both with regard to the status of Western preconceptions in Africa and with respect to the motives and ambition that led them into the field in the first place. Even if we were to assume the worst in the religious motives of missionaries and see them as colonialists in pious garb, there is no question but that they were often engaged in agonizing self-scrutiny, turning the searchlight on themselves in self-revealing ways. That principle of scrutiny, of cutting into oneself and exposing the motive springs of action, is the dynamo of historical construction. As a result, the records of missions are suffused with a rigorous, contemporary appeal. The documents they have bequeathed to us are not mere transcripts of clever manipulation but affidavits of the most scrupulous inquiry. These stern athletes of Jacob's angel who tussled so gallantly with Africa's venerable serpent had not self-deceptive enough blinkers to leave us records of what only they thought, said, and did. Consequently, from missionary records it is possible to construct as authentic a picture of Africa's heritage as we are likely to get from other sources. For those Africans who took an active part in this clash of wits, the threshold of self-understanding and self-appreciation was raised, and the ancient barriers of tribe and clan were significantly lowered. Crucial for our reappraisal is acknowledgment of the creative part the missionary interest played in the religious and intellectual awakening of Africa, helping to bring the continent into the family of nations through projects of indigenous self-affirmation.

The evidence for such awakening is as impressive in scope and volume as it is remarkable in quality and detail, although we can offer only a few examples here. The modern Zulu scholar, Professor C.L.S. Nyembezi, in a public lecture at the University of Natal, commented that the missionary cultivation of Zulu language and literature was a significant force behind general Zulu awakening. After acknowledging that the great pioneers of the people's language and literature were missionaries and the Africans they trained, Professor Nyembezi went on to say that the missionary interest extended beyond the narrow issue of religious affiliation. It was not simply that "missionaries concerned themselves primarily with grammars, dictionaries and the translation of the Scriptures (but that), some of them recorded folklore, proverbs and valuable historical material" (Nyembezi, 1961:3).

The missionaries followed a vigorous policy of vernacular development, promoting African languages as complete and autonomous vehicles for bringing God's revelation to the people, with the obvious effect of making Western languages, including Greek and Latin, of limited usefulness in religious appropriation. Zulu received its share of attention in this regard. In 1850 Hans Schreuder published a grammar of the language, as did Bishop Colenso in 1855. In 1859 Lewis Grout of the American Board for Foreign Mission also produced a grammar of Zulu. Similar attention was devoted to the production of dictionaries: in 1857 Perrin's dictionary of Zulu was published, and in 1857 J. L. Dohne of the American Board came out with his Zulu dictionary. Bishop Colenso wrote his dictionary of the language in 1861, and in 1880 Charles Roberts produced a similar work.

Colenso was instrumental in having the first account in Zulu by mother tongue speakers published. On a visit to the Zulu king, Mpande, in 1859, Colenso was accompanied by two Zulu boys and a schoolteacher. As a record of their visit, the three Zulu companions produced an account in Zulu of their impressions, thus leaving a landmark in the history of the language (Nyembezi, 1961:3–4).

These linguistic endeavors were accompanied by detailed investigations into Zulu religion, with Canon Callaway setting a model of meticulous research and comprehensiveness. His monograph on the subject is a stunning achievement in retrieval and rehabilitation even by the standards of the time. (Calloway, 1870). These and other efforts ensured that a revitalized Zulu world would be the indispensable context for the new order under Christianity.

Missionaries were as conscious of the relevance of a revitalized Africa for the enterprise as were Africans themselves, and often it was missionaries who set the pace. Such was the case with Rev. Johannes Christaller in Ghana, the former Gold Coast. Christaller arrived in the Gold Coast in the 1850s, serving the Basel Mission there from 1853 to 1868. He finished a translation of the Four Gospels into Twi in 1859, the New Testament in 1864, the Psalms and the Book of Proverbs in 1866, and the whole Bible in 1871 after he returned to Europe. In 1875 he completed his monumental work, the *Dictionary of the Akan Language,* which was published in 1881 and acclaimed by experts, both Ghanaian and others, as a masterpiece of scholarship.

Christaller went on to crown his labors with an invaluable and methodical compilation of Twi proverbs and idioms, numbering in all 3,600. He came to acquire a deep and abiding love for the Akan, a love that was reciprocated. In the preface to the collection he appended a sort of manifesto to the vernacular, encouraging educated Africans to cultivate the genre for itself. He wrote:

> May this Collection give a new stimulus to the diligent gathering of folk-lore and to the increasing cultivation of native literature. May those Africans who are enjoying the benefit of a Christian education, make the best of the privilege; but let them not despise the sparks of truth entrusted to and preserved by their own people, and let them not forget that by entering into their way of thinking and by acknowledging what is good and expounding what is wrong they will gain the more access to the hearts and minds of their less favoured countrymen. (Cited in Danquah, 1944:186)

In 1883 Christaller also helped found *The Christian Messenger,* a paper devoted to the promotion of Akan life and culture. From 1905 to 1917, when it was transferred from Basel to Ghana, it published articles in Twi, Ga, and English, and covered local as well as international news. In that regard it reported the Russo-Japanese War of 1904, an event in which Ghanaians took great political interest, Halley's comet in 1910, and the sinking of the Titanic in 1911. The *Christian Messenger* belongs as much to the history of modern African journalism as it does to missionary contributions to Africa. The use of the vernacular by *The Christian Messenger* to report and reflect on world events was a remarkable example of the range missionaries afforded to the indigenous heritage in the emerging world order.

The testimony of Dr. Danquah, considered by the Ghana Academy of Arts and Sciences a giant, was immortalized with a distinguished annual lectureship, the Danquah Memorial Lecture. Danquah was an intellectual founding father of Ghanaian nationalism, a committed and articulate defender of his people's culture and destiny. He spoke in very thoughtful and lavish terms of the achievement of Christaller. Christaller, he said, might be considered the first dispensation for the Akan, the Old Testament canon by which Danquah's own work should be judged a continuation. Furthermore, Danquah insisted, Christaller ensured that the Akan people would bring forward their contribution as part and parcel of the general heritage of humanity (Danquah, 1944:184ff).

Such evidence as this still leaves critics of mission retiring from the field of controversy with a political flea in their ear, and to that theme we must therefore turn once more. The missionary who embodied the politico-religious ambiguity of missions was Dr. David Livingstone (d.1873), a towering figure over the entire course of the missionary movement. Livingstone arrived in Africa in the 1840s, and died there. He formulated what has come be known as the three "Cs" for the missionary motto: commerce, civilization, and Christianity must go together as partners. Not only that, but Livingstone had an explicit political agenda that he wished mission to carry out. In a confidential letter to Professor Sedgwick of Cambridge University, Livingstone spoke of his "secret ambitions," which he said he would not divulge in public. In that letter he said he was setting out for Africa not for the mere sentimental reasons of serving the African but for the tangible reason of advancing the interests of his own country. He continued: "I take a practical mining geologist to tell us of the mineral resources of the country, an economic botanist to give a full report of the vegetable productions, an artist to give the scenery, a naval officer to tell of the capacity of river communications, and a moral agent to lay the foundation for anything that may follow . . . I hope," he concluded, "it may result in an English colony in the healthy high lands of Central Africa" (Kirk, 1965:309).

The course of subsequent events on the ground in Africa altered Livingstone's ideas in remarkably radical ways, and his elevated Anglo-Saxon strategy gave way to the basic reality of African needs and aspirations. Livingstone is justly accliamed for his scientific discoveries in Africa, and for the astute historical enquiries by which he explored inter-ethnic relations and customs. Unfortunately, however, his intellectual contributions tend to be overclouded by popular religious eulogizing. Victorian sentimentality was in this regard a major source of the difficulty. The Victorians painted him in colors of extreme sanctification, displaying him in stained glass to become a visible target for rock-throwing critics.

Livingstone's real significance lies not in the strategies of Whitehall, in spite of his influence there, nor in the colorful portraits of popular adulation in spite of pockets of genuine appreciation in that sphere. His significance lies on the ground in Africa and in the hearts of Africans.

This was the verdict of one modern secular writer who toured the Africa that Livingstone knew and met the dwindling ranks of people who knew Livingstone, or else knew the people who knew him. "The best way to make contact today with David Livingstone," the account states, "is simply to talk to Africans. You could do this anywhere, but perhaps best in Nyasaland (Malawi), his beloved land by the lake, where his influence remains most profound" (Keatley, 1963:124).

One example should suffice to show the depth of impact on Livingstone of his African experience. He came to acquire a deep interest in the work of his father-in-law, Robert Moffat, who began work in Bechuanaland in the 1820s. Livingstone spoke of his admiration for the Sichuana language of which Moffat had been the brilliant pioneer. Livingstone spoke of its richness, its copiousness and subtlety. Some European students of the subject, he cautioned, may imagine there would be few obstacles in mastering the tongue of a so-called primitive people, but his experience was different.

> In my own case, though I have had as much intercourse with the purest idiom as most Englishmen, and have studied the language carefully, yet I can never utter an important statement without doing so very slowly, and repeating it too, lest the foreign accent . . . should render the sense unintelligible . . . The capabilities of this language may be inferred from the fact that the Pentateuch is fully expressed in Mr. Moffat's translation in fewer words than in the Greek Septuagint, and in a very considerably smaller number than in our English version. (Livingstone, 1857:114)

Livingstone argued that language was the most cogent proof of human intelligence and sensibility, and its development among Africans is warrant of their humanity, too. "Language," he reflected, "seems to be an attribute of the human mind and thought, and the inflections, various as they are in the most barbarous tongues, as that of the Bushmen, are probably only proof of the race being human, and endowed with the power of thinking (Livingstone, 1857:114).

These theoretical reflections are designed to show that field experience in Africa affected deeply Livingstone's motives and intentions, whatever these might have been. He had come to Africa perhaps to build a new frontier in continuation with Britain's imperial destiny. Now, however, he was spokesman for the heritage of the vanquished, or soon to be vanquished. In relation to the political and economic schemes by which Africa was being tied to Britain, Livingstone forged links of a different kind to mobilize African aspirations and encourage self-responsibility.

His political counterpart in Africa was Cecil Rhodes, "the empire-builder in the hard political sphere" (Keatley, 1963:124).

Cecil Rhodes' motto was "philanthropy and five per cent" in contrast to Livingstone's "commerce and Christianity." Both men dominated Central Africa, but Rhodes left a legacy of white settler domination, and the bitter strife with Africans that created, while Livingstone opened the path for rising African aspirations. The clash of values represented by the two pioneers came into the open in the 1950s with the abortive Central African Federation, which grouped together Nyasaland with Northern and Southern Rhodesia, with power in white minority hands. It was a clash between "the Exploiter tradition of Cecil Rhodes, with the settler-politicians as its guardians, and the Tutor tradition of Livingstone," with its guardians in the Kenneth Kaundas, Joshua Nkomos, the Kamuzu Bandas, and the missionaries of St. Faith's Mission in Southern Rhodesia and the Church of Scotland Mission in Nyasaland (Keatley, 1963:467). The forces that menaced the political dream of Cecil Rhodes were "the spiritual heirs of the other empire-builder, David Livingstone" (Keatley, 1963:121). In a passage of prophetic significance, Patrick Keatley, then the Commonwealth correspondent of the *Guardian* newspaper, said in 1963 that "it is not particularly difficult to predict which of the two empires will last the longer, for Livingstone chose much the sounder foundation" (Keatley, 1963:121).

After Livingstone died, his African companions, Susi and Chuma, as an act of pious regard, removed his heart and buried it deep in the earth before carrying the body across 1,500 miles of difficult, treacherous terrain on foot to the coast whence it was taken to England for burial at Westminster Abbey. Thus, Africa and England each retained a token of the missionary, each allowing the other a share in that heritage. It was cross-cultural encounter of the profoundest kind.

The point worth stressing in the missionary involvement with political questions in Africa is the role they enabled Africans to play vis-a-vis the advance of European power, rather than the role they envisaged for themselves, although even that was increasingly seen as a complement to the African role (Oliver: 1952:247). Undoubtedly, major and lasting changes were introduced by missionaries in the nature and composition of tribal Africa, but it would be a stern critic who would insist that all of it was to the detriment of the people. For instance, in Nyasaland, missionaries were instrumental in fomenting a sense of awakening among the people. They mediated successfully in the wake of the devastation that followed the massive upheavals of the Zulu-Angoni wars. In 1887 a peace treaty was negotiated between the invading Angoni and the native Atonga. The missionaries followed it up with the adoption of the language

Lamin Sanneh

of the Manganja people, Chi-Nyanja, employing it as the lingua franca of the country. Chi-Nyanja did a lot to create a sense of cohesion and self-identity and was a productive channel for the emergence into modern history of the Nyasas. As one testimony affirms, "the missionaries gave to the Nyasas a heritage of national unity and of deep regard for learning that was to serve them well in the political battles of the 1950s and 1960s" (Keatley, 1963:129).

A surprisingly large number of missionaries saw the extreme ambiguity of European designs on Africa, and felt unconvinced that the advancing worldwide system of colonial rule held any prospects for the future of the cause. Few described that ambiguity as eloquently as the pioneer missionary in East Africa, Rev. Dr. J. Lewis Krapf. He remarked

> Expect nothing, or very little, from political changes in Eastern Africa . . . Do not think that, because the East-Africans are 'profitable in nothing to God and the world,' they ought to be brought under the dominion of some European power, in the hope that they may then bestir themselves more actively and eagerly for what is worldly, and, in consequence, become eventually more awake to what is spiritual and eternal. On the contrary, banish the thought that Europe must spread her protecting wings over Eastern Africa, if missionary work is to prosper . . . Europe would, no doubt, remove much that is mischievous and obstructive out of the way of missionary work, but she would probably set in its place as many, and perhaps still greater checks. It is a vital error to make the result of missionary labor dependent on the powers that be . . . Whether Europeans take possession of Eastern Africa or not, I care very little, if at all; yet I know full well that missionary labor has its human phase, and that it cannot, as if by magic, without any outward preparation of the people for its reception, grasp the life of a nation. But many persons vastly overrate this human phase of our work, and, like the Jew, wish to see the bottom of the water before they cross the river . . . It is not missionaries, but those who are not missionaries, who see impossibilities in the way of the regeneration of Eastern Africa. (1860:416–417)

Conclusion

We cannot expect to lay to rest the political view of missionaries as the religious surrogates of colonialism, for it is built rock-solid into the self-image of the West. This self-image encourages the idea of mission as the driving force of the European imperialist impulse.

Yet we can show by a different interpretation of some of the same evidence the profound impact it had for the emergence of the new Africa. If, in the light of the colonial takeover, we can speak justifiably of African capitulation, and, in that setting, of missionary assault on the old order, we can, in the light of vernacular agency of missions, speak equally plausibly of African resistance to the forces of subjection, aided and abetted by missionary sponsorship of projects of cultural and social renewal. Considering that the principle of deepened self-understanding lies at the heart of such renewal, we can say that missionary development of vernacular resources, whatever the motives or expectations that fueled it, instituted a central pillar of the modern dispensation in Africa. Thus, Africa's participation in the worldwide system would occur in the context of vernacular specificity as that was developed by Christian missions. One implication is that the Western missionary tradition has facilitated exposure to the world, and that it is mistaken to conclude from that a hegemonic conspiracy.

Notes

1. The "omnipotence of thought," and occurs in Sigmund Freud's *Totem and Taboo* (1913 Geman edition) as a symptom of neurotic patients. It has come to be employed as a shorthand for the idea of mind over matter.

2. Monica Wilson (1969:266) describes what amounts to "enclaving" for missions in South Africa. She says: "Acceptance of Christian teaching implied a radical change in the manner of life of converts." Consequently, the missionaries "expected their converts to wear a Western style of clothing; to build square houses rather than round ones; to settle in a village round church and school rather than in scattered homesteads; to change the division of labour between men and women, and to abandon ancient festivals, such as the traditional initiation dances, which were judged by whites to be lewd, and became illegal west of the Kei." Elsewhere Wilson gives details of changes that resulted from the introduction of Christianity among the Nyakyusa but that Nyakyusa converts themselves had in many critical respects adapted Christianity to indigenous ideas and categories. For example, missionary rebukes of African morality were perceived by the Nyakyusa as a form of the traditional curse. See Monica Wilson, 1959.

References

Callaway, Canon
1870   *The Religious System of the AmaZulu*. London: Trubner.

Danquah, J. B.
1944   *The Akan Doctrine of God*. London: Lutterworth Press.

Hutchinson, Bertram
1957 "Some Social Consequences of Nineteenth Century Missionary Activity among the South African Bantu." *Africa* 27, No. 2 (April).

Keatley, Patrick
1963 *The Politics of Partnership: The Federation of Rhodesia and Nyasaland.* Harmondsworth, England: Penguin Books.

Kirk, John (ed.)
1965 *Zambezi Journals and Letters.* Vol. 1. London: Reginald Foskett.

Krapf, J. Lewis
1860 *Travels, Researches, and Missionary Labors.* Boston: Ticknor and Fields.

Livingstone, David
1857 *Missionary Researches and Travels in South Africa.* London: John Murray.

Nyembezi, C. L. S.
1961 *A Review of Zulu Literature.* Pietermaritzburg: University of Natal Press.

Oliver, Roland
1952 *The Missionary Factor in East Africa.* London: Longman.

Philip, J.
1828 *Researches in South Africa.* London: Vol. 2.

Sanneh, Lamin
1983 "The Horizontal and Vertical in Mission: An African Perspective." *International Bulletin of Missionary Research,* vol. 7, no. 4.

Wallis, J. P. R. (ed.)
1945 *The Matabele Mission.* London: Chatto and Windus.

Westermann, Diedrich
1949 *The African Today and Tomorrow.* 3rd edition. London: Oxford University Press.

Wilson, Monica
1959 *Communal Rituals of the Nyakyusa.* London: Oxford University Press.
1969 "Co-operation and Conflict: The Eastern Cape Frontier." In Monica Wilson and Leonard Thompson (eds.), *The Oxford History of South Africa: South Africa to 1870.* Oxford: Clarendon Press.

9

World Order and Mainline Religions: The Case of Protestant Foreign Missions

Michael A. Burdick and Phillip E. Hammond

While it is safe to say that world order (or world system) theory has had most to say about economic actions and processes, religious reverberations from world-order changes have also been noted. (See, e.g., Wuthnow, 1978; 1980; 1987; and Robertson, 1985a; 1985b; 1987 for general theoretical statements.) The following broad assertions would seem to summarize the current outlook with respect to this relationship: (1) A nation-state's position in the world political economy is reflected in its religious institutions; (2) During shifts in the world order, ideological reformation is likely, including religious "unrest and diversity" (Wuthnow, 1978: 72); (3) In nation-states experiencing ascendency and hegemony, "establishment" religion will gain in popularity, while during periods of decline, such religion will lose in popularity (Smith, 1986).

Empirical arguments advanced in support of one or more of these theoretical assertions include explanations for: (1) the worldwide cult explosion in the 1960s and 1970s, (2) the renewed vigor of evangelical Protestantism in the United States, (3) Vatican Council II and attendant changes in Roman Catholicism such as the charismatic movement, (4) the feminist movement in religious organizations, and (5) the *havarot* movement within Judaism.

The most focused empirical effort to date to relate world order changes to changes in religious institutions, however, is Peter Smith's endeavor to show that:

> periods of national dominance have also been periods of religious florescence for those churches which cater for the middle and upper

classes. Correspondingly, one of the corollaries of loss of dominance is a decline in such socially established religiosity. (Smith, 1986: 88)

In a general way, Smith bases his argument on evidence that: (1) "Major Protestants" membership in Great Britain rose from about 1830 to about 1900, then started a decline that continues today, a process correlated with Britain's changing position in the world economy, and (2) American church membership experienced an overall (if uneven) increase from early in this century until the mid-1960s, then a decline, especially in the "elite" Protestant denominations, a process corresponding to America's changing position in the world economy.

The virtue of Smith's study not generally shared by other empirical studies of religion and world order is that its proposition linking independent and dependent variables is clearly stated and the evidence is quantitative and longitudinal. Other studies have tended toward anecdotal evidence, often for a single time period and/or have been less clear regarding just *how* a change in the world order has effected a change in the religious situation. Such shortcomings do not negate these other studies, of course, but they do highlight the singular character of Smith's article.

Unfortunately, Smith's article is open to serious challenge, especially its American half. The challenge comes in two ways: (1) Most palpably, it can be shown that, while American church membership peaked in the 1960s, that is true of total church membership, not establishment membership ("catering for the middle and upper classes"), which — by one important standard at least — had peaked *before* the United States began its world system ascendency. (2) Less damaging to Smith's article, but more challenging to the world-system theory from which it derives, is the fact that changes in the most international aspect of establishment religion — foreign missions — not only do not conform to the world-order model but seem, indeed, to contradict it. We discuss these two challenges in order, and then conclude with a discussion of how they might be resolved in a manner that could leave world-order theory relatively intact but sensitized to some subtleties in the religious situation.

Regarding American Church Membership

Nobody would question that Anglicanism in Britain is and has been the establishment religion.[1] Until very recently at least, with nonconformist Margaret Thatcher and her nonconformist cabinet, the Church of England was rightfully called "the Conservative party at prayer." For Smith to track the vitality of establishment religiosity in relationship to

Britain's ascendency, dominance, and then decline in the world's political economy has a certain intuitive merit, therefore.[2]

What of American establishment religion, however? Congregationalists, Episcopalians, and Presbyterians certainly catered to the middle and upper classes during the colonial period, but, while their membership rolls grew in absolute numbers as the American population grew, their *share* of the church-belonging public peaked early in the nineteenth century! In other words, other denominations—the Baptists and Methodists especially—grew even faster. Did not those two denominations then become part of establishment religion? The answer is "In due time, yes," but then the Methodists' share of the church-belonging public peaked by 1920; American Baptists, not too long after (Finke and Stark, 1989).

The implication is clear: what was reached in the mid-1960s in the United States was not just the apex in sheer numbers of membership figures in churches serving middle and upper classes but also the saturation of the religion market. In relative terms, however, establishment religion had already started to decline. The continued success at penetrating this market after the 1960s by evangelical Protestantism is precisely that, therefore—the continuation of a 200-year-old process by which nonestablishment religions have been gaining a larger and larger share of the church-belonging public. Not until the overall population growth slowed down and not until so-called mainstream Protestant denominations failed to retain their youthful generations, however, was the latter's long-term market loss exposed (see table 1; Roof and McKinney, 1987).

Of course, it might be argued that even if sectarian, evangelical growth rates were greater than those of establishment denominations, the latter have remained large in absolute terms and have truly dominated the Protestant religious scene. They founded and still help operate the elite colleges and seminaries, write the religious histories, and send their members to Congress in disproportionate numbers. (George Bush is the fourteenth Episcopalian to be elected president, even though Episcopalians are only about 1 percent of the American population.) While this argument may be correct in its facts, it nevertheless contradicts the Peter Smith thesis—which is that establishment religion flourishes and then declines *because* it is establishment religion. If nonestablishment religion flourishes even more during the period of world order ascendency, and then continues to flourish while both nation and establishment religion decline, some revision in the thesis seems called for.

Regarding Foreign Missions—Great Britain

A more telling challenge comes from a quarter not considered in the Peter Smith article—the involvement of establishment religion in foreign

TABLE 1

Percentage of U.S. population who are religiously affiliated (Line A);
percentage of U.S. Christians who are affiliated with established Protestant churches (Line B);
percentage of U.S. Protestants who are affiliated with established Protestant churches (Line C).

(For selected years)

		1890	1906	1923	1940	1947	1954	1960	1965	1970	1975	1980	1985
Line A:	*Religiously Affiliated* Total Population	22%	36%	43%	49%	57%	59.5%	64%	64%	62%	62%	60.5%	59.5%
Line B:	*Established Protestants* Total Christians	35%	35%	33%	31%	28%	25%	22%	25%	24%	22%	20%	17%
Line C:	*Established Protestants* Total Protestants	52%	58%	55%	49%	45%	41%	41%	43%	42%	37%	36%	30%

Sources: Census, 1890, 1906; NCCC yearbooks.

missionary activity. It would seem logical in the world-system theoretical framework to expect that the links between a nation-state's destiny in the world's political economy and its efforts at evangelizing other parts of the world would be even closer than its links to domestic religion. As Brian Stanley has shown, a convergence existed between British missionary and free trading expectations in the mid-nineteenth century: " . . . the years 1857–1860 were crucial in the process whereby the evangelical understanding of empire in terms of providence, natural law, and trusteeship became the established framework of British imperial thinking" (1983: 94). The mission field is a kind of "market," after all, and sellers and buyers make it up. We expect the participants in this market to be especially responsive to their uneven positions in the world economy, whether they are sending or receiving missionaries.

Figures for Great Britain's Anglican missionary program can be seen as support for this perspective (see table 2). From a total of 687 in 1854, missionary personnel sent to foreign lands by the Anglican church rose to 1,042 in 1890, 2,107 in 1900, 2,411 in 1905, and still maintained a figure of 2,538 in 1938, dropping to 925 in 1980. While the years of ascent and descent do not coincide closely with Britain's political-economic destiny, if we allow for the fact that adding to and then dismantling foreign mission operations probably requires a lead time longer than domestic changes, these figures then add credibility to the Smith thesis.

However, there is a set of facts not anticipated by the theory if one considers the foreign mission efforts of Britain's non-Anglican Protestants. Not only were the latter already slightly more numerous than the Anglicans in 1854, but by 1905 they had more than double the number of

TABLE 2

Great Britain Foreign Missionary Personnel Deployed by
Anglican and Other Protestant Agencies

(For Selected Years)

	1854	1890	1900	1905	1925	1938	1973	1980
Line A: Number of Personnel (Anglican)	687	1043	2103	2411	2186	2538	936	925
Line B: Number of Personnel (Other Protestant)	679	1352	2461	5381	4140	4255	4105	4209

Sources: ATS, 1900; Beach, 1925; Bliss, 1891; Brierly, 1975, 1981; Newcomb, 1854; Parker, 1938; Wright, 1905

Anglican personnel, maintaining that superiority in 1925 and 1938, and now (1981) outnumbering Anglicans by a 5:1 ratio. This pattern is not at all what system theory would predict; it is not establishment foreign mission emissaries going out on behalf of an empire in greater numbers but their domestic challengers. Moreover, like the continued growth of American evangelicalism after overall national growth is halted, British nonconforming mission personnel appear to keep increasing. Changes in a nation-state's position in the world system may still be reflected in its religious institutions, but — if the foreign mission enterprise is the focus (and a perfectly logical focus it is) — clearly more explanation is needed than simply the rise and fall of world political economic position.

Regarding Foreign Missions — American

American foreign mission history more severely challenges the Peter Smith thesis, however. Arthur Schlesinger, Jr., puts the matter succinctly:

> . . . one must begin by acknowledging the autonomy of the missionary impulse. . . . Whatever links the missionary enterprise might develop along the way with traders or bankers, politicians, generals, or diplomats, however much it might express in its own ways the aggressive energies of the West, the desire to save souls remains distinct from the desire to extend power or to acquire glory or to make money or to seek adventure or to explore the unknown. (1974: 342)

The fact is, American foreign mission activity by establishment Protestantism did follow a pattern of growth, hegemony, and then decline, but this entire cycle occurred *before* the United States reached hegemonic position in the world's political economy. The brazen assault by America's mainline Protestant missionaries peaked in the 1920s, had clearly changed strategies by the post-World War II period, and — by the mid-1960s — had become a disappearing pattern.

The dominant aim of American Protestant missionaries throughout most of the nineteenth century was religious, not cultural imperialism. As Rufus Anderson, secretary of the American Board of Missions, 1832 – 1866, insisted, the goal was to "convert souls" not argue the superiority of American culture. A mission station, he said, was *not* to become an agency of social or political reform. Anderson sought no agricultural experts or mechanics, and he called for the Gospel to be preached not in English but the native tongue (Schlesinger, 1974:350–1).

After the Civil War, this "Gospel alone" mentality underwent revision. Domestically, as a response to the problems created by urbanization and industrialization, a Social Gospel theology developed, and in the foreign mission field this revisionist thinking took the form — for example, in China — of missionary attacks on concubinage, foot-binding, opium, and naturapathic medicine. In China and elsewhere, mission energy thus shifted to social, medical, educational, and agricultural efforts. Just as the newly articulated postmillennialism led domestically to church resolve to bring in the kingdom *before* Christ's return, so in foreign missions the emphasis shifted away from the salvation of individual souls and toward the salvation of entire societies by use of American technology.

Premillennialists — those who thought individual souls must be converted as quickly as possible before Christ's return and the eventual end of history — were still represented in foreign missions, though decreasing among the cadres associated with mainline Protestant churches. The latter had shifted mission strategy to one that — not unlike that of their Peace Corps counterparts of the 1960s and 1970s — harbored feelings of Western cultural superiority: only the water supply could be unpolluted, the schools reach more children, better nutrition be supplied to pregnant women, etc.

Ironically perhaps, convinced of Western (American) superiority in these cultural institutions, American missionaries during the waning years of the nineteenth and first years of the twentieth centuries sanctioned greater cultural imperialism than they had before or have since. Military assistance by American armed forces to protect and foster American missionary "good will" was even encouraged in such places as Turkey (1894–5) and China (1900–01). Likewise, the expansion of American "interests" in Cuba, Puerto Rico, and the Philippines after the Spanish-American War (1898) allowed United States Protestants to engage in missionary work in the newly acquired territories under a denominational comity arrangement, surely in the belief that advanced American ways were superior to the natives'.

By the 1920s, however, the American Protestant establishment missionary thrust peaked in the deployment of personnel. Mission theorists, having seriously questioned the nineteenth-century notion of theological superiority, now questioned the subsequent assumption of cultural superiority. Daniel J. Fleming, a professor at Union Seminary in New York and a former missionary to India, articulated the new theory. America, like all societies, was "less-than-Christian," and hence, "the whole world is the mission field." Also, Fleming redefined the objectives of missionary activity—away from conquest of land masses—to defeating "nationalism, materialism, racial injustice, ignorance, war, and poverty," wherever they are to be found (Hutchison, 1987: 152).

Whether theological or cultural in form, imperialism was being attacked, most notably from within the American foreign missionary establishment itself. As Schlesinger describes pre-World War II Protestant missiology:

> Missionaries now retreated from the view that faith could be served by force or that missions shared a common cause with national states. Confronted by anti-Christian riots in Nanking in the 1920s, missionaries opposed American military intervention and, by calling for a revision of the unequal treaties, signified a readiness to renounce specific diplomatic protection. By the 1930s the Hocking Commission said it was "clearly not the duty of the Christian missionary to attack the non-Christian systems. . . . " In 1935 a professor at the University of Chicago Divinity School could even write a piece for *The Christian Century* stirringly entitled, "I Don't Want to Christianize the World." (1974: 359)

It is difficult to overestimate how great an ideological shift this was. Not too many years before, just prior to World War I, a British mission pamphlet was published with a vivid color illustration showing the Cross, British flag, and United States flag side by side (Hutchison, 1987: 138). No longer would that be possible for American (or British) establishment religion. If, in the enthusiasm of earliest twentieth century, the ecumenically minded American Protestants could have the goal of "evangelizing the world in this generation" (Handy, 1984: 113), by the 1920s, revisionist thinking was articulating a new agenda for world missions.

The watershed for revisionist mission theory was the report (funded by J. D. Rockefeller, Jr.) entitled *Re-Thinking Missions: A Laymen's Inquiry After One Hundred Years* and written under the leadership of a Harvard philosopher, William Ernest Hocking. Presented in 1932, the message, while meeting mixed reactions among American Protestants, nonetheless said what knowledgeable missiologists already knew: Christianity, though encouraged to continue evangelizing anywhere it might choose, should no longer claim religious or cultural superiority:

> For a part of the life of any living religion is its groping for a better grasp of truth. . . . We desire the triumph of that final truth: we need not prescribe the route. It appears probable that the advance toward that goal may be of the immediate strengthening of several of the present religions of Asia, Christian and non-Christian together. . . .

He [the Christian] will look forward, not to the destruction of these religions, but to their continued co-existence with Christianity, each stimulating the other in growth toward the ultimate goal, unity in the completest religious truth. (1932: 44)

The *Laymen's Inquiry* consisted of seven volumes, but the one-volume summary favored Hocking's personal agenda for the collaboration of world religions. His underlying concern was to find a "world faith" to counter the growing secularization of the times. Critics chastised the report for this perspective, claiming that it would undermine the uniqueness of the Christian faith. Nevertheless, changes internationally and domestically had altered the parameters of and motivations for missionary work, and Hocking merely offered a rationale.

From the peak year of 1925, when the establishment denominations holding membership in the Federal (now National) Council of Churches maintained 6,794 foreign missionaries, the number has dropped until now (1985) only 2,467 remain. Differences of opinion are held regarding why this decline occurred (see Burdick, 1986), but irrespective of which opinion is correct, none conforms to a world-system perspective or the implied Peter Smith thesis. Great Britain may have been the last empire that could missionize in accordance with its world political-economic position, but, whether or not the United States could, it is certainly the first major player in the game that *failed* to do so. The simplest explanation would seem to be—to cite Schlesinger again—"the autonomy of the missionary impulse"; American mainline churches changed international strategies long before their country's political and economic elites changed theirs.

Schlesinger cites two kinds of evidence that show how the American, Protestant, establishment missionary movement did not coincide with America's world-system position. First, he shows that the deployment of foreign mission personnel held no correlation with patterns of United States imports and exports (1974: 421). He does this for 1840, 1880, and 1900; we have checked more recent years and found the same lack of relationship. The second kind of evidence is really Perry Miller's, whom Schlesinger quotes:

'. . . the peculiarity, more striking in America than anywhere else in Christendom, of a continuous admonition to the merchant classes, who contributed the finances for missionary endeavors, that they were at heart the secret foes of the sacred enterprise.' In short [Schlesinger goes on], at least in particular times and places, missionary zeal was strongly at war with the secular interests in acquisition and exploitation. (1974: 344)

Even more than in the British case, therefore, the rise and fall of American establishment religion's foreign missions operation simply do not accord with the world-order model.[3] As has been shown, the rise and fall of mainline Protestant missionary activity occurs well before the ascendance and then challenge to America's hegemonic position in the world's economy. Hutchison, noting that the real changeover occurred in the 1920s and reverberated for a few more decades, points to: (1) theological innovation, (2) organizational restructuring, (3) the emergence of a world culture, and (4) the rise of nationalism in the Third World as accounting for this change (1987: 161). As Wuthnow has pointed out (1978: 77), the world itself increasingly set the agenda for North American churches, which in some sense undercut the liberal religious rationale for evangelizing that world.[4]

In addition to such ideological challenges to American mission theory, one can note the creation of the World Council of Churches in 1947 and its later Commission on World Mission and Evangelism. Not only was a worldwide, ecumenical structure thereupon available as a conduit for denominational participation, but — more importantly perhaps — Third World nations, especially their Christian leaders, had an organized opponent to combat. By the 1970s, therefore, infused both with rising nationalism and theologies of liberation, these leaders called for a "mission moratorium." Missionary colonialism had long since lost its usefulness, they claimed. As one Indian church leader declared: "The mission of the church is the greatest enemy of the gospel" (Verghese, 1970: 1118). Though never really implemented, this moratorium symbolized the completion of a transition by American mainline Protestant churches. Begun in the nineteenth century with the goal of *conversion,* their mission strategy had become, by the 1920s, one of *compassion.* Now, by 1970, these churches, if they were to remain in the mission field at all, had to become *companions* to those to whom they would minister (Hartley, 1987: 273 – 285).

Regarding American Foreign Mission (Nonestablishment)

If establishment Protestantism's systematic dismantling of its foreign missions, beginning in the 1920s, calls into question the world-system perspective, the missionary thrust by nonestablishment Protestants offers an astonishing contrast. If the modern world occupied the ecumenical, mainline mission theorists, evangelicals adamantly adhered to older theological priorities: the primacy of the supernatural, a definitive social orientation, an open hostility to modernity, and thus a continued conviction that conversion of others to Christianity was their chief objective. Schlesinger's notion of "the autonomy of the missionary impulse" is amply, if ironically, illustrated by the evangelicals' dominance of foreign missions since World War II.

About the time (1925) so-called mainline American denominations were at maximum personnel strength, other American Protestant bodies had reached parity and then continued a remarkable growth that has yet to stop. Put another way, in 1890 the denominations that were to become members of the National Council of Churches outnumbered their competitors by a 7:1 ratio. In 1985, those competitors enjoyed a 14:1 lead (see table 3). Just as nonestablishment, sectarian, evangelical religion has continued its penetration of the domestic religious market, so has its share of the foreign religious market shown few signs of slowing down. While this growth was most pronounced between World War II and 1968 — a trend commensurate with the world-order model — the growth continues, a fact that does not accord with that model.

Evangelical mission agencies can be subdivided by their "affiliated" or "unaffiliated" status. Affiliated groups belong to either the Evangelical Foreign Missionary Association or the Interdenominational Foreign Missionary Association. Unaffiliated groups many times operate independently of national churches, and the largest growth is seen among them.[5] Perhaps not surprisingly, it is especially these newer unaffiliated groups that are viewed as a threat to the respective cultures they evangelize. In Latin America, for example, the mainline Protestant churches — with their long history of coexistence on the Catholic continent — are no longer the perceived threat they once were, but the *evangelistas* have now become the focus for vehement national sentiments.

In the case of Argentina during World War II, heightened anti-Americanism included a virulent hostility towards Protestantism.[6] The government's neutrality was a ruse to conceal their pro-Axis sympathies. By March 1945, fearing postwar isolation, Argentina's military government declared war against Germany and signed the Act of Chapultepec, the Pan-American agreement. Prominent right-wing Catholic nationalists — feeling betrayed by the military for their capitulation to the "colossus of the north" — wrote that Pan-Americanism was based on "the messianic protestantism of the Pilgrim Fathers and the Masonic enlightenment of the XVIII Century" (Navarro Gerassi, 1966: 191).

Protestants, liberals, Masons, and Jews were repeatedly blamed for the ills that had befallen the country. As late as 1959, a pastoral letter issued by a leading bishop stated: "To be Argentine is to be Catholic; to deny Catholicism is to deny the Fatherland." The Second Vatican Council, however, ushered in a new era of ecumenical relations. The traditional Protestants of the country were welcomed, at least begrudgingly so. A new "enemy," however (after Marxism that is!), threatened the fatherland.

TABLE 3

U.S.A. Foreign Missionary Personnel Deployed by Establishment and Nonestablishment Protestant Agencies

(For Selected Years)

		1854	1890	1900	1905	1920	1925	1938	1952	1960	1968	1980	1985
Line A:	Number of Personnel (Establishment Denominations)	756	2331	3001	3411	4945	6764	5852	5541	5249	5454	2511	2467
Line B:	Number of Personnel (Nonestablishment Denominations)	5	357	497	1216	3877	6843	4699	7896	11,968	23,533	32,078	35,079
Line C:	Established Denominations	15	6.5	6	2.8	1.3	1	1.2	1.4	2.2	4.3	12.7	14.2
	Nonestablishment Denominations	1	1	1	1	1	1	1	1	1	1	1	1

Sources: ATS, 1900; Beach, 1925; Beach, 1920; Bliss, 1981; Coote, 1982; Dayton, 1986; Newcomb, 1854; Parker, 1938; Wright, 1905.

The *sectas* that have "invaded" Argentina range from the Moonies to the Mormons, from the electronic church to Latin America's own Tradition, Family and Property (an ultraconservative Catholic group founded in Brazil). Over 1,900 non-Catholic religious bodies are registered in the country. The prominent North American groups are perceived—even by moderate religious observers—as a cultural extension of the domination over peripheral countries by the United States. An editor of a progressive Latin American Catholic journal stated: "We share ... in the challenges that confront us, from the international usury of the external debt to the invasion of the sects, both are the destruction of our ethos. ... " (Methol Ferre, 1987: 3). Latin American Catholics fear the loss of their religio-cultural heritage. Most Argentines, moreover, are acutely sensitive to their country's position in the world political economy.

Another journalist offers a more strident analysis for Latin America's predicament. After the 1960s' upsurge of left-wing nationalist movements, the "oligarchy"—acting in consort with United States imperialist policies—implemented widespread repression. In addition to state-sponsored terror under the aegis of the National Security Doctrine, "hundreds of sects and individualistic and apocalyptic credos [belief systems] were implanted. The memory is the strength of the people and what better than religion to erase that conscience" (Silletta, 1987: 145). The *sectas*—like the International Monetary Fund—symbolize the continued erosion of their nation's political sovereignty, economic independence, and cultural heritage.

A Possible Resolution

No reasonable alternative theory comes to mind that retains the world-order perspective as outlined here and *also* explains: (1) American establishment Protestant missionary decline before the 1960s and (2) American nonestablishment missionary growth since the 1960s. One obvious adjustment is to change the world-system theory regarding religious institutions, but if that would bring order out of disorder in these materials, we, at least, do not see the way to accomplish it.

Another kind of adjustment is possible, however, and that is to revise our notions of what is establishment religion. Perhaps one of the lessons to be learned from table 1 (which shows that so-called mainline churches have been losing proportionately to sectarian competitors throughout the twentieth century) is that mainline churches are no longer so mainline, and so-called sectarian churches are assuming increasingly representative status. While such an adjustment does not solve all the discord we have encountered here, it nonetheless alerts us to what may be a significant change in the religio-political nexus in today's America.

Actually, our point is more easily made if we start from another perspective — that of "civil religion." Peter Smith himself noted that by establishment religion he meant something approximating the concept of civil religion. . . .

> [It] may also be thought of as the religious element in . . . the 'dominant ideology,' that is, the ideological framework by which the coherence of a dominant or ascendant social class is maintained. (1986: 91)

Perhaps the label *legitimating myth* is the clearest rendering we can offer of this concept.

Certainly America had had a legitimating myth, and certainly America's churches have participated in that myth's creation, content, promulgation, and modification. (See Albanese, 1976; Bellah, 1967; Hammond, 1976, for illustration.) Without doubt, moreover, the enthusiastic missionary thrust by the mainline churches in the nineteenth and early twentieth centuries, and the continued domestic growth of *all* churches in America until the mid-1960s, reflected the vitality of that myth. As Robert Wuthnow has recently written, the core of the myth — "the millennial future of America" and its role as beacon and harbinger — came under increasing challenge until, by the 1960s, its unifying power was gone. In its place: "Religious conservatives and liberals offer competing versions of American civil religion that seem to have very little of substance in common" (1988: 244).

Another way to describe this process is to say that, until the 1960s, presidents, other leaders, and perhaps even people in general, were able to blend together, or at least hold in tension, the disparate elements of a single legitimating myth. After the Vietnam protests, the collapse of the civil rights movement, and the rise of the counter-culture as examples on the domestic front, and after our defeat in Vietnam, the turnabout in the export-import ratio, and the spread of nuclear weaponry as examples on the international front, such containment in a single myth was no longer possible. Instead, *two* renditions of the legitimating myth have emerged. While the links of each rendition to class, partisan politics, and general policy dimensions are not all that clear yet,[7] the links to Protestantism are rather obvious: there is a conservative Christian right and a liberal, erstwhile mainline Protestant left. The one is chiefly concerned domestically about returning America to an earlier, "better" time and, internationally, has few qualms about holding out this nation as still the world's leader.[8]

The other is chiefly concerned domestically about extending equal rights and, internationally, seeks peace and commonality. The first of these views, needless to say, engages in foreign missionary activity with increasing fervor; the second, just as obviously, has either given up on the foreign mission field altogether or severely redefined it as a "partnership of equals."

The implication is clear, even if it cannot be adequately documented here: Evangelical Protestantism in its several forms is replacing liberal Protestantism as the establishment religion of America. (See table 4.) Only in the South did liberal denominations gain members during the decade of the 1970s, no doubt in part because of the in-migration of non-southerners. Everywhere else those denominations declined significantly, while evangelical denominations, especially those with roots in southern culture, rose spectacularly. Evangelical religion has dominated the South for a long time, of course, but who would have thought it had

TABLE 4

Change in the Number of Members of Liberal and Evangelical
(Southern and Nonsouthern) Denominations, by Region, 1971–1980[1]

	Liberal[2]	Southern Evangelical[3]	Other Evangelical
Northeast	−6.1% (422,000)	76.7% (108,000)	−0.9% (6,000)
North Central	−8.4% (951,000)	26.9% (396,000)	1.4% (56,000)
South	7.3% (674,000)	13.3% (1,797,000)	17.6% (231,000)
West	−9.5% (312,000)	39.5% (371,000)	11.6% (158,000)

[1]These data are from the Glenmary Research Center Publications, as analyzed by Mark Shibley in an M.A. thesis, Dept. of Sociology, University of California at Santa Barbara, 1989.

[2]Liberal denominations are those referred to as liberal or moderate by W. C. Roof and W. McKinney, *American Mainline Religion* (New Brunswick, N.J.: Rutgers University Press, 1987). They include Episcopalian, United Church of Christ, Presbyterian, Methodist, Lutheran, Disciples, American Baptist, and Reformed.

[3]All other Protestant groups with clear evangelical style were then divided by whether their history and/or current headquarters trace to the South.

more than a quarter the strength of liberalism in the Northeast, nearly half the strength in the Northcentral region, and approaching double the strength in the West? (See Egerton, 1974; Streicker and Strober, 1972.)

To the degree such evangelicalism is becoming established, therefore, something of the world-order perspective on religious institutions with which he began this discussion would seem to be upheld. As the United States gained its leadership position in the world economy, so was there an increase in the number of missionaries going out from the United States. These missionaries were going out under the sponsorship not of the old establishment religion but on the new. Similarly, throughout this period of ascendancy and hegemony, this new establishment religion gained disproportionately on the domestic front as well. Were Peter Smith's proposition fully supported, decline, not continued growth of evangelical religion should have set in during the past two decades. Decline has not occurred, however; therefore we can assume that only part, not all, of the world-order perspective on religion needs revision.

Notes

1. Kenneth Medhurst writes: "The presence of its [the Anglican church's] leaders on State occasions, their membership of the House of Lords, and the survival of chapels directly under Royal jurisdiction, all witness to the persistence of time-honoured links with the Crown . . . Indeed, this legacy is reflected not least in the extent to which 'top people' in Britain still manifest a Christian adherence to an exceptional degree when compared with that of ordinary citizenry'' (1988: vii–viii).

2. For reasons not clear to us, Smith tracks only other major Protestants, not Anglicans, as indicative of establishment religiosity. This correction changes the percentages but not the relationship. Using the same source material and combining Anglican and other major Protestant figures, the percentage would be 27.4 percent (1870), peaking at 28.9 percent (1900) and then declining. In addition, Smith does not account for the momentary increase in church membership that occurred in the 1950s and early 1960s, a phenomenon corresponding to the American experience (see Table 1).

3. One might note a possible exception: the correlation following World War II between the United States government's rising position in the world's political economy and its growing involvement in a church activity analogous to foreign missions. The United States (partly through the United Nations) was increasingly extending relief to refugees and famine-stricken populations. To a significant degree, such aid was given through already existing agencies of main-

line Protestant, Catholic, and Jewish organizations. Cold War objectives were perceived to be taking precedence over humanitarianism, however, which led to a cutting back by many of these mainline groups in their cooperation with the government. By the late 1960s, "The work of Christian and Jewish agencies overlapped with less frequency; differing views over the proper disposition of the Palestinian refugees created underlying tensions. Mainline Protestant and Catholic efforts were styled differently from the often brash efforts of evangelical Protestants. And the expanding work of secular agencies such as Save the Children, the International Rescue Committee, Oxfam, and others diminished the pride of place religious agencies had long held in the field" (Nichols, 1988: 116). Therefore, establishment church cooperation with the United States government in these efforts peaked (just as Peace Corps volunteers peaked) in 1966–67, probably for the same reasons. The United States, it could be argued, had lost its hegemonic position, but, just as clearly, other forces were at work, too.

4. Without doubt, the most telling example was the grant of $85,000 by the World Council of Churches' Committee to Combat Racism to the Rhodesian Marxist rebels. Whatever else it meant, it certainly meant revisionist thinking in any mission theory dating from early in the century.

5. In 1985, unaffiliated personnel numbered 17,961; combined total for IFMA and EFMA, 14,457; and 4,349 for Department of Ministry-National Council of Churches in the United States of America.

6. Protestantism has a long history in Argentina. As British investments aided the development of the country, Anglican and other Protestant missionaries ministered to the expatriate community and missionized the indians of Tierra del Fuego. Also, Welsh settlers had inhabited the Chubut valley of central Argentina, bringing with them their Protestant religion. In 1986 the Argentine Methodist church celebrated its 150th anniversary in the country.

7. These issues foretell a possible realignment in the American political parties, most notably by Republican inroads on white southerners and labor union members. No such clearcut switching into the Democratic column has occurred in recent presidential elections, but it is worth noting that the so-called eastern bloc of the Republican party may, in due time, be seeking a new home. Columnist Richard Reeves identifies the underlying issue in his image of a future "American troika, with a middle party made up of people who now consider themselves moderate Democrats and moderate Republicans. The old Democratic Party, heavily black, would become a true party of the left. The old Republicans would become a country-and-western band, a populist and religious party of the right" (syndicated column of 10/2/88).

8. Wuthnow (1988: 247) quotes from Jerry Falwell: "We have the people and the resources to evangelize the world in our generation," thus echoing the sentiments of his liberal counterparts of three-quarters of century earlier.

References

1900   *Ecumenical Missionary Conference*. 2 vols. New York: American Tract
       Society.

Albanese, Catherine
1976   *Sons of the Fathers*. Philadelphia: Temple University Press.

Beach, Harlan P., and C. H. Fahs, eds.
1925   *World Missionary Atlas*. New York: Institute of Social and Religious
       Research.

Beach, Roderick, ed.
1920   *Foreign Missions Yearbook of North America*. New York: Foreign Mis-
       sion Conference of North America.

Bellah, Robert N.
1967   "Civil Religion in America." *Daedalus*, 96 (Winter): 1–21.

Bliss, Edwin M., ed.
1891   *The Encyclopedia of Missions*. 2 vols. New York: Funk and Wagnalls.

Brierley, Paul W., ed.
1981   *UK Christian Handbook: Overseas*. London: Evangelical Missionary
       Alliance.

Burdick, Michael A.
1986   "Overseas Mission: Failure of Nerve or Change in Strategy? In *Liberal
       Protestantism*, edited by Robert S. Michaelsen and Wade Clark Roof, 102–
       114. New York: Pilgrim Press.

Carroll, Henry K., Special Agent
1894   *Report on Statistics of Churches in the United States at the Eleventh Cen-
       sus: 1890*. Washington, D.C.: Government Printing Office.

Coote, Robert T.
1982   "The Uneven Growth of Conservative Evangelical Missions." *Interna-
       tional Bulletin of Missionary Research*, 6 (July): 118–123.
1982   "Supplement." Private correspondence.

Currie, Robert, Alan Gilbert and Lee Horsely
1977   *Churches and Churchgoers*. Oxford: Clarendon Press.

Dayton, Edward R., ed.
1986   *Mission Handbook: North American Protestant Ministries Overseas*. 13th
       edition. Monrovia: MARC.

Durand, E. Dana, Dir.
1910   *Religious Bodies: 1906*. Washington, D.C.: Government Printing Office.

Egerton, John
1974   *The Americanization of Dixie.* New York: Harper's Magazine Press.

Fairbanks, John K., ed.
1974   *The Missionary Enterprise in China and America.* Cambridge, Mass.: Harvard University Press.

Finke, Roger, and Rodney Stark
1989   "How the Upstart Sects Won America: 1776–1850." *Journal for the Scientific Study of Religion* (March).

Hammond, Phillip E.
1976   "The Sociology of American Civil Religion." *Sociological Analysis,* 37, No. 2 (Summer): 169–182.

Handy, Robert T.
1984   *A Christian America.* (second edition.) New York: Oxford University Press.

Hartley, Loyde H.
1987   "Popular Mission Philosophies and Denominational Mission Policy." In *Yearbook of American and Canadian Churches, 1988,* edited by Constant H. Jacquet, Jr., 273–285. Nashville: Abingdon Press.

Hocking, William Ernst, et al
1932   *Re-Thinking Missions: A Laymen's Inquiry After One Hundred Years.* New York and London: Harper and Brothers Publisher.

Hutchison, William R.
1974   "Modernism and Missions: The Liberal Search for an Exportable Christianity, 1875–1935." In *The Missionary Enterprise in China and America,* edited by John J. Fairbanks, 110–131. Cambridge, Massachusetts: Harvard University Press.
1987   *Errand to the World.* Chicago: University of Chicago Press.

Jacquet, Constant H., Jr.
1987   *Yearbook for American and Canadian Churches.* Nashville: Abingdon Press.

Medhurst, Kenneth, and George Moyser
1988   *Church and Politics in a Secular Age.* Oxford: Clarendon Press.

Methol Ferre, Alberto
1987   "Editorial." In *Nexo* No. 13, Montevideo (September): 3.

Navarro Gerassi, Marysa
1965   "Argentine Nationalism of the Right." In *Studies in Comparative International Development,* I: 181–194.

Newcomb, Harvey
1854   *A Cyclopedia of Missions*. New York: Scribners.

Nichols, J. Bruce
1988   *The Uneasy Alliance*. New York: Oxford University Press.

Parker, Joseph I., ed.
1938   *Interpretive Statistical Survey of the World Mission of the Christian Church*. New York: International Missionary Council.

Robertson, Roland, and J. Chirico
1985a   "Humanity, Globalization, and Worldwide Religious Resurgence." *Sociological Analysis* 46, No. 3 (Fall): 219–242.

Robertson, Roland
1985b   "The Sacred and the World System." In The *Sacred in a Secular Age*, edited by Phillip E. Hammond, 347–358. Berkeley and Los Angeles: University of California Press.
1987   "Church-State Relations and the World System." In *Church-State Relations*, edited by Thomas Robbins and Roland Robertson, 39–51. New Brunswick, New Jersey: Transaction, Inc.

Roof, Wade Clark, and William McKinney
1987   *American Mainline Religion*. New Brunswick, New Jersey: Rutgers University Press.

Schlesinger, Arthur, Jr.
1974   "The Missionary Enterprise and Theories of Imperialism." In *The Missionary Enterprise in China and America*, edited by John K. Fairbank, 336–373. Cambridge, Mass.: Harvard University Press.

Silletta, Alfredo
1987   *Las Sectas Invaden la Argentina*. Buenos Aires: Editorial Contrapunto.

Smith, Peter
1986   "Anglo-American Religion and Hegemonic Change in the World System, c. 1870–1980." *British Journal of Sociology*, 37: 88–105.

Stanley, Brian
1983   "'Commerce and Christianity': Providence Theory, The Missionary Movement, and the Imperialism of Free Trade." *The Historical Journal*, 26: 71–94.

Streicher, L. D., and G. S. Strober
1972   *Religion and the New Majority*. New York: Association Press.

Verghese, Fr. Paul
1970   "A Sacramental Humanism." *The Christian Century*, 87 (September, 27): 1118–1119.

Wright, Henry Otis, ed.
1905   *The Blue Book of Missions*. New York: Funk and Wagnalls.

Wuthnow, Robert
1978   "Religious Movements and the Transition in World Order." In *Understanding the New Religions*, edited by Jacob Needleman and G. Baker, 63–79. New York: Seabury.
1980   "World Order and Religious Movements." In *Studies of the Modern World System*, edited by Albert Bergesen, 57–75. New York: Academic Press.
1987   "America's Legitimating Myths: Continuity and Crises." In *America's Changing Role in the World System*, edited by Terry Boswell and Albert Bergesen, 235–255. New York: Praeger.
1988   *The Restructuring of American Religion*. Princeton: Princeton University Press.

Part IV

American Religion and Civic Culture

10

A World Polity Interpretation of U.S. Religious Trends Since World War II

George M. Thomas

The changes in religion since the end of World War II appear dramatic and complex, matching the complicated pattern of change generally during this period. The purpose of this paper is first to delineate several major trends identified by observers of United States religion and second to interpret these trends in the context of world dynamics. The interpretation proposed here is admittedly tentative, primarily intended to present important elements that I believe are necessary for an adequate account of some of the more important and more discussed changes. I will identify features of the argument that would seem to be general to the relation of national cultures to the world context, and thus applicable to other countries provided that the particulars of each country are taken into account.

Religious Trends Since 1945

Religious denominations entering the 1950s largely were not organized to make demands on the state, and in this sense were apolitical. Nevertheless, they had the goal of affecting civil society and were quite optimistic about their prospects. Conservative and evangelical groups were active especially in parachurch organizations, including ministries to the military and colleges. Most denominations participated in national organizations and associations; liberal denominations were the most visibly active in such formal organizations. Religious book publishing grew throughout the period, and evangelical publishers and book dealers formed national associations. A national network emerged comprised of pastors, writers, and speakers (see Handy, 1984; Roof and McKinney,

1987; Wuthnow, 1988). While denominational identifications were still strong, all of these factors tended to downplay the importance of denominational doctrine, ecclesiology, polity, and history (as well as these subjects generally). By the mid-1950s the general condition of religion was described as a revival (Handy, 1984), and if there was a lull in the early sixties it soon was forgotten with increased religious activity, attention, and intensity later in the decade, which included new religious movements, the Jesus movement, and a takeoff in conservative evangelicalism.

The content of United States religion during this period was marked by an increase in individualism. Certainly Christianity in the United States has been marked by ever-increasing individualism in fits and starts from the colonial period. In the 1950s there was an increase if not qualitative change in the rise of "harmonial religion" (Ahlstrom, 1972) that focused on inner peace and security. In particular, religious discourse was brought to bear on the subjective—the inner needs, desires, processes, and experiences of the individual. Postwar themes of peace, tranquility, and harmony were later reworked and integrated into a more assertive psychological framework that included prescriptions for self-esteem, inner self, self-actualization, and getting in touch with one's self, which became integral to theological and, certainly, pastoral discourse during the sixties and seventies.

Salvation became associated with psychological and physical health as well as power and successful action. Salvation was both an inner search and outward actualization; it was something material — health, wealth, success, and power. It also was an experience. Experience took different forms and was discussed differently. It might be an emotional conversion. It might be the baptism of the Spirit and speaking in tongues. It might be the dramatic effect of high liturgy. It might produce healing and health; it might produce greater religious commitment, or it might empower. Even social action was discussed in psychological and experiential terms. The discourse, forms, techniques, and behavioral expectations varied across denominational groupings, and I will explore these differences, but experience—that is, having an experience—was a powerful theme that cut across denominations.

A focus of attention on inner processes, subjectivity, and experiences was prevalent throughout culture (Campbell, 1982). In the churches, people did not have to be taught this emphasis, although they struggled to master the diverse techniques, disciplines, and discourses. From liberal to evangelical congregations, if there was any natural and spontaneous predisposition, it was toward this type of individualism.

This focus was reinforced by parachurch organizations, which replaced doctrine and distinctive denominational elements with individual concerns.

By the late 1960s issues emerged within the churches that became associated with national cleavages (Roof and McKinney, 1987; Wuthnow, 1988). While there were exceptions, these became defined as liberal versus conservative or evangelical — biblical inerrancy, creationism, abortion, homosexuality, the equal rights amendment, and family issues. A notable exception was the growth of charismatic factions within churches and the issue of speaking in tongues: Evangelicals were as opposed to this practice as much if not more so than mainline liberals, but because charismatics are theologically conservative in the fundamentalist tradition, they were grouped with evangelicals. In this manner, the liberal-conservative cleavage, while in fact fluid and situational, was maintained as a hard and fast boundary.

Inerrancy is an extremely strong boundary differentiating liberals from evangelicals. Denominations and congregations can be classified rather easily as liberal, moderate, and conservative according to their stance, and much emotional charge is associated with these distinctions. For example, in a Ted Koppel television interview after the televangelism scandals of the eighties with, among others, Rev. Jerry Falwell, the issue of biblical inerrancy was raised. Rev. Falwell, in a raised and firm tone, recited a highly formulized evangelical position. The audience *en masse* applauded, cheered, and stood for an extended time (Harding, 1988). Such response is not merely the result of a socioemotional excitation, although it is that; it is the observance of a symbolic boundary.

Yet, even with inerrancy, we find a fluidity in practice that is unexpected from such boundary maintenance examples. One finds many in a liberal congregation reading their Bibles in a commonsensical literal manner, despite the intellectual stance of the leaders. Moreover, pastors and teachers in evangelical churches seem always to struggle in their Sunday school classes with an innocently recalcitrant flock that questions the importance of finely nuanced doctrinal statements. Learning these boundaries as a congregation can be an arduous and divisive process (Warner, 1988). By the eighties, most congregations had come to observe these boundaries and knew which side they collectively were on, sometimes at the expense of dissenting factions, sometimes with an uneasy internal pluralism.

Thus, what we see is a tendency toward individualism with a strong focus on individual subjectivity and experience, and laid over this commonality are issues increasingly national in scope that congregations came to learn. Associated with national orientation was an overall increase in religious activity and intensity in the late 1960s. The intensification of religion after 1965 was not experienced uniformly across denominations. Growth rates in part were associated with the stances on these issues, as well as different forms of individualism. Specifically, conservative denominations have grown steadily since 1965 while liberal ones have declined (Hunter, 1987; Kelley, 1972; Roof and McKinney, 1987)

A final important trend is the politicization of religion in the seventies, not coterminous with the resurgence of the late sixties but a short time after. As noted, all types of denominations since 1950 were political in the broad sense of being oriented to affecting civil society. Conservative churches acted for the most part when their interests were directly involved. Notable examples include the mobilization of black churches (in some respects more moderate than conservative) in the civil rights movement (Morris, 1984), the countermobilization of many white Southern Baptist congregations, and the antidesegregation pronouncements of many fundamentalist leaders (who later would moderate with increased national status in the seventies). Liberal denominations were most involved in "social action" but even here rarely mobilized to make claims on the state. During the sixties, liberal denominations were socially active in civil rights, antiwar, and student movements. In the seventies they continued to be open to politically liberal programs and greater state authority in the name of equality, justice, and human rights. Yet, these movements seemed to diffuse the liberal impulse. A whole generation of youth from these churches pursued such goals within secular movements or new religious movements, some as a disenchantment with but others as a fulfillment of their liberal upbringing. Many continued their search through these movements to a conservative evangelicalism.

Initially, the apolitical nature of resurgent evangelicalism at the beginning of the seventies was a postliberal nearly Anabaptist critique of political social action. By the late seventies, however, conservative groups were being mobilized around national moral issues. The national networks of pastors and speakers, book publishing, television, and electronic mailing corporations, coupled with local congregations already highly active religiously, provided a strong basis for political mobilization. Pastors allowed representatives of social action to use their pulpits or to dedicate a particular meeting to the issues. Films were shown; books were discussed in small groups previously described as home Bible studies. Thus, there was a continuity of social organization. There also was a continuity of goals: the evangelization and creation of a moral society. If there was a change in goals that marked politicization, it was the more explicit focusing on morality distinct from religion. By entering the political arena, conservatives to varying degrees downplayed religious particulars, reduced religion to morality, and single-mindedly pursued consentual moralism (Handy, 1984).

Religion, Symbolic Boundaries, and the Nation-state

Any religious system includes statements about what is real. This has been referred to as a worldview (Berger and Luckmann, 1966; Geertz, 1973). I will also refer to it as an ontology (a theory of existence) or ideology (a theory of polity and society) that is taken for granted by adherents and contested within the broader polity by different groups. An ontology is cognitive because it is a theory of reality; it also is moral in the sense that the given structure of reality is assumed to be what should be. Symbolic boundaries, to follow Wuthnow (1987), are moral boundaries. I use *symbolic boundaries* to refer to the entities and structure of the ontology in order to avoid confusion with a second set of statements—an ethos or morality. An ontology as a classification of reality compellingly defines morally binding attitudes, moods, and behavioral imperatives (Geertz, 1973). Looking at this process from the opposite direction, we note that morality, or any particular moral issue, is embedded in an ontology. Morality defines and preserves in practice the integrity of types of entities that are assumed to exist, they symbolic boundaries, and the very structure of being.

Thus, we may speak of a structured reality and moral rules defining that structure in practice. For example, Mary Douglas (1966) in a now classic work argued that the Levitical dietary laws concretize and preserve within everyday life the structure of creation as described in the first chapters of Genesis. Symbolic boundaries are defined and observed through rules of everyday life. If there is a strongly contested moral issue or set of issues within a polity, it is likely that what is at stake is a fundamental definition or boundary about reality, and thus the collective's meaning and identity.[1]

The construction, expansion, and intensification of nation-state authority is embedded in an ontology structured around primary entities of nation and citizen, the dynamic reality and value of individual action (including economic action), and collective goals of economic prosperity, justice, and progress. The broad meaning of the nation-state as a moral project is defined in terms of these entities and ends. Rules and myths, which are institutionalized and observed, define and elaborate the nation, the individual, action, and how rational, moral individual action is related to collective goals (see Thomas, 1989; Thomas et al., 1987; Wuthnow, 1987). Sociocultural change causes redefinitions or shifts in the interre-

lations of entities and their relations to collective ends. Change in symbolic boundaries can include an elaboration of entities and a concomitant
intensification of their boundaries or it can refer to shifts in those boundaries. For example, one of the arguments that follows is that the intensification of nation-state authority results in greater rational, moral, and
subjective complexity of the individual. Cultural work on defining increased individual subjectivity might shift the value of the individual
from equality to liberty or vice versa.

Within the ontology of the nation-state, a set of religions is defined
as acceptable. The broader the set is, the more pluralistic the nation-state
is said to be. Boundaries are put on what is acceptable in religion; a universe of different religious beliefs are defined and pluralism is tolerated
within those limits. Thus, Protestantism and then Christianity and then
Christianity and Judaism defined the boundaries of pluralism in the
United States. Religious pluralism very often assumes pluralism on ontological statements but a consensus on moral ones, this has been especially true of the United States. There rarely has been complete moral
consensus, but claims for one morality are acceptable, not to say appreciated. Temperance, Sabbatarianism, abolitionism, prohibitionism, sexual moralism, and public prayer are behaviors that were so contested.

I propose the interpretation that increases in what I will refer to as
global density (including nation-state involvement in the world polity),
and concomitantly greater nation-state authority and status, are the context of religion. These variables increased throughout the post-World
War II period, marked by discrete jumps and events. These events were
latched onto and constructed as crises by movements, the public, and social scientists, but these events functioned more as markers and meaningful referents than as causal agents. A long-term increase in global density
and nation-state involvement and status results in increased competition
and conflict over the nature of symbolic boundaries and the moral constitution of nation and citizen. There is a concomitant intensification (resurgence, revival) of religious discourse and activity as an integral part of
that reconstitution, conflict, and debate. Moreover, global effects on the
symbolic boundaries of the nation are direct, as well as indirect through
state expansion and sociocultural heterogeneity.

World Order and Symbolic Boundaries of the
United States through 1965

Religion in the United States characteristically has defined the nation as a special people. While this distinctiveness was defined in terms
of being a Christian nation, it was manifested and more universally dis-

cussed as being a moral people. Indeed, the "reduction" of religion to morality is one of the characteristic marks of religion in the United States (de Tocqueville, 1945; Weber, 1946; Lipset, 1963; Handy, 1964). Symbolic boundaries and collective purpose were displayed in moral rules governing and defining personhood and action.

We can relate waves of moralistic religious movements in the United States to increased status of the nation, formation and bureaucratization of the state, and the nation-state's increased incorporation into the world market and polity. For example, the optimism of peaceful growth after 1815 and the subsequent economic takeoff and prosperous involvement in the world political economy were marked by revivalism, abolitionism, and temperance movements (Ryan, 1981; Thomas, 1989). In the last quarter of the nineteenth century, state formation (including bureaucratization and a formal school system) along with increased political-military action in the world were accompanied by large-scale religious issues and cleavages from the liberal-fundamentalist split on both theology and modernity to the emergence of the Pentecostal-holiness movements (Marsden, 1980). The refusal of the United States to take world leadership after World War I and its resolute isolationism probably accounts for the lack of new movements in the 1920s and 1930s. Moreover, the failure of prohibition contributed to a "disestablishment" of Protestantism from defining and managing public morality. While this resulted in a shift in strategies and a more cautioned optimism, Protestantism after World War II was still clearly in the business of shaping public morality (Wuthnow, 1988).

With the close of World War II, the United States accepted and pursued a position as the center of global political economy and culture. From the various financial reconstruction plans and military presences in Europe and East Asia to continued political dominance in Latin America, the United States used its economic, political, and military resources to create a hegemony or what has been referred to as the *Pax Americana*. Within the country, a cautious optimism prevailed. Above all, this optimism was nationalistic, not essentially in a psychoemotional sense but in the sense that the war dramatically increased civil society's orientation to and participation in the national occupational structure, economy (and economic indicators), and institutions, all in the context of the state's role in the world. Moreover, there was a larger United States state entering the 1950s, measured in terms of revenues, bureaucracy, symbolic presence, and status in the world.[2] Optimism was predicated on the nation's self-confidence in its democracy and goodness. The presence of the Soviet Union as the "other" that was nondemocratic and atheistic tempered the optimism but heightened the importance of the United States as a moral project.

The characteristics of religion during the 1950s, as described, were part and parcel of the nation-state's increased incorporation, centrality, and status in the world community after the war. The "promise and peril" (Wuthnow, 1988) tone of religion during this period reflected, shaped, and channeled the optimism of greater national stature but also the greater caution resulting from global and national complexities as well as from the "second disestablishment." Thus, through the nationalism, mobilization, and world involvement of the cold war, denominational religion thrived through the early sixties. The construction of parachurch organizations, national associations, book publishing, and a national speaker circuit provided larger-scale platforms by which to shape the greater orientation to national and international structures. In this light, the assessment of Handy (1984) that this social action was a denial of the reality of the second disestablishment that would catch up to Protestants a few decades later seems incorrect. Such action was a natural adaptive increase in scale of organization, issues, symbols, and discourse to the increased importance of national symbolic boundaries. This interpretation further suggests that the intensification of religion after 1965, especially but not only for conservative churches, and subsequent politicization reflected and shaped the symbolic boundaries of the United States nation-state in the context of global dynamics.

Global Density, Heterogeneity, and the Nation-state, 1965–

The importance of the national center increased throughout the last half of the century, and by the mid sixties various global factors intensified national mobilization. After the Cuban Revolution, the United States was more involved than ever in supporting regimes in Latin America through financial aid, military excursions, and the designing of land reform programs. Its military continued in the Pacific, increasing its involvement in Southeast Asia. The Soviet Union's increased technology as symbolized by Sputnik satellites and the emergence of China as a major power presented increased political-economic competition. The movement of newly independent African democracies toward dictatorships and one-party regimes also created ideological competition and increased threats to a Western hegemony. Moreover, a new international system was being constructed, characterized by international regimes or organizations. For example, the average number of intergovernmental organizations to which the ten richest noncommunist countries belonged was about forty in 1940, rising dramatically with the formation of postwar pacts and the United Nations system of organizations to about seventy-five in 1950, leveling off to about sixty in 1960, and jumping to over eighty by 1966

(Demmitt and Thomas, 1987). The level of global incorporation, competition (military, economic, and ideological), and participation in formal transnational structures can be summarized as global density.

Global density increases the importance of the nation-state as a country's central authority and increases sociocultural heterogeneity. Both of these involve the intensification and at times reconstitution of nation and citizen (Robertson, 1985). I first look at heterogeneity; then, the state, and then, their interaction. I describe these dynamics in some detail in order to establish the interpretive frame for religion since 1965.

Heterogeneity results directly from competition in the world system and not solely from immigration and urbanization because heterogeneity is as much cultural as demographic. The political and economic control of a tribe with an indigenous local religion might have little effect on an industrialized country aside from sparking curiosity and possibly a new academic discipline (such as anthropology in England and France). However, confrontation with a rich and productive country with a different world religion has profound effects on the adequacy of cultural boundaries. For example, the oil crisis of the mid seventies, which demonstrated United States dependence on the policies of other nation-states, the buying of major United States corporations by wealthy Arabs, as well as large numbers of Muslim students studying in the U.S. forced the presence of Islam into the United States religious universe. The political mobilization of Islam throughout Sahara Africa and Asia as a shaping force of nation-state policy has similar effects. The infusion of millions of dollars to fund Islamic centers in universities from Oxford to large state ones in the United States concretely manifest this increased heterogeneity.[3]

Heterogeneity has profound effects on the boundaries of pluralism. First of all, it stretches the outer boundaries of acceptable religious ontologies. As noted, in the United States the boundaries have been pushed outward to include different systems. In the 1960s and 1970s they came to include Eastern and Native American religions,[4] and in the eighties it is being extended to include Islam. Second, heterogeneity calls into question a moral consensus, especially as more divergent ontologies are fit into the polity. These two effects have broad implications for the very meaning of the polity. What religions and moralities are acceptable within the boundaries of the pluralistic universe define the larger meaning and project of the nation-state. It defines "us" versus "them." Civilization cannot mean Christian morality and civility if the polity includes Islam. Consequently, the good society cannot be the millennium. Third, as a religion is accepted within a polity, it syncretizes cultural elements and becomes less dissimilar. This is the flip side of heterogeneity: As diverse religions are incorporated within a polity, each tends to take on elements of the whole, resulting in increased homogeneity. For example, Hinduism, Buddhism, and even Islam are "Americanized." This results in factions within the religion, some reinforcing accommodation, others resisting secularization. Overall, the polity witnesses increased religious action, discourse, mobilization, and conflict.

Global density affects culture, symbolic boundaries, and religion also because it increases the status of the nation-state in the world system and its authority, legitimacy, and status vis-a-vis society.[5] The state claims and is given greater power and authority, usually through conflict. It makes greater claims on society and reinforces national definitions, identities, and orientations. For example, increased national mobilization in the early sixties was manifested in the redefinition of education and science as the crucial basis of national strength and the assurance of United States optimism. This change was reflected and intensified by military mobilization for the war in Southeast Asia and the student movement.

Movements increasingly orient themselves toward making claims on the state in a world context; their success further heightens the state's status and authority as well as world discourse. For example, the civil rights movement was reinforced by African independence movements, and its claims on the federal government reflected both historical particulars of United States federalism and the increased status of the nation-state. The movement reinforced the federal state as the source and manager of individual rights and dignity and as the arena for collective action; it also elaborated world ideology of nonviolence and human rights. Likewise, the student movement used worldwide categories of global responsibility, world ecology, global humanity, national self-determination, and a will to power in national politics. Thus, world factors directly affect the symbols and claims of movements and indirectly affect them through the increased authority and status of the nation-state.

State expansion within the world polity reshapes a society's ontology. In the contemporary world culture the nation-state is made sacred as the center of power and value (Ellul, 1975). It is the agency by which the good society, progress, justice, equality, and other broadly accepted collective goals are pursued. Put another way, the value that derives from such ends flows into society through the state and nation. Groups and organizations that link up to those flows, whether as means to their ends or as defining structures, gain in legitimacy. That is, the closer the linkage to the nation-state, the greater the legitimacy. Yet it is necessary to address the diverse effects that different types of linkages might have.

Ellul (1975) documents that the profaning of the nation-state in the form of revolution or opposition generally is also sacred. This is so because while it is counter to the regime in power, it is a dialectic of the state, making use of the same logic of power and control to define the structure of the nation-state. Successful overthrow tends to increase state power (e.g., Thomas and Meyer, 1987). Thus, movements oriented toward the nation-state are prone to be sacralized and to use religious symbols because, first of all, they are working on and constituting symbolic boundaries and, second, because they are the opposition that promises "the new way." This dialectic can be referred to as a state-revolution axis.

In this process, the individual also is made sacred. Historically, the state has gone hand in hand with increased individualism, freeing the individual from traditional moral constraints (Durkheim, 1972; Boli, 1987). State expansion tends to transform symbolic boundaries rooted in kinship, local community, and traditional religion.[6] With greater symbolic moral stature of the nation-state, there is a concomitant increase in individual identification with national citizenship. There are increased levels of individualism, including not only rights ideology but also a general cultural focus on the construction of self and life course and the middle-class goals of comfort, security, and the good life (Ellul, 1967; Lasch, 1979; Meyer, 1987). This relationship can be referred to as a state-individual dialectical axis.

The expansion of nation-state authority and status (internal and external) affects national symbolic boundaries in several ways. First, the definitions of corporate meaning and the constitution of the nation become more important. The "us" versus "them," on the one hand, is made problematic through heterogeneity and global interdependence; on the other hand, this boundary becomes more central. As value flows through the state into society, there is a greater demand for defining the meaning of the nation and delineating influence over and access to the state. Crisis theories tend to emphasize the problematics of old boundaries. The present interpretation emphasizes the mobilization around the construction of new ones that are generated out of the increased symbolic significance of the center (Young, 1970; Robertson, 1985). This process increases the value of member units—the individual citizen, and as noted it increases the mobilization of collective action toward the center. Thus, much work takes place on the moral definition of citizenship and individual and subcultural identities from religion to ethnicity. As part of the process, movements define change as a crisis that can be met only by their claims. In the United States during this period this process is manifested in the redefinition and mobilization of education and individualism.

A second and related effect on symbolic boundaries is that the state increasingly becomes the authoritative source of social ontology and public morality. I do not mean that the state as a bureaucracy or professional class consciously legislates such things, although this can occur. Rather, I mean that the organization and mobilization of the polity has the structural effect of defining the nation-state as the carrier of moral excellence and the means of attaining progress, justice, liberty, and equality. Geertz's (1980) description of Negara in nineteenth-century Bali as the exemplary center is in some sense an applicable conceptualization of the twentieth-century nation-state. State policy and the rational legal order institutionalize moral definitions and rules, shape the collective ontology, and set the boundaries for acceptable competing religious ontologies. For example, the loss of a Protestant consensus at the turn of the twentieth century in part was due to immigration and urbanization; it also was due to the construction of a more authoritative federal bureaucracy and increased importance in the world. This state formation can conflict with a society's religious tradition, which has direct consequences for the course and degree of subsequent conflict.

In the case of the United States by the late 1960s, the state was more assertive in its specifying rationalized ontology into law, especially its elaboration of citizenship. By the seventies it was becoming more directly involved in managing rules and institutionalized identities of individuals primarily through the overlapping discourses of rights and psychology within national institutions such as schools, courts, and welfare bureaucracies. This encroachment was not into a "privatized" sphere of morality and religion. For one thing, morality has always been public, even after the failure of prohibition. Also, we have noted already that religion was not completely privatized. The greater management of morality was more of a collision between the state and a revived and socially active evangelicalism. The timing here is important: Conservatism and evangelicalism prospered since the fifties with a clear agenda to affect public values and morality. Their takeoff occurred in the late sixties at the same time as increased state mobilization. The collision in the form of explicit politicization occurred several years later in the mid seventies: the result of a natural discursive and organizational development of evangelical mobilization and competition with the state.

A third effect of increased nation-state authority and status is greater heterogeneity, counter to the common notion that centralization homogenizes culture and groups into one mass society. This does occur under certain conditions, and the acceptance of a religion within a culture tends to decrease that religion's distinctiveness. Nevertheless, state mobilization as often increases heterogeneity. This is due partly to the mobilization of more diverse groups more completely and partly to the use of more diverse cultural symbols. The increased incorporation of the state within the world polity almost requires that it incorporate more diverse groups and symbols. There consequently is an interactive effect between heterogeneity and state expansion; the global dynamics that increase one also increase the other.

This interaction has profound effects on cultural definitions that give meaning to the nation. To summarize the effects of heterogeneity noted previously, America cannot be equated with Christian moral civilization or the millennium if it includes Buddhism and Islam. Moreover, the set of acceptable religions defines what religions and groups can make claims on the state, increasing the potential for conflict. Precisely as the center becomes more important, there is greater competition over influencing the center's symbols, boundaries, and underlying ontology or ideology.[7] This is not secularization but intensification.

One major consequence is a movement from pluralism to a syncretism. The increased status of the state and national institutions, including schools and a rationalized legal order, presents a unified moral political order. There is a concomitant tendency to extend pluralism to an all-encompassing relativism, which can provide a basis for structural integration. This often takes the form of syncretizing specific beliefs and practices, often abstracting out similarities — the lowest common denominator approach. The latter has been especially prevalent in the West and seems to continue (e.g., Bellah, 1970). Put another way, there is an increase in substantive rationality (Weber, 1946): A haphazard, untidy collection of deities that characterize a broad pluralism of ontologies is viewed relativistically as a set of different manifestations of one abstract high God or the diverse expressions of humanity and as different specifications of one underlying reality.

This syncretism produces factions — usually labeled liberal — within a religious tradition that celebrates this higher or more developed universalism. This in turn produces factions that resist these developments, drawing on traditional symbols to depict them as secularization. One consequence is the resurgence of traditional factions competing not only with each other but with the secular state. However, this resurgence tends to focus on morality rather than ontology. These very movements, in making coalitions against the moral relativity of the state, might themselves generate this abstraction and syncretism of ontology.

In summary, the denser world culture and more competitive political economy tend to expand the authority and status of the nation-state. This results in the increased importance of influencing the state at the same time that both global density and nation-state expansion increase heterogeneity. The result is greater competition within the national polity and the emergence of specifically religious movements in competition with each other and in some instances with the state for influence over the symbols, ontology, and moral order underlying the polity. Many of these movements draw on historical traditional symbols, with the result that state expansion becomes associated with a resurgence of seeming traditionalism. Other movements more fully embrace the symbols and identities of world culture or experiment with other traditions. Some focus on the state-revolution axis: the use of power to oppose or even overthrow the state regime; others focus on the state-individual axis: individual empowerment, health, and security; some might move from the axis of individualism to that of political power, or combine the two, as for example the politicization of evangelicalism in the seventies.

Religious Constituting of Citizen and Nation, 1965–

Religion in the United States has, since the nineteenth-century revivals, defined citizen and nation. Because of the intensification of symbolic boundaries in the 1960s, religious discourse took the form of social movements reworking those definitions. They elaborated theories of the individual and shaped moral issues that defined the nature and meaning of the nation and citizenship. Religious content and movements became more oriented to national-level discourse. Importantly, nationally recognized liberal and conservative religious stances evolved, defining individualism and morals differently, but nevertheless sharing the underlying cultural structure.

Constructing and Empowering the New Citizen and Nation

During this period, liberal and conservative groups elaborated very different versions of individualism that became associated with different growth rates, conservative evangelicalism growing rapidly. At the core of evangelicalism is a personal conversion experience while at the core of liberalism is a personal choice and commitment of will. In conservativism a personal God is active in current affairs and history; humans are not sovereign, and history is open to the intervention of the transcendent and is moving toward the *eschaton*. Within liberalism, God is less directly active and is more immanent in the actions of individuals who choose to construct symbols of commitment, act on that commitment, and take control of history. Conservativism makes piety open to public discourse and exhortation requiring accountable individual action; liberalism views piety as private, although usually emphasizing identification with or commitment to corporation action.[8] Within conservatism there is an emphasis on naive faith and belief despite whatever science might say; in liberalism there is an emphasis on critical faith shaped by human knowledge through the self-conscious construction of symbols. Liberalism makes extensive use of global symbols and the categories of other traditions, celebrating the diversity-commonality of human responses to the cosmos, and thereby extending collective moral boundaries to global humanity; conservatism tends to view such discourse as syncretism and instead makes extensive use of traditional symbols.

These are profound differences, which can be summarized as a historical realism (Symbols have an ontological referent, and human history is sacred history.) versus symbolic realism (Symbols are constructed with no larger ontological referent, but they are real and valid constructions by humans.) (Bellah, 1970). Also, evangelicalism tends to articulate the state-individual axis while liberalism tends to work on the state-power axis.

Despite their differences, both religions define the nature of the individual and symbolic boundaries generally. Consequently, there are many similarities underlying the differences. Put another way, a broad cultural order is a common context and cuts across denominations and the conservative-liberal cleavage. For example, both versions build on a subjective faith: Conservatives posit an irrational belief against scientific knowledge while liberals claim an existential will to power. Both emphasize experience, power, technological control of reality, and instrumentality: For conservatives this might be the baptism of the Spirit, speaking in tongues, health, wealth, or success; for liberals it might be something very similar or possibly effective social action or political-economic empowerment. Both value human happiness, self-esteem, and fulfillment and develop different techniques for creating them. Both abstract the characteristics of God to an impersonal loving force. This is stronger and more explicit among liberals, but even evangelicals do so: They de-emphasize the autonomous will of God and focus on His desire to bless as the individual sees fit; they focus on morality that will mechanically produce blessing; certainly the Holy Spirit tends to be viewed as a power source. Some movements spread across denominations. For example, the charismatic movement emerged in the early sixties in the Episcopalian church and spread dramatically in other mainline liberal churches as well as within Catholicism; it also had an effect within Protestant parachurch organizations, which swelled traditional Pentecostal denominations. Their emphasis on intense emotional experience makes liberals and conservatives open to mysticism — individuals using techniques to experience deeper levels of self and higher levels of the sacred. The appeal of Eastern mysticisms and techniques might have been confined to liberals of a particular generation, but Western mystics and mystical writings generally are being rediscovered by a cross-section of people. Finally, since the mid seventies, both liberals and conservatives assert the absolute importance of political action as the enactment of faith.

Recent trends in evangelicalism might bring about even greater similarities (Hunter, 1987; Marsden, 1987). For example, one of the distinguishing marks of evangelicalism is its emphasis on missionary work that preaches that salvation is only through Jesus. Ironically but understandably, missionaries have been the most syncretistic of evangelicals and have emphasized more humanistic elements such as individual autonomy, freedom of will, and special revelation apart from the Bible. Recently this syncretism is being expanded in the targeting of Islamic populations. Much work is being done to highlight the similarities if not identity of Jehovah and Allah, often by assuming that to experience the holy is an underlying human search. On one hand, much of this work has the effect of purging parochial American culture from transcultural, transhistorical Christianity. On the other hand, it increases the abstractness of God and makes piety more subjective, in not a completely dissimilar way than in liberalism.

The point of listing these similarities is to show that both of these distinct and conflicting groups are specifying a broad cultural structure. This culture defines the individual as a central unit of the nation-state, collective goals in terms of the well-being, happiness, and autonomy of the individual, and rational moral action as the guarantor of progress. In short, both sets of movements are constructing the modern citizen and nation, albeit in significantly different ways. For this reason, both sides have broad appeal across occupations and levels of education and income.

National Moral Issues and Shaping of the Cleavage

Religious ontologies and ideologies of national moral boundaries are specified in national issues. Different types of individualism become concretized and dramatized in different stances on moral rules. The long tradition of defining the United States as a Christian civilization is invoked by focusing on a small number of moral issues. This is not new, and there is much continuity with the nineteenth century, when issues of temperance, slavery, and Sabbatarianism were national issues similarly used to define the moral citizen.

Significantly, issues cluster around family and schools, the central institutions constructed and used in nineteenth-century nation-building to define the moral and Christian uniqueness of the United States and its citizenry (Ryan, 1981; Meyer et al, 1979). Discourse centers on constructing crises: Evangelicals focus on the crisis in the family and schools with the state and liberal humanism as the agents of the crisis; liberals alternately define as the source of the crisis a narrow, unenlightened tradition-alism or the impersonality and exploitation of modern schools. Some-thing as simple as one minute of silence in a grade school takes on immense proportions — by both sides. Its emotion-charged importance derives from it location at a symbolic boundary: Schools symbolize as much as any other institution the project called America. Moreover, the promise of progress, civilization, and prosperity is linked to the schools for it is believed that it is primarily up to them to instill in the next gener-ation technical skills, rationality, knowledge, virtue, and morality. The question then is whether this project, symbolized in the school, is sub-mitted to the Creator or is freed from tradition. A seemingly innocuous ritual has historic and cosmic significance.

Issues also cluster around the core tenets of Christianity in appro-priating them as vehicles for reconstituting symbolic boundaries. De-nominational distinctions had long ago been decoupled from the meaning of the United States and, therefore, could not be used to this end. The prevalence of premillennialism since the turn of the twentieth century made it difficult to explicitly invoke the millennial role of the United States as a redeemer nation (cf., Tuveson, 1968). Issues concerning the very boundaries of Christianity itself seem necessary to define the boundaries of a Christian nation. There are a large number of such issues, from the virgin birth to the Trinity. Many of these have little direct rele-vance to morality. Inerrancy of scripture and new birth are both central elements almost taken for granted in orthodox Christianity. Both are har-nessed to define Christians versus non-Christians in the mobilization for a moral nation. On one side, the more publicized one, inerrancy and being born again are the necessary realities to rejuvenate and empower the na-tion: the first providing a moral guide and the second, an empowered moral, rational citizenry. They are traditional positions but not ones at-tempting to return to an idyllic past. They are used to reconstitute the United States in the complex global dynamics of the seventies and eighties. On the other side, a Bible with errors and individuals neverthe-less committed to some of its ethical themes and symbols are taken as the marks of maturity, strength, and a human will to power that would pro-vide the basis for the United States to take a more humanitarian lead in the world rather than a parochial traditional militaristic one. The former stance is embedded in a historic realism and the latter in a symbolic re-alism, but both define moral boundaries of the nation, individual, and action.

There seems then to be a natural selection of content in terms of scale. Only expansive issues can mobilize around national boundaries and identities. Only such issues can be used to take advantage of parachurch and cross-denominational organizations and networks.[9] For example, in the Ted Koppel interview, Rev. Falwell asked a member of the audience who raised a biblical question what Baptist church he was from. Mr. Koppel, seemingly bewildered, asked the significance of Falwell's question. The latter replied that the church the man belonged to did not believe in biblical inerrancy. There was then immediate recognition of the issue that set the stage for Rev. Falwell's previously cited statement (Harding, 1988).

Thus, the general spread and intensification of individualism in the late sixties coincided with the emergence of national moral issues and their organization into nationally recognized liberal and conservative stances. Largely through the crystallization of this cleavage over moral issues, rather than over abstract arguments over different types of individualism, were the differences between religious liberalism and conservatism dramatized.

Conservative evangelicals quickly moved beyond their disagreements with religious liberals. In fact, conservatives rarely attack religious liberals publicly. Their main target is secular humanism or state policy (Liebman and Wuthnow, 1983). They are out to shape changing America, and they focus on the secular political forces generating change, rather than on a competing religious frame. The result is politicization.

Politicization

Different types of individualism are politicized as a natural evolution of movement organization in the context of the nation-state. Symbolic boundaries have been affected by the increased status of the nation-state, and they are defined, dramatized, and contested in the arena of national politics. Thus, any movement working on those boundaries will evolve toward participation in that arena. It takes time, resources, and particular conditions to move from gradual growth to a surge in growth to organizing for political action. Abstractly, this is an integration of the two axes of individualism and political power. In many cases such an integration is never accomplished.

The success and quickness of evangelical mobilization from the late sixties to the mid seventies in part was due to the presence of organizations from the grass-roots to national parachurch structures and networks. Few organizations of the fifties and sixties became directly political. Rather, new ones were constructed that disseminated information and mobilized individuals and resources through the organizations and networks already in place (Liebman and Wuthnow, 1983). The state's encroachment into moral issues certainly helped this mobilization. Yet, this encroachment as a crisis is more the construction of political mobilization than its cause.

There was a collision between the state regime and evangelicals who since the fifties were oriented toward social influence but now increasingly so. For example, the rising costs of parachurch and social activities coupled with intense competition threatened the viability of many organizations. In particular, private schools, day-care centers, nursing homes, counseling services, and inner city organizations, whether religious or secular, were more dependent on federal funding. The disqualification of a religious organization for such funds either because it could not comply with hiring standards or because it used religious discourse put it at great disadvantage. In short, the two clauses of the First Amendment — to neither establish nor destroy religion — came to be zero sum. Mobilizing to make claims on the state was one option. To further decouple moral issues from religion was another.

One aspect of politicization has been that evangelicals have increased social action and developed more sophisticated responses to change, partly due to the fact that to varying degrees they have come to view political and social action as being intertwined with spirituality. For example, the organizations and congregations within the pro-life movement have mobilized people and resources to provide safe secure care for single women who decided to carry their child to term. Others, few in number but significant nevertheless in their survival and growth, have integrated such issues with those of economic and political justice. For example, some argue that a consistently pro-life agenda would include limits on military spending, attention to ecology, and different responses to the Third World.[10]

Schooling, Legitimacy, and Growth Rates

Education has complicated associations with religious liberalism and conservatism during this period. Education within nation-states is institutionalized in schools. Because the term *education* is so value-laden, it is difficult to talk of the more versus less educated without connoting evaluations. Thus, it is important to speak more precisely of the effects of schooling. Schooling appears to be a persistent difference between liberalism and evangelical fundamentalism. Cross-sectional descriptions, especially when one compares mainline liberal denominations with narrowly fundamentalist ones, show that liberals on the average have more schooling (Roof and McKinney, 1987). Furthermore, looking across denominations, individuals with greater schooling tend to report more liberal religious (and political) beliefs and forms of participation (for a summary see Wuthnow, 1988).

These effects, as with educational effects in general (e.g., Meyer, 1977), are institutional and cultural in nature. It is not that entering freshmen are convinced intellectually in an introduction to sociology or to philosophy class that liberal beliefs are more reasonable, rational, aesthetically pleasing, or factual. Rather, schools throughout the West, as the result of near universal sociopolitical contests over education, have been linked to the cultural tradition of the enlightenment and ideals of humanism and progress. This linkage is manifested generally in the relation between the state and education (Ramirez and Boli, 1987).

In the United States this linkage was manifested especially in pragmatism's shaping of public education, but it was less complete in the United States, even after the Scopes event. For example, even by the 1950s greater schooling was associated with greater religious participation. The redefinition of education, science, and technology in the early 1960s intensified schooling's linkage to the nation-state, democracy, progress, and humanism. It also was reinforced by the fact that liberal denominations were visibly more schooled through the fifties than conservative ones. One result was the greater decrease in religious participation among the new generation of college graduates, and especially those in liberal denominations.

Yet, even with intensification, these associations are not perfect. Conservatives and neoconservatives were present and vocal in the universities even in the sixties. Evangelicalism is appealing and credible to a broad population base, including a sizable portion of the college educated. This is due to sophisticated critiques of the schooling-education-enlightenment nexus and to effective buffering by the "plausibility structures" of evangelical campus organizations. When taking into account the lower schooling and income of fundamentalists, largely in the South, after World War II, the levels of schooling for contemporary conservative evangelicals is quite impressive (Roof and McKinney, 1987; Wuthnow, 1988). Moreover, small evangelical denominations that have grown since the early seventies have many of the characteristics of the "new class": the more schooled, professionals, engineers, and civil servants. For example, the Evangelical Free Church, which nearly tripled in size from 1970 to 1985 (Wuthnow, 1988:192), and other evangelical denominations are consistently closer to the liberal mainline on several variables, including schooling, than are other fundamentalist groups (Roof and McKinney, 1987).

Apparently, there is greater schooling throughout society and across denominations; nevertheless, there are persistent schooling effects on individuals to be more liberal even when committed to an evangelical congregation. For example, the more schooled evangelical groups also tend to be slightly more liberal on religious and political issues. These effects vary greatly in content and size, and they distinguish people within denominations and congregations as much as between them. Wuthnow (1988) argues forcefully that internal cleavages between schooling levels are greater than external ones.

Another general effect is that the schooled are the most mobilized, whether conservative or liberal. This in part is due to the process whereby the schooled are certified and empowered to take leadership. The institutionalized effect of education, in the United States especially since the sixties, is precisely to orient people toward citizenship and national issues to produce greater empowerment and levels of participation. In liberal denominations, it is primarily the more schooled that support the social action of the clergy (Wuthnow, 1988).

In evangelical denominations the relation is slightly more complex. The more schooled evangelicals tend to be more liberal than others in the same congregation and denomination; yet, some are among the most conservative. What emerges then is not only a split between the more versus less schooled but also among the schooled; the most active in the process of orienting a local congregation to national issues are the schooled. The more liberal ones are in a precarious position of attempting to construct an integration of stances on issues that are defined as inconsistent in the broader religious-political environment (e.g., pro-life, pro-welfare, antimilitarism). In some sense there is a contest among the schooled elites, vying for the allegiances of a congregation initially less oriented to such issues. With increased external resources in the seventies (cultural and material from conservative organizations, media, publishing, and other networks), the more conservative faction often is able to gain power. It is no wonder that negative stereotypes between liberals and conservatives are greater among the more schooled and no wonder that the more schooled evangelicals are more likely to switch to a liberal mainline denomination (Wuthnow, 1988).

Given their formal educational advantage early in this period, liberal denominations had greater resources, both material and intellectual, to more fully experiment with different symbol systems and ontologies. There was not a consensus in these denominations and congregations concerning experimentation or social action, but there was relatively little mobilized dissent. With the support of the more schooled, the clergy and other officials enjoyed an autonomy from the larger congregation. This was reinforced by the corporate theories of these denominations. The action of a congregation was defined as the action of the clergy or the official action of denominational leaders; people saw themselves as involved even when they in practice were not. This meant that the pastor could sermonize on what "we" stand for and what "we" should do without a strong need to mobilize the individual to act. High visibility of global aid organizations and knowledge to which part of the church budget or special offerings went reinforced corporate identification. The use of facilities by diverse social groups also established this corporate social action. Consequently, the teachings, practices, and direct social action of these churches were not primarily the product of coalitions and compromises. Rather, they were built into denominational structures at the highest levels.

This interpretation has another side: The liberals' advantage locked them into direct corporate social action. They seemed limited in their ability to adapt to changes, resulting in declining memberships. The symbolic realism of the liberal mainline coincided with the predominant culture through the mid sixties. As Roof and McKinney (1987) put it, those denominations closest to the "post World War II cultural integration" were the hardest hit in the change of the sixties, resulting in a decline in adherents. New religions and evangelicalism emerged as alternatives to a delegitimated structure. This is insightful and calls into question any simple proposition that the closer to the center a religion is the more legitimate it is. Clearly, if the center is undergoing crisis, any institution closely linked to it will experience similar crisis. Yet, this line of thinking needs to be qualified. After all, the liberal mainline is still the mainline.

The issue might not be religious liberalism's loss of legitimacy as much as its inability or reluctance to mobilize. It appears to be a noncontester in the political arena. It is not that symbolic realism is less suited to politicization for these denominations are active politically, and it would be gross amnesia to say that historical realism and fundamentalism are especially suited to politicization.

Religious liberalism appears to be a noncontester for several reasons. First, I suggest that it is so interwoven in the cultural fabric, so institutionalized in the social structure (Parsons, 1963) that is is a constant backdrop but not a movement. This admittedly is tenuous and *post hoc,* for certainly this level of institutionalization under certain conditions could facilitate growth. Yet, in fact it seems that liberal denominations, while frantically searching for clues to rejuvenate growth, consistently put forth an order that is taken for granted in the larger culture. The relativism, pluralism, open-mindedness, and civility of the liberal agenda is much more legitimated throughout the population and within national institutions than is the conservative stance. People in public discourse routinely use liberal symbols and themes, without being members. Moreover, liberal influence is more institutionalized and invisible. For example, conservatives might mobilize enough letter writers and voters to force a president or a senator to address their demands, but the president and senator are more likely Episcopalians than evangelicals — Jimmy Carter not withstanding.

Second, liberalism's institutionalized definitions of individual and corporate action tend to inhibit mobilization. It was noted that mobilization was confined largely to the upper bureaucratic levels, clergy, and the more schooled laity. With its emphasis on a person's private determination of subjective religious commitment, it is very difficult to mobilize individuals. Within its conceptions of corporate action, the congregation or denomination is defined as acting when the officials do so. Generally, they continued to use social action strategies of the fifties and sixties, not adopting the mass-mobilizing style of the seventies and eighties. When religious liberals do use mobilizing strategies it tends to be in society, to mobilize the poor for example, and this then is accounted as a secular movement.

Third, liberal groups tend not to have autonomous symbolic resources to shape their own discourse. Rather, their upper bureaucracy is closely linked to and depends on the cultural nexus of the state and global structures. Moreover, their religious framing of symbolic boundaries is more closely linked culturally and organizationally to worldwide definitions and identities. There is the already noted emphasis on the diverse religious forms that emerge out of a common humanity and that point to a common destiny. While implicitly working on the symbolic boundaries of the United States, there are fewer religious symbols that can be mobilized explicitly. As an example, the most powerful symbols of the United States polity is Christian America and the Christian-non-Christian distinction; these are largely rejected by the liberal mainline.

The noncontester status of the liberal denominations is reflected in the flow of members in and out of them. It seems that the less active conservative members are more likely to move to a liberal mainline denomination (Roof and McKinney, 1987). Those who leave liberal denominations are more likely to become unchurched. Now these shifts might be of individuals and they might be across generations. In either case, it is possible that the more schooled in conservative denominations who tire of battles over national issues or who are pressured by internal politics will view the more peaceful symbolic realism as more attractive and possibly more Christian.

Many commentators (and not all of them otusiders) long have noted the rather bland and boring nature of liberalism. This, of course, is ironic given its emphasis on existential struggles, individual subjectivity, and grand liturgical worship. It might derive in part from the noncontester status of the religion. It might be worth exploring the possibility of a sociology of the bland and boring as a valid religion in such a political-cultural context. It is very possible that this blandness will be short-lived. The symbols and discourse that speak of diverse religious responses within a common existential humanity could very easily play a major role in framing world culture and movements. If indeed liberalism has suffered because of a crisis in American religious-political integration, its links to world culture increase the likelihood that it will reemerge as a viable contester. Yet, the abstractions of evangelical missionary activity might be moving in a similar direction but having the advantage of both national and world imagery.

Implications for Comparative Religion

A global perspective for interpreting a country's religious change suggests cross-societal, cross-traditional comparisons; also, such comparisons are necessary for critically evaluating the perspective. I briefly sketch some lines of comparative reasoning and research. First, because of a common world cultural and economic environment and because of similar logics of nation-state authority within that environment, we should find similar processes operating in other countries. The specifics, such as type of individualism and nationalism, will vary according to different religious traditions, historical development of the state and its relation to religion and society, class structures, and a country's position in the world stratification system.

Second, the interpretation developed here suggests that global density increases heterogeneity and nation-state authority (and the various consequences of each) resulting in social movements that work on national symbolic boundaries specified in moral imperatives. These movements will define the nature of the individual as citizen and of the nation as meaningful project. Moreover, religious elites will tend to mobilize local populations resulting in national cleavages. Factions will vary according to their degree of politicization toward making claims on the state. In Third World countries, these cleavages tend to be more pronounced and radicalized because of dependency, a conservative landed elite, and authoritative bureaucratic states.

Third, the axes of state-opposition and state-individualism also seem to be a useful general distinction between moments. Comparative studies show that across a wide range of societies there are two major types of responses to nation-state authority and capitalist markets (Lincoln, 1984). One centers on healing, health, and security, includes various millennarian movements, and in the Christian tradition focuses on the return of Jesus. There usually is a set of such movements that syncretize traditional animism and spiritualism with a world religion. Specific forms vary from syncretism in Pentecostal bodies in Africa to burnt offerings on street corners in Sao Paulo to the relative success of Pentecostalism among Sufi. The rapid growth in conservative Protestantism and Pentecostalism in Latin America is also an example. Such movements tend to be apolitical by not being oriented toward making claims on the state, but it is a mistake to assume such movements are inherently apolitical or that they are mere escapes from change and oppression. They as much as state-oriented movements are working on the definitions of the polity and their degree of politicization will vary across societies and over time.

The second type of response is to mobilize and make demands on the state. Like liberalism in the United States, these movements support and overlap with otherwise secular political movements, and they appropriate symbols and identities broader than the nation. However, they tend to be more radical (in the broad sense of the term), to use national identities, and to adopt more mobilizing strategies. For example, liberation theology combines national mobilization and global identification. The new individual is one that identifies with humanity and human history, one who takes his destiny into his own hands. It is the liberated citizen who will accomplish national liberation, which will be the basis for global historical liberation. Shi'a Islam is an example of a conservative religion that is highly politicized and radical in its claims on the state. The interplay between Pentecostalism and liberation theology and that between Shi'aism and other branches of Islam in their respective contexts would need to be studied to further assess the present interpretation of United States religious trends and to see which if any aspects are general.

Notes

1. There is not necessarily a one-to-one correspondence between the two levels for groups presupposing fundamentally different ontologies might agree on a moral issue. For example, feminists who might be atheistic fight pornography as an oppression of women while an evangelical, who might agree that it is oppressive, is primarily oriented to its displeasing a holy God. The different ontologies become apparent by looking at the ideological rationale of the moral stances and stances on a number of other issues. In this case, the issue of abortion would discriminate the different justifications and the fact that one ideology is anchored in the inviolability of individual liberty while the other is rooted in the law of a holy God.

2. We know that mobilization for war generally does not revert to the level of societal mobilization before the war. For example, governmental expenditures infrequently drop to prewar levels. This was the case in the nineteenth century in

the expansion of state authority, bureaucracy, and military after the civil war. The increase during and after World War II was furthered by the immediately prior policy shift of the New Deal. Moreover, women and blacks experienced greater incorporation, and again the declines after the war marked overall gains.

3. In the case of Japanese ascendancy in the eighties, Buddhism and other Eastern religions already had made inroads into the West in the sixties for somewhat different reasons. Shintoism has to date not diffused as had Buddhism and Islam. One reason might be its particularistic civil religion aspects.

4. Both native American and Eastern mysticisms are immanental. Immanentalism, and mysticism have powerful affinities with postmodern society and the educated middle class in particular (see Campbell, 1978, 1982; Troeltsch, 1931), in part accounting for their acceptance in the West.

5. Global density actually has complicated contradictory effects on nation-state authority. The world polity of states is the strongest support for the nation-state. Nation-states actively participate in and construct the system in part to constitute themselves as legitimate actors. On the other hand, as rules and identities are elaborated at the world level, the nation-state is undermined in important ways. It is seen as parochial and the source of wars. Sovereignty begins to be located at the world level. Nevertheless, the undermining effects during this period are outweighed by the supportive effects. Moreover, the limitations of nation-state sovereignty are felt much more in Europe than elsewhere. As these dual effects are worked out, we see as in the case of heterogeneity that sovereignty and symbolic boundaries are made problematic precisely as they are made more important.

6. Popular convention, intellectual observers, and sociological theory have assumed that traditional structures will totally disappear from public life. Instead, they are transformed and often are reworked in order to mobilize claims on the center. For example, there continue to be religious movements as well as a resurgence of ethnic nationalisms throughout the world, including industrialized core countries.

7. The Islamic state is an example of one religious group winning control of the state. While the group now can define ideology and morality, the contradictions of state power and individualism with traditional religious categories are now built into state structure and policy, often affecting the religion in power.

8. This distinction is related to different mobilization styles: conservatives are able to make stronger claims on individual action while the personal commitment of liberals is not open to such exhorting. The greater corporate identification of liberals allows each person to identify with the action of the congregation while conservatives tend to insist on individual action.

9. This process parallels similar ones in the reemergence of ethnicity. For example, tribal identities tend to be glossed over in the interests of mobilizing as one native population to make claims on the nation-state.

10. Social action also has come to focus on lower levels of organization, sometimes using the concept of vocation. Lawyers might set up legal services for the poor; doctors might start a clinic; mothers might start a program for mothers of preschoolers. All of these in some sense go against the trend toward higher levels of organization to make claims on the state. They do address national issues, but through local organizations aimed at addressing local problems. It will be interesting to see what the fruit of this might be and whether these also will be mobilized at larger levels or swamped by the economies of scale and lack of federal funding.

References

Ahlstrom, Sydney
1972   *A Religious History of the American People*. New Haven: Yale University Press.

Bellah, Robert N.
1970   *Beyond Belief*. New York: Harper and Row.

Berger, Peter, and Thomas Luckmann
1966   *The Social Construction of Reality*. Garden City, N. Y.: Doubleday.

Boli, John
1987   Human Rights or State Expansion? Cross-national Definitions of Constitutional Rights, 1870–1970. In G. M. Thomas, J. W. Meyer, F. O. Ramirez, and J. Boli. *Institutional Structure*, 133–149. Newbury Park, Calif.: Sage.

Campbell, Colin
1978   "The Secret Religion of the Educated Classes." *Sociological Analysis* 39:146–156.
1982   "The New Religious Movements, the New Spirituality and Post-industrial Society." In E. Barker (ed.), *New Religious Movements: A Perspective for Understanding Society,* 232–242. New York: Edwin Mellon Press.

Demmitt, Kevin, and George M. Thomas
1987   "State Formation and Global Involvement: An Analysis of Intergovernmental Organizations." Paper presented at the annual meeting of the American Sociological Association, Chicago.

Douglas, Mary
1966   *Purity and Danger.* London: Routledge & Kegan Paul.

Durkheim, Emile
1972   *Selected Writings.* Ed. by A. Giddens. Cambridge: Cambridge University Press.

Ellul, Jacques
1967   *Metamorphose du Bourgeois.* Paris: Calmann-Levy.
1975   *The New Demons.* New York: Seabury Press.

Geertz, Clifford
1973   *The Interpretation of Cultures*. New York: Basic Books.
1980   *Negara: The Theatre State in Nineteenth-Century Bali*. Princeton: Princeton University Press.

Handy, Robert
1984   *A Christian America: Protestant Hopes and Historical Realities*. 2nd. ed. Oxford: Oxford University Press.

Harding, Susan
1988   "Televangelism." Presentation at the Institute for Advanced Study, Princeton.

Hunter, James Davison
1987   *Evangelicalism: The Coming Generation*. Chicago: University of Chicago Press.

Kelley, Dean
1972   *Why Conservative Churches are Growing*. New York: Harper and Row.

Liebman, Robert, and R. Wuthnow, ed.
1983   *The New Christian Right: Mobilization and Legitimation*. Chicago: Aldine.

Lincoln, Bruce, ed.
1985   *Religion, Rebellion, Revolution*. New York: St. Martin's Press.

Lipset, Seymour Martin
1963   *The First New Nation*. Garden City, N.Y.: Anchor Books.

Marsden, George
1987   *Reforming Fundamentalism: Fuller Seminary and the New Evangelicalism*. Grand Rapids, Mich.: Eerdmans.

Meyer, John W.
1977   "The Effects of Education as an Institution." *American Journal of Scoiology* 83:340–363.

Meyer, John W.
1987   "Self and Life Course: Institutionalization and its Effects." In G. M. Thomas, J. W. Meyer, F. O. Ramirez, and J. Boli. *Institutional Structure*, 242–260. Newbury Park, Calif.: Sage.

Meyer, John W., D. Tyack, J. Nagel, and A. Gordon
1979   "Public Education as Nation-building in America." *American Journal of Sociology* 85:978–986.

Morris, Aldon
1984   *The Origins of the Civil Rights Movement*. New York: Free Press.

Parsons, Talcott
1963 "Christianity and Modern Industrial Society." In E. Tiryakian (ed.). *Sociological Theory, Values, and Sociocultural Change.* New York: Free Press.

Ramirez, Francisco O., and John Boli
1987 "On the Union of States and Schools." In G. M. Thomas, J. W. Meyer, F. O. Ramirez, and J. Boli. *Institutional Structure,* 173–197. Newbury Park, Calif.: Sage.

Robertson, Roland
1985 "The Relativization of Societies, Modern Religion, and Globalization." In T. Robbins, W. Shepherd, and J. McBride (eds.). *Cult, Culture, and the Law,* 31–42. Chicao, Calif.: Scholars Press.

Roof, Wade Clark, and William McKinney
1987 *American Mainline Religion: Its Changing Shape and Future.* New Brunswick, N.J.: Rutgers University Press.

Ryan, Mary
1981 *Cradle of the Middle Class: The Family in Oneida County, New York, 1790–1865.* Cambridge: Cambridge University Press.

Thomas, George M.
1989 *Revivalism and Cultural Change: Christianity, Nation Building, and the Market in the Nineteenth-Century United States.* Chicago: University of Chicago Press.

Thomas, George M., and John W. Meyer
1987 "Regime Changes and State Power in an Intensifying World-state-system." In G. M. Thomas, J. W. Meyer, F. O. Ramirez, and J. Boli. *Institutional Structure,* 92–110. Newbury Park, Calif.: Sage.

Thomas, George M., J. W. Meyer, F. O. Ramirez, and J. Boli.
1987 *Institutional Structure: Constituting State, Society, and the Individual.* Newbury Park, Calif.: Sage.

Tocqueville, Alexis, de
1945[1835] *Democracy in America,* 2 vols. New York: Vintage Books.

Troeltsch, Ernst
1931 *The Social Teaching of the Christian Churches.* New York: Macmillan.

Tuveson, Ernest
1968 *Redeemer Nation: The Idea of America's Millennial Role.* Chicago: University of Chicago Press.

Warner, R. Stephen
1988 *New Wine in Old Wineskins: Evangelicals and Liberals in a Small-Town Church.* Berkeley: University of California Press.

Weber, Max
1946　*From Max Weber: Essays in Sociology.* Translated and edited by H. Gerth and C. W. Mills. Oxford: Oxford University Press.

Wuthnow, Robert
1987　*Meaning and Moral Order: Explorations in Cultural Analysis.* Berkeley: University of California Press.
1988　*The Restructuring of American Religion: Society and Faith Since World War II.* Princeton: Princeton University Press.

Young, Frank
1970　"Reactive subsystems." *American Sociological Review* 35:297–307.

11

Globalization and Theology in America Today

Max L. Stackhouse

Recently, a team of scholars of which I was a part published a study of "globalization, contextualization and mission in theological education " (Stackhouse et al., 1988). Many motivations were behind that study, not the least of which was the recognition that the world is shrinking. In our seminaries the clergy of tomorrow are puzzled and confused by the new pluralism on the horizon at the same time as they are becoming more aware of those ecumenical and Catholic strains of the theological heritage that have attempted, at least, to reach to the whole inhabited earth. My remarks can be seen as reflections on the near side of that project in view of changing conditions and the specific questions of this conference. I will thus identify three distinct dimensions of globalization, turn to implications and perceptions of contemporary world systems theory, and identify some implications for theology in the context of American religion.

Deprovincialization

Part of the puzzlement and confusion of globalization comes from the shock of deprovincialization. For those who have had little exposure to anything but a specific tradition or a denominational faith or a religion-saturated local or national culture, an introduction to the world religions and to cosmopolitan cultures makes certainties less stable.

It is not new to theology to broaden horizons. Over the centuries, theological education has introduced succeeding generations to aspects of tradition or biblical history that stretch over long centuries and that manifest shifting accents, multiple meanings, and constantly revising patterns of piety and practice. However, modern historical and develop-

mental views, including theories of progress, have allowed the processing
of historical variety without placing strain on mind or soul or social imagination.

Today, it is less often deprovincialization by the awareness of history or the emersion in classical texts, which much of education had
brought in the past and which is now a lost possibility for many, than deprovincialization by interreligious and cross-cultural exposure. Not all of
this is intentional or formal. The pastors of the twenty-first century become acquainted with the great faiths of the world in a myriad of ways
well outside the classroom. Islam is on television, Hinduism is in the religious section at the book shop. Confucians are among the members of
the Parent-Teacher Association. The daughter of a church member mar-
ries a Buddhist; a relative converts to Judaism; a lay leader in the church
becomes fascinated with the Samurai sense of duty to a corporate unit—
which threatens both his sense of the superiority of the Protestant ethic
and his job, while his wife signs up for yoga class, and his son becomes a
Marxist.

Future pastors in America are meeting in their communities and
among their friends what the explorers, the missionaries, and the anthro-
pologists of the nineteenth century made familiar to the world of scholarship: great, complex, civilization-forming religions other than Protestantism or Christianity in any form or Judaism, for that matter, that are
intellectually, spiritually compelling, and accessible. People we know believe them.

In the past, Christianity expanded primarily by the encounter with,
the evangelization of, the indigenization into, and in some cases the
overcoming of what Milton Singer called the "little traditions." This process was not without ambiguity. There surely were conscious or precon-
scious elements of imperialism in it, although contemporary historians
are clear that many fulminations of the anticolonialist period against missions have overstated the case (Hutchison, 1987; Hutchison and Christensen, 1981).

Indeed, missions frequently brought, as Lamin Sanneh has persua-
sively argued, the simultaneous revitalization of societies far from the
centers of world history by selective affirmation and selective modification of key dimensions of culture in contexts where Christianity did not
originate. All of this deprovincialized the missionary as often as it deprovincialized the missionized (Sanneh, 1989).

In many lands, tribal peoples, marginalized segments of the population, and troubled civilizations have found in Christianity a way of dis-
covering their own dignity, of relating to the wider world, and of incorporating a broader theological and civilizational vision than had been
previously available — much as other peoples at other times have found

similar possibilities in, for examples, Islam, Hinduism, and Buddhism. Meanwhile, the reports back home about what the "natives" are like prompted the formation of the sciences of anthropology and comparative religions (Eliade, 1987).

Christians continue to encounter the so-called little traditions as they exist at the margins of global history, sometimes under the umbrellas of the "great traditions." This encounter occurs in several ways. Occasionally they appear as a rejection of biblical and theological traditions and a celebration of neopaganisms (of which the name Shirley McLaine can stand as a popular symbol and Matthew Fox as a more theological one). The Druids are apparently alive and well in America's new pluralism. Sometimes, they appear in contemporary missiology as advocacy work to defend the core of the cultures of marginalized, dispossessed, and alienated peoples, or when efforts are made to deprovincialize what some white, male North Americans have totemically represented as "authoritative." Sometimes it appears under the guise of "contextualism" and romantically identify the divine with the quaint traditions or current events in subcultures (Costa, 1988).

More striking, however, is the increased recognition that tomorrow's leaders shall have to encounter the great traditions that have shaped civilizations at least as complex as the European heritage. Eurocentrism in faith is simply not possible. Nor have the efforts to evangelize Muslims, Confucians, and Buddhists been notably successful. Those who did not learn from the "comparative religion" or "history of religions" scholars of the last two centuries that non-Christian religions were out there, and were at least as subtle, coherent, and devoutly held as anything homegrown, and those who did not learn from World War II and the decolonial period not to identify cultural-linguistic traditions with Christianity, are learning from contemporary cross-cultural exposures that many things thought to be unique are in fact quite common.

Each may have a preferred example. Consider this one: Christians might think that the intimate dynamics of grace and faith in human salvation could only be worked out in Christianity — until they learn of the parallel discussion, for example, about the intricate debates between the "cat doctrine" and the "monkey doctrine" in Bhakti Hinduism. The mother cat, wanting to save a kitten under threat, takes it by the scruff of the neck and moves it to a new place; it is helpless by itself, although it trusts. While the baby monkey, hearing the warning cries of its elders, clings to the mother as she moves, and is thereby graciously saved. In the moment of true enlightenment, both occur.

The shock of deprovincialization makes us aware that Christianity is not the only great religion with many features that Christians think are peculiarly their own. This often ends, in students, with a tenuousness about what they do believe—an insecurity of faith, a doubt about the propriety of having strong convictions about anything, except as a purely personal commitment. The last thing anyone would ever want to do is to impose a view on someone else. Such an effect can bring about a proper modesty. It can also evoke a systemic loss of confidence that produces poor preachers with nothing to say beyond psychobabble or sociojargon. In mass cultures, a "wimp faith" also may evoke a militantly postured confidence—which we sometimes call fundamentalism.

In scholars, deprovincialization takes a more subtle form. Often it appears in symposia about the relative incapacity of anyone to say much of anything with security about God because everything we can say is a perspectival construction conditioned decisively by the sociohistorical situation from which one comes—a view that, oddly, always seems to be coupled with a plea to discuss the matter a lot more, which seems silly if it is true. Sometimes it takes the form of inventive explorations of polytheism (by other names, of course, because theism of any kind is not terribly fashionable in academic circles) with minimal wrestling with pertinent classical traditions. It is intriguing, for instance to see how little leading proponents of pluralism have engaged the doctrine of the Trinity, which long ago defined most of the problems of diversity and unity (Hick and Knitter, 1987).

Whatever we may think of these responses, however, the theological community today has come to substantive agreement on this point: isolated ignorance of other faiths is both socially irresponsible and religiously foolish. Max Mueller was surely correct when he said that whoever understands only one religion understand none. Indeed, the Association of Theological Schools is presently sponsoring programs to intensify the experience of and reflection on the deprovincialization that is already a fact of our times.

Those who work in theological education, however, are aware that we must also avoid intellectual or spiritual tourism—the tendency to explore the range and quaintness of the world's wondrous variety, without asking about the truth claims of various cultures, without attempting to discern the relative justice of alternative social practices, or without seeking commonalities that may overarch multiple lands and religions (Cox, 1988; Kueng, 1988).

Internationalization

Beyond deprovincialization, beyond discovery and wonder at the variety and pluralism at home and abroad, is the second feature of globalization, the fact of internationalization. This term points to the reality that some aspects of modernity have transcended national and cultural boundaries and require a new awareness of interdependency and new levels of commonality — aspects of which are likely to destroy much of the variety we have known and produce new varieties of cross-cultural and transnational interaction.

Arend van Leeuwen argued in his greatest work a quarter of a century ago that the sociohistorical forces of technology, urbanization, democracy, and human rights, as worldly effects of prophetic Christian presuppositions, were in fact spiritual forces in secular garb, bearing with them deep implications for social transformation. They would shatter all the particular qualities of hierarchy and traditionalism in Asia and Africa, as they had begun to do in the West. That would both open the horizon to evangelization and would facilitate the development of global community (van Leeuwen, 1974).

His views were severely criticized at the time; they remained highly controversial for more than two decades and may well be in need of modulation still. Those who defended the nobility of the great civilizations of Asia, for instance, resisted his views; those who were hostile to the emerging patterns of technology, urbanization, democracy, and human rights to which Christianity allegedly led were often incensed; and those who saw both these developments and Christianity as masks of individualism or capitalism or sexism or cultural imperialism were positively outraged.

Subsequent global developments, however, suggest that he may not have been entirely misguided. As we face the twenty-first century, not only blue jeans and soft drinks are exported from the West to the exploding cities of the globe; technology is eagerly pursued wherever people can get access to it. By technology, I refer not only to machines or pills or techniques but to the central praxis of modernity — the most consistent and self-consciously methodical way of using contemporary science in engaged action/reflection to alter the natural order so that it will serve human desires and needs. The most remarkable thing about the international embrace of technology is that modern humanity has agreed with Christianity that we have a right, indeed a duty, to change the world — a notion many cultures do not swallow easily.

In the bookstores of south India, where I teach as often as possible and for which I have a great love, the racks near the front no longer are filled, as they were a scant decade ago, with volumes dedicated to the preservation of village life, or to the intellectual, cultural, or social history of South Asia, or to the writings of spiritual and political leaders calling the people to overcome imperialism and colonialism. They are filled with books on technology, computers, management, and business.

In the villages, the rice paddies are plowed while transistor radios next to the field broadcast to the elders and children working the fields the changing prices of oil, which influences fertilizer and marketing costs, along with the latest pop music from all over the world. Oxen are still used for plowing; water may have to be carried from the tank, and *pujahs* are still said at the local shrine. However, the oxen are tied with nylon rope, not hemp; the water is carried in plastic, not earthenware or brass, pots, and the donations for *pujah* are broadcast on a public address system. The young adults are not to be seen; they are gone to the city — to technical school if they are lucky, bright, and have family support.

Nor are Indian farmers the only ones to be plunged into a technological, global future. Indiana farmers listen to the weather reports from Asia on their transistor radios in their barns. The news shapes their purchase of fertilizer and marketing also. Their sons and daughters are also gone to the city for training to become technicians, computer experts, managers, or engineers. They watch television preachers in the evening if there is no basketball game.

We need not rely only on examples from farming. Most news programs broadcast the changing prices on the stock exchanges of Tokyo and London as well as New York. The gold, bond, and financial markets are global and continuous. Law, medicine, education, and business methods are no less international or less dynamic. Similar developments can be found in the arts. The materials and styles used in paintings on display at the Museum of Modern Art in Delhi are indistinguishable from those on display in Boston, although some of the themes are distinct. At the New England Conservatory of Music, more than half the entering class was of Asian extraction, and teachers there are regularly asked to come to developing countries to help set up music schools. To be sure, ethnomusicology is a growing field of enquiry, studying what has been before it is lost, but around the world people want to hear Bach, Mozart, and Beethoven — or Michael Jackson, Bruce Springsteen, and Tracy Chapman.

As important as these indicators of internationalization are, more remarkable developments, fateful for international life, can be found in still other sectors — entirely against the forecasts of the best minds of the past several decades. Gorbachev followed his earlier initiatives on the reduction of nuclear weaponry by announcing to the world two things of momentous import: socialism does not work economically, and democracy is the road to the future politically.

We do not know whether he will be able to lead the Soviet Union in new directions or not in the long haul, but it is more than remarkable that world leaders have celebrated his efforts by declaring the end of the cold war. Both "mixed economy" nations everywhere and socialist nations in developing countries are privatizing industry as fast as possible, as well as trying to reclaim democracy.

Further, during the week of this consultation, most of Europe, east and west, along with other major nations concluded a new treaty in Vienna on human rights—this one compromising the sovereignty of the signatory nations in unprecedented ways.

These developments can, in some regards, only be compared to the end of the religious wars in European history, and, in other regards, only be seen as the beginning of the end of a long chapter in political history that began with the rise of the sovereign nation-state in the late Middle Ages — a development that, as it ran its course, eventuated in colonialism. A corrective to international anarchy, which was the effort of many wars, of balances of power (and of terror), of bilateral and regional agreements, of the League of Nations, of the United Nations, and of all dreams of a world under law, is potentially at hand—although the road to any gain of this magnitude is filled with mines, pits, and barriers, and the weight of human history does not easily induce optimism.

These developments are not unambiguous for the United States. For one thing, the Gorbachev initiatives mean that while the pattern of dualistic enmity is reduced, the United States is likely to become the uncontested police force of the world. This is likely in a context in which state power is less important than in the past, precisely because of supranational arrangements. The United States will have to work, for example, with the consent of its allies more fully than it has before, for the Economic Common Market of Europe will go into fuller effect in 1992; Japan is already creating, along with the "little dragons of Asia," ties to China that signal a gigantic center for development well beyond America's control, and Latin America will remain as suspicious of any North American ascendancy as any opposition party has ever been. Further, both the Mideast and South Africa remain explosive, and no one particularly likes cops. The use of any authority that comes to the United States now by default will require as full a measure of steady, constrained prudence as this adolescent nation can command.

For another thing, every failure to defend human rights at home or abroad, or to nurture the conditions under which neglected or oppressed or excluded peoples can claim and exercise civil and political rights will discredit the moral legitimacy of leadership. Every use of coercive power that cannot be clearly defended as just before the court of international opinion will breed charges of imperial arrogance.

A powerful victor in a historic conflict such as the world has been through must not gloat or sack or become slack but must steward all the more carefully those principles that stand at the core of its deepest sense of responsibility. That means, especially, that the principles of human rights must be reflexively applied, stringently, to our own institutions as well as to our foreign policies.

Nevertheless, what all these developments signal is essentially a process of globalization beyond deprovincialization in the twin senses of the emergence of new, clearly interdependent, international structures for every sector of society, and the emerging of an international consensus about what the good society might look like in the twenty-first century — or, to be more modest about it, a temporary vision of what is *not* likely to work and a willingness to adopt and adapt at least features of the West's technological, pluralistic, democratic capitalist experiment.

If this is so, internationalization poses the question of whether the United States as a nation has the depth of character to model and to guide what is likely to be, at least for a time, a global *Pax Americana*.

Universality

No civilization can endure for long if it is built on technological prowess, business acumen, political power, military might, or mass-culture artistry only. It may well be that no civilization can exist without them, but peace cannot be established on these bases alone, and none of these can, by themselves, discern truth or assure justice. The various sectors of society depend, in the long run, on a deeper foundation, on the type and quality of religious orientation that prevails in a civilization. That is what forms the cognitive/emotive skeleton to which the deepest loyalties of the people adhere, and that is what shapes the institutions on which they depend.

The social sciences may well teach us which kinds of social institutions are necessary to the survival and well-being of societies. They also reveal that even the most necessary social institutions can be variously structured, and this variety depends on the "metaphysical-moral vision," usually religious, by which people grasp, more or less, the reason for life and its activities. On this basis, people decide, often in minute decisions made over time and discernible only in the aggregate and cumulatively — hence, the special vocation of sociology of religion, how they think the social institutions of technology, politics, family life, business, education, law, the arts, and medicine ought to be, so that life is meaningful. Theology, working with the social sciences, is the discipline that tries to analyze whether this sense of meaning is intrinsically valid.

If the civilization of which we are a part is, in the foreseeable future to guide the destiny of the world, we should be rather clear that it will not only take the greatest prudence we can marshal in all these sectors of modern life, it will also make demands on our social science and on our religious life. It is not clear that American theology is fully prepared for such a task.

Of course, in several very significant ways, neither religion nor theology is about such matters. Religion is not, in the first instance, transcendentalized politics, left or right, cosmopolitan or local. Religion finds its core falsified when it becomes only propaganda manipulated for even decent social ends. A theology geared essentially to such matters leads only to a lie in the heart, a betrayal of justice, and a denial of God.

On the contrary, profound religion at its center is about the relationship of the soul to the divine, the relationship of the deepest dimension of human selfhood to that which is held to be most holy, most powerful, and most worthy of devotion, sacrifice, and commitment—unto death. Those who share a conviction about what this relationship really is, form communities of commitment from which generations can be nurtured—even if some show their loyalty only by not overtly denying the validity and import of that primal relationship.

If it is the case that civilizations are, in their roots, dependent on the quality of religion, and if it is the case that America, by the cunning hand of providence, has been thrust into the leadership of a global civilization, it may well be the case that we should attend to the question of whether or not the religion that guides the leading superpower of the new global system now emerging is genuinely universal. This, indeed, becomes the central question for any theology done in America today that hopes to influence the common life — one for which we are only marginally prepared.

We are not fully prepared for this task for several reasons. For one thing, many of our deep structures were shaped by the strands of Christianity that derive from the sixteenth century, and that century was divided against itself—not only were Roman and anti-Roman parts of the church separated, but on both sides we see pressures toward a Protestant element and a Reformation element.

The one side is essentially based on "protest," the element of negating by refutation, satire, and debunking false claims to universality in the name of particularity. This is a marvelous instrument to undercut pretense and expose fraud. It can demystify domination and exploitation. It gets us out from under Pharaoh, from feudalisms, from slaveries, from patriarchies, from all the Babylonian captivities to which nations, empires, and human hearts are heir. It is the theme of every hermeneutic of suspicion, every resentment of heteronomy, every drive for emancipation, every theology of liberation. Protest, centered in freedom, is a great tradition, now allied, against its earlier intent, with the dynamics of the free market (Campbell, 1987).

But it has a fatal flaw. It knows no other norm. It cannot, finally, order, reconstruct, and build. Freedom has no architecture, no design, no plan by which to guide the interaction of systems so that they do not destroy one other, or by which to contain the whims of the free who are strong. Freedom is a river without a channel; a story without a plot; a vitality without a form. Where it is not nihilistic, it is anarchic.

That is just the point. The other side of American theology, of the Reformation and of Christianity generally, is essentially based in "form," in the recovery and actualization of a normative vision of eternal truth, justice, or righteousness to which it wants to return a soul, a society, or a civilization that has lost its moral and spiritual grip on its intended pattern. This is the notion of moral law, based in some relatively secure knowledge of how, so far as humans can know these things, God wants things to live. This is the motif in our heritage that forms a covenant for those wandering in the wilderness after their escape into freedom. This is what turns protest into reconstruction. According to Troeltsch, it transmutes the autonomy won in the struggle against heteronomy into the discipline and restraint of theonomy. According to Tillich, it weds the Protestant principle to Catholic substance. In other words, presuming freedom, this side is governed by a normative vision of universal truth and justice by which it secures, structures, and guides freedom.

This element of re-*form*ation is, however, in poor repair today—especially among ecumenically oriented Christians who, in priciple, would seem to be the logical custodians of this heritage. This element contains presuppositions about which many have doubts. It contains, for example, the suggestion that, by the grace of God, humans have a serious capacity to recognize in scriptures, traditions, or experiences what is universally true or false, just or unjust.

Further, it suggests that we ought to, we have a right to, indeed, we have a duty to, draw our own freedom into a disciplined constraint, on a universalist basis—even if, or perhaps *especially* when, we are not constrained to do so by others. Such a theological perspective has philosophical parallels among those positions held, over the years, by platonic, Stoic, Cartesian, Kantian, and structuralist strands of Western thought (as well as by great reformers of other traditions), although this is precisely the sort of thing that has been under sharp criticism during the last few years for being idealistic, abstract, dualist, or unhistorical. It is forsaken entirely only to our peril.

In a recent work, Bruce Kucklick claims that the philosophical theology of the Puritan heritage is "the most sustained intellectual tradition the United States has produced,'' in spite of the fact that it is frequently slandered (Kucklick, 1985). This heritage does contain both the element of freedom and protest and the element of norm and reform. The protest side has, in recent years been most triumphant—so much so that it may have deprived us of connections with precisely those dimensions of our most immediate traditions that most nearly approximate genuine universality and appear to be most necessary in the present context.

In the wake of this heritage, one side focuses on the sociohistorical-interpretative character of everything humans know. All that we think about is reputably an interpretation shaped by our place in society, by our historical epoch, and by the models generated out of the crucible of practical experience. We can share these perspectives with others by developing modes of interaction in a common environment with them (Byrnes, 1985).

In our heritage, however, we can also see a side of this Lockean-Calvinist tradition, which says that some common ontic structure is necessarily presupposed in the fact that we can interact in a common global environment, just as common epistemic structures are necessarily available or we could not discuss old texts cross-culturally or engage in dialogue in ways that made sense, and as common ethical patterns govern us all, else we could not recognize the scoundrel at home or the saint abroad (Diggins, 1984; Mouw, 1989).

These two sides of our heritage have become split into opposing schools of thought in much contemporary thought — with one side protesting constrictive rationalisms of all sorts in the name of freedom, and the other resisting all plunges into the historicist relativism brought by modernity's flight from ''reason.'' In most serious theology, and the best sociology of religion, however, the mutually rejecting tendencies of Dionysius and Apollo or of Rousseau and Kant or of faith and science are not taken with ultimate seriousness. The deepest orthodox, the widest Catholic, the most Reformed, and the best new world theology does not see opposition but complementarity in the voluntarist and intellectualist dimensions of life. Today, in America, it will be enough to try to regain a decent balance. If we remain Puritans, it must be as ecumenical ones, in conversation with both other religions and the social sciences. They had many things right; they were just unreasonably narrow about some of them.

World Order?

One of the themes that makes this book interesting is that out of the sociohistorical, interpretive side of the Western intellectual heritage, we now find the emergence of world systems theory. (See the papers in this volume especially, by Robert Wuthnow, George Thomas, and James Davison Hunter, and the critique by Michael Burdick and Phillip Hammond.)

When modern social science was being developed by the late-nineteenth-century giants, many simply tried to imitate the natural sciences. Others drew a distinction between the historical sciences, that is, those that dealt with the arenas in which human agency could make a difference, and the natural sciences, which held that aspects of human agency were simply determined. The purpose of the historical sciences was said to deal with the idiographic, the unique and particular events and developments in human societies, whereas the purpose of the natural sciences was to deal with the nomothetic, the constant patterns or repeating occurrences of the biophysical order.

Some philosophies of history attempted to develop ways of treating the idiographic in terms of the nomothetic—as are most familiar to us in the thought of Hegel, Marx, Compte, and the social Darwinists (up to and including E. O. Wilson and his proposal on "sociobiology"). These matters have seemed, to many, to be too deterministic and too schematic, even if heroic, in the attempt to grasp the whole of things. In contrast to these efforts, much research and much theory in anthropology, economics (particularly microeconomics), political science (especially when it deals with political culture), and all interpretive sociology has protested the artificial character of these earlier efforts and tried instead to understand peculiar aspects of human history, belief, or social formation on their own terms.

What is fascinating about the newer world systems theory is that it emerges in part from the protests against deterministic and schematic renderings; yet it tries to see the larger patterns that encompass and illumine, even where they do not fully explain, the particularities, the varieties, the uniquenesses of human historical experience.

It is not long since the informed person was inclined to say, in response to any claim about "universals" for instance, that such ideas are but passé residues of an "onto-theo-logical" past. Modern social science "proves," it was widely held, that variety, particularity, and change are reality, and that generalities are humanly constructed artifacts, possibly for reasons of ideological sanctification of a class, a clique, or a religious prejudice. They are certainly not discovered or revealed.

If the world systems theorists are correct, we would have to say, instead, that very complex and quite dynamic, but clearly objective, nomothetic patterns exist in social history that, on the surface, only appear to exemplify variety, particularity, and uniqueness. The "bloomin,' buzzin' confusion" of life has a form, and that form can be known. There is a logos in the *socius* of all cultures after all. Whirl is not king; we do live in a universe, a historical and social as well as a biological and physical one, an extremely variegated one that we do not understand terribly well, but one which has a *nomos*.

The significance of such an idea is obvious. It is comparable to, possibly an echo of, and partly a confirmation of the discovery of monotheism in the face of ancient, radical polytheisms: the discovery of "nature," beyond the customs of the peoples, by the Greeks. It is at least a modern rediscovery on this side of historical consciousness of what Troeltsch called relative natural law, and what the theologians of old called orders of creation, now modulated by the results of both the contemporary sense of change and new capacities to cross-culturally tabulate social-scientific information.

Here we find a convergence with the tradition, and the current needs, of theology in America. Everything cannot be simply perspective, decision, and multiplicity. That leads to arbitrary anomie and anarchy, all the more dangerous when held among those who have great power and little sense of history or of global responsibility. The only God worth worshiping liberates, but on the other side of liberation, calls to order—to a universalistic order.

Ecumenically open theology has historically found its best allies among those who attempted to wrestle with the most universal patterns in the nature of things. It may be, says Christianity and all the great belief systems that we classify as "salvation religions," that the fundamental order of the universe is obscured by sin, by disobedience, by ignorance, or by corruption. All these also believe, however, that there is a primal or ultimate order (at least in the mind of God) that has been unveiled (revealed or discovered) and that we can understand things, including some things about history and religion, in these terms.

At this point, of course, the great theologies also depart from such theories as those given in world systems thought. They do so for one critical reason: finding a form is not necessarily finding a norm. The way things are is not necessarily the most universal way of thinking about reality. Indeed, the way things are is not the way things ought to be, and the more universal way of thinking includes imaging how things ought to be changed so that they are more true, more just, more compassionate. The high religions generally, and Christianity particularly, are, at this point, dualist, not monist. There is another order beyond the world system that can and should comprehend the world system.

For this reason, we must turn more to a theology of society than to a sociology of religion, even if the theology to which we turn will be the ally, not the enemy of world systems theory. It may well be that the analytical tools generated by Weber and Durkheim, Geertz and Dumont,

Berger and Bellah, and now, with a new voice, world systems theorists, will play the role of beloved companion in modern theology that Plato and Aristotle, Cicero and Boethius, Kant, and Locke have played in the past. It was, finally, not the platonic elements that made Augustine able to shape civilization, nor was it Aristotle that made Thomas so distinctive and influential any more than it was the Stoic jurists that gave Calvin's understanding of law such potency to change the world. It was in each case and many others a theological world vision that allowed them to adopt and adapt the realities of the world to a more universal vision.

Toward a Global Theology

It far surpasses the purposes of this paper to detail how we might build on our partially forgotten American memory and integrate it with modern world systems theory to articulate a global vision, although I have attempted to do something like this in a recent study (Stackhouse, 1984). Beyond such efforts we also would have to take into account non-American scholars who are working at this task already, either by trying to grasp the whole or by trying to see how decisive parts relate to one another (Kulandran, 1981; Smith, 1981; Balasuria, 1984; Koyama, 1985).

What we might look for in both our own past and in discerning encounters with others is important as we try to go beyond our present situation and face the theological task of the next, inevitably global, century. Above all, our theology will have to engage in a quest for norm beyond freedom and beyond description of how things are, but there is more that is needed both for the sake of theology and for the salvation of the world. Every effort will have to be made to see that:

1. Our theology is public; our guiding faith must be based in moral realities beyond private interest and beyond the privileged insights of our unique historical experience. The public, which it addresses and for which it speaks, cannot be that of particularity alone. If we may draw elements from these, we have to indicate why we do so beyond the fact that they accord with our interests and experience; the criteria for such assessments have to be open and accessible to those who are not part of the experience and do not benefit from it. "Public" attached to theology means "worldwide" in a normative sense, or it is simply political.

2. To this public, we can make a case for our faith, beyond merely the confession of it. We should not expect anyone to take us seriously if we cannot do so. The dogmatic method in theology is very useful in proclaiming the faith to those who already (or al-

most) believe it; in a global society, however, we shall have to take up the apologetic method again. We shall have to make the substantive case for that which we hold to be true in the face of those who really do not know, and cannot quite imagine, what we are talking about—especially if we expect our faith to have some bearing on how we conduct public business. We shall have to enter into philosophical and cultural-linguistic systems other than our own and show *in those terms* that what we intend makes sense, or that that system is in itself confused on its own terms, and that we are prepared to abandon our beliefs if they cannot make sense in other viable systems and, hence, are not universal in significance.

3. Our faith leads ethically to the formation of inclusive, compassionate communities beyond particular solidarities. Communities, for instance, based on class, caste, and clan exclude any who are not of the "proper" physical condition—economically or genetically or sexually. They are, by self-definition, not universal and are structured to resist universal equity and rights. They produce a pluralism, but it is a pluralism of exclusion not of mutuality and care. Solidarities of interest may have temporary roles to play in some moments of life, but communities of compassion reach beyond them and break barriers that exclude persons from participation in the common life.

If these aspects of religion can be nurtured by theology into the conscience and character of America, it is likely that God—the only real basis of all that is universally true and just—will be served. If these are vital and alive in our interactions with the peoples of the world, and if we are called to global leadership as is likely to be the case, we may assume this temporal vocation with fear and trembling but perhaps also with a touch of grace.

References

Balasuria, T.
1984   *Planetary Theology*. Orbis.

Byrnes, T. A.
1985   "H. Richard Niebuhr's Reconstruction of Jonathan Edwards Moral Theology." *Annual of the Society of Christian Ethics*.

Campbell, C.
1987   *The Romantic Ethic and the Spirit of Modern Consumerism*. Blackwell.

Costa, R., Ed.
1988   *One Faith, Many Cultures*. Orbis

Cox, H.
1988   *Many Mansions: A Christian's Encounter with Other Faiths*. Beacon.

Cragg, K.
1986   *The Christ and Other Faiths*. Westminster.

Diggins, J. P.
1984   *The Lost Soul of American Politics: Virtue, Self-Interest and the Foundations of Liberalism*. Basic Books.

Eliade, M.
1987   "Missions/Missionary Activity." *Encylcopedia of Religion*. Macmillan.

Hick, J., and P. Knitter, Eds.
1987   *The Myth of Christian Uniqueness: Toward a Pluralistic Theology of Religion*. Orbis.

Hutchison, W. R.
1987   *Errand to the World*. Chicago.

Hutchison, W. R., and T. Christensen
1982   *Missionary Ideologies in the Imperialist Era*. Ed. with T. Christensen. Aros.

Koyama, K.
1985   *Mount Fuji and Mount Sinai*. Orbis.

Kucklick, Bruce
1985   *Churchmen and Philosophers from Jonathan Edwards to John Dewey*. Yale.

Kueng, J.
1988   *Christianity and the World Religions*. Beacon.

Kulandran, S.
1981   *The Concept of Transcendence*. CLS (Madras).

Mouw, R. J.
1989   "The Christian Sources for 'Lockean Individualism.'" Society of Christian Ethics.

Sanneh, Lamin
1989   *Translating the Message: The Impact of Missions on Culture*. Orbis.

Smith, W. C.
1981   *Towards a World Theology*. Macmillan.

Stackhouse, Max L. et al.
1988 *Apologia*. Eerdmans.

Stackhouse, Max L.
1984 *Creeds, Society and Human Rights: A Study in Three Cultures*. Eerdmans.

van Leeuwen, Arend
1974 *Christianity in World History*. Scribners.

12

Realism, Just War, and the Witness of Peace

Jean Bethke Elshtain

Consider the following: several years ago I delivered a seminar to the Columbia Women's Studies Seminar in New York City. My topic was realism, just war, and pacifism and the implications for feminism of each of these complex political and ethical theories. This was an initial formulation of the considerations that later emerged in my book *Women and War*. I talked about the dominant image of the man and his capacity as war fighter, a character I tagged the "just warrior," and I discussed as well his female counterpart, the "beautiful soul," a collective representation embodying the values and virtues of home life once domesticity had been definitively sealed off from concerns with the wider world.

I was careful to lay out the central concerns and premises of just war thinking. I did so because I wanted those who were listening to recognize that justifying war from a narrowly strategic or realpolitik perspective and assessing whether war is just or justly waged are different kinds of activities; these activities structure the moral and political universe in dissimilar ways. I was not successful in this effort. My audience assumed that the just war position was little more than a patina on crudely fashioned realpolitik; moreover, that hard-line Machiavellianism was preferable to all this moral glossing of violent realities. An eminent feminist philosopher, who was that evening my interlocutor and who discussed my essay in wise and discerning ways, shared my frustration. She, too, tried to convey a sense of what just war had meant historically and what it might mean, or might yet come to mean, for our own times, but we found an unreceptive audience. Our listeners were determined to collapse any distinction between realism and just war. They assumed that just war was and always had been a weapon fashioned by the powerful in order to justify any and all wars the powerful sought to fight, to oppress persons in other societies, and to legitimate continued congealment of male/female identities. It was a frustrating night.

A second moment, this one is from teaching. For several years, I have taught a course called "Issues of War and Peace in the Nuclear Age." My students are interested, lively, concerned, skeptical, and irreverent, the best sorts of students. As part of this course I use films, both Hollywood war films of the classical genre, for example, John Wayne's *Iwo Jima,* and antiwar films that have become classic, for example, Ingmar Bergman's *Shame.* But I also turn to films made by our own War Department, now the Defense Department, in various eras, including World War II. One of these is a striking film directed by John Huston called *The Battle of San Pietro.*

The film conveys the terrible life and death struggle to capture one hillside leading to one small village during the American campaign being waged up the Italian boot towards Rome. In and of itself the village of San Pietro was not terribly important, but it overlooked the Liri Valley; the Germans had dug themselves in, and it was deemed important to get them out. Casualties were extremely heavy. The film shows young frightened men trying to slog their way up the hillside against sniper fire and, from time to time, we see one of these men crumple, collapse like a rag doll tossed to the ground by an angry child. The film's conclusion is haunting, for the Italian villagers, to escape the depredations of their German captors, had dug themselves into a mountainside. Many had been living for months in caves. They emerged tentatively from the caves into the light — ragged, filthy, gaunt, ill, barefooted. They greeted the American GIs with great affection, as liberators. The Americans are then shown delivering supplies to the village, helping to detonate leftover mines and other incendiary or explosive devices before moving on to the next engagement.

In the discussion that followed the film I was shocked that many of my students, from a stance of hardened cynicism, no doubt on the underside of which lies crushed idealism, said that they considered the film a hoax. They didn't think the deaths were faked or the bullets were unreal but that the reaction of the Italian villagers to the presence of American soldiers was fraudulent. How could Americans be greeted as liberators? They simply couldn't believe it. They didn't believe it in part because they could not accept the possibility of just war. War for them was definitively encapsulated in the word Vietnam.

Reading from *that* standpoint back into history, they could see in scenes of GIs helping to clear rubble, to deliver food, to protect an area so that villagers could sow seeds in their fields and return to peaceful life, only media chicanery. For them the image of Americans and villagers in time of war is represented by My Lai, not San Pietro. They had forfeited the notion of just war, at least as a possibility for the United States, past or present, even as many of these same students vociferously proclaimed the justice of "Third World revolutionary struggles."

Finally one additional sign of the times. In a recent piece in *The New York Times* (November 2, 1988) by Janusz Glowacki, a Polish playwright and novelist, we find a discussion of the dozens of ways that Shakespeare's *Hamlet* has been played. As "a criminal melodrama, a drama of metaphysics, a lesson in Viennese psychoanalysis, or an internal passion play." Glowacki offers the suggestion that at the end of the twentieth century, "Hamlet once again looks beyond the man to the state of the nation and seethes with politics." Reviewing several recent representations of *Hamlet* with the political theme held foremost, the Oedipal theme downplayed, he notes that in the shocking final moments of a recent production of *Hamlet* by Ingmar Bergman, Fortinbras' army "enters by demolishing the back wall of the stage, carrying machine guns and boom boxes that blast a deafening roar of hard rock. On their heads they're wearing black helmets with protective plexiglass shields. They're a cross between Middle East terrorists, New York crack dealers, and South American guerillas. Expertly they toss corpses into a common grave followed by the furniture." Glowacki observes that when he watched the play with a largely student audience at the Brooklyn Academy of Music, this entry of Fortinbras' army was received with "carefree laughter" from the audience. Why? Because America "has not had any experience of the loss of independence, foreign armies, or occupations." Glowacki, who has had such experience, didn't laugh. "Not me," he says, "I belong to the nervous generation."

The happy laughter of that student audience is a mirror image of the cynicism of my students. They are secure in the knowledge that our power protects us even as they revile that which is done to sustain this power. So, on the one hand, they are laughing, safe, protected; on the other, they are convinced that we live in a world in which the rule of force is dominant, and all else pales beside it.

It has been an object of curiosity to me for a long time how a cynical construal of war and war fighting, particularly when Americans engage in it, may go hand in hand with support of armed struggle in other arenas. One frequently hears celebrations of the possibility of a future of peace if only those who now wield power in unjust ways are bested, curbed, and curtailed. The dream is that those who have defensively engaged in armed struggle will no longer find it necessary to do so, that pacifists will have won the day with their insistance that we can solve problems if we just talk *to* rather than past one another, and that an era of peace and non-exploitation will have been ushered in. Current views on the part of the young, then, often seem an amalgam of fragments of Realpolitik, just war, and pacifist hopes.

I propose to explore our current discontents with this clash and melding of perspectives in mind, asking whether we can recapture just war thinking for our time, and, if so, what it would look like and what it might do for us that other ways of approaching these dire and solemn matters cannot. What is demanded of us as citizens if we take seriously a just war perspective? Is just war a viable civic philosophy, a robust way to structure the thinking of contemporary American citizens on issues involving war and peace in a time of changing world order?

First, I will discuss current alternatives to just war, setting these options as ideal types, hence necessarily exaggerated. Then I will go on to show the ways in which modified versions of each of the positions I will reject make contact with and help to enrich a just war framework.

The first alternative to just war is that of pure war. A hard-line, so-called realist posture that tracks its genealogy from the Athenian generals telling the representatives of the Island of Melos in Thucydides' *Peloponnesian Wars,* "We're not interested in arbitration. We're not interested in negotiation. We've got the power. We are prepared to use force. You are undone." The might makes right posture.

Essential to the pure war stance is the following: Between Athenians and all others—foreigners—the rule of force comes into play. Limiting instances of that rule are possible: one might negotiate; one might arbitrate, but one is not required to do so if force is more certain and effective. The only requirement is to look out for one's own strategic concerns and to pursue with the greatest economy what will guarantee the most favorable outcome to oneself. Easier, then, to kill the men of Melos, take the women and children captive than to sit down over time and to work out some kind of agreement, not knowing, of course, whether they will keep their end of the bargain, not knowing whether or not they may then go to strike some deal with Athenian enemies. In pure war, we find a world of war as politics, politics as war, a stance that has fed bellicist imperatives throughout the history of the West.

Within the world of pure war, the other, the foreigner, is *always* an enemy *in situ* or actual. The world is, as Colonel Oliver North repeatedly said, a dangerous place. Those dangers are understood in a particular way, in and through the notion that the other or *all* others are either enemies or potential enemies. The hard-line realist, as a theorist of pure war, makes of *disorder* an absolutized given, the natural condition of humankind. Anarchy is the defining feature both of relations between states and, as well, of domestic or internal affairs until order is imposed. That order is inherently unstable, however. One must be constantly on guard. War is the primary way that states have relations with one another. War is as natural as the disorder that requires it. Heraclitus deemed war the father of all things, arguing that it is through strife alone as a natural law of being that anything is brought into being.

This concept of pure war helps to make possible the concept of total war or holy war in which the other is fit only to be obliterated or quelled and all *right* is on one side only. To move from pure war to justifications of holy war requires ideologies, doctrines, alas many of them historically religious, that promulgate a universe of Manichean absolutes: the believer, the infidel. Engrafted upon notions of we versus the barbarians, amalgams of pure war with right, with religious and ideological conviction, invite and have invited total and holy wars, but there is a version of contemporary realism that I will draw into contact with just war discourse. My reference point is a particular text, Michael Howard's, *The Causes of War* (1984). Framed with a horizon set by realist assumptions, Howard nevertheless rejects a pure war, bellicist stance.

He argues that the contemporary realist must look at the political circumstances out of which conflicts arise. He finds two forms of abstract war thinking extremely dangerous. One, contemporary nuclear strategic doctrine, has separated itself from reality in a terribly dangerous way. He expresses his bewilderment as he reads the "flood or scenarios in strategic journals about first strike capabilities, counter-force or countervailing strategies, flexible response, escalation dominance, and the rest of the postulates of nuclear theology." He indicts this kind of thinking as something Clausewitz, who remains the greatest theorist of war, would oppose because it is divorced from any coherent political context.

Howard insists, the leaders of the European peace movement, and I think he would add the American peace movement, are also living in an abstract dream world. Many believe problems of power would melt away were it not for the vested interests of various rogues—governing classes, arms manufacturers, or other easy to indict, specific forces that block the road to what Kant called perpetual peace. Howard carves out a realist position as an alternative to abstracted realism run amok, pure war, which ceases, therefore, to be realistic *and* to a peace politics untethered as to historic reality and possibility.

He insists that state war fighting is not pathological: it is a particular kind of conflict, the way collectivities have dealt with one another for better or for worse. States can and have moderated or eliminated conflict within their borders, but states or peoples will continue to find reasons to fight, either to preserve or to acquire a capacity to function as independent actors in the international system.

War is inherent in the structure of the state; states historically have identified themselves by their relations with one another, asserted their existence and defined their boundaries by the use of force or the imminent threat of force. So long as the international community consists of sovereign states, war remains a possibility. We can mitigate; we can mute; we can and should negotiate. What is at stake is not just *raison d'état* but also *raison d'system*. This means having a stake in preserving a diverse international community. There is here an imbedded ethic, an ideal of a world of autonomous states that can and should attempt to resolve conflicts. However, this is not at all times and in all places possible, and one's commitment to a diverse international community composed of multiple loci of power may require, sadly, and for limited ends and aims only, going to war.

To those who find this an unpalatable argument, Howard asks: what is the alternative? Continuous eruption of murderous local conflicts, whether tribal, familial, ethnic, or religious wars that were enormously destructive and repressive prior to the formation of states? The state is the guarantee of internal order; it has eliminated much of that conflict. The only realistic alternative available to us is the breakdown of the nation-state, hence the loss of internal order. Balkanization, a term that always comes up in these discussions, or, perhaps, in our own time better put, Lebanonization, would be the result. He says: is this what you want, because that is what you are going to get if we move away from or seek to defeat or to undermine or to erode the power of nation-states and the always present possibility of war.

It is important to be clear here. Howard's is neither a pure war nor a holy war perspective. He opposes crusades. Indeed, he would argue that holy wars historically have been made possible not because of the wily maneuverings of realists, but because of the stalwart convictions of idealists, those who set the world up in and through highly moralized categories, including visions of peace that are parasitic upon a totalized image of war. For if pure war is a story of absolute conflict, we find a vision of peace as a world of perfect harmony, perfect order, as its mirror image.

Just as there is a strong version of pure war there is a similar narrative of pure peace. I will now discuss the paradigmatic case of pure peace, explore why it is problematic, and elaborate a modified version. Within the horizon made possible by these two elaborations, I will argue that just war discourse can function as a compelling and vital civic philosophy.

Visions of perfect peace draw upon Christian dreams of the kingdom of God. These, in turn, were parasitic upon mythologies of a lost Golden Age of fructifying harmony and full transparency in which none was an enemy to the other. The Christian Gospel proclaims peace as the highest good, arguing that peace is not reducible to the terms of any earthly order. This Christian New Jerusalem was balm for the weary but proved over time a vexation for the impatient determined to bring peace to earth, the sooner the better. The high point of utopian peace hopes, prior to our own epoch, were sixteenth and seventeenth century utopias, and all contrasted the disorder they found with the perfect order, the world without conflict that they sought. Peace discourse seeks to bring the trancendental down to earth in supreme confidence that human beings might enact eschatological feats. As I argued in *Women and War* (1987), this peace is an ontologically suspicious concept. It never appears without its violent *Doppelgänger,* pure war, lurking in the shadows. Peace is inside, not outside, a frame with war in its most powerful and absolute expressions. War is threatening disorder, peace is healing order; war is human beastiality, peace is human benevolence; war is discordance, peace is harmony.

The apogee of proclaiming peace as an absolute good and an absolute possibility within our own tradition was the political philosopher Immanuel Kant's essay "On Perpetual Peace" (1983), Kant absolutizes order, denying the very possibility of conflict. He celebrates republican commonwealths: if we are going to have peace, every society must be ordered internally in identical ways. Peace that is not perpetual is a mere truce; a genuine peace must nullify all existing causes of war. Any and all disorder, for Kant, is a falling away from preternatural wholeness. The peace that follows in his schema is a dream that can exist among like kinds and equals only, making of the mere existence of otherness a flaw in the perfect scheme of things. It is not so much that the lion will lie down with the lamb, as that the distinction between the lion and the lamb will no longer even interest us, will not be an occasion for any kind of concern or reflection.

As in pure war, difference itself is a block to the end of peace. It is a source of danger that must be denied or eliminated. Peace is a series of ontological endorsements that project a world of ongoing equilibrium, harmony, and perfect order.

There are feminists historically who have been attracted to this vision of peace. For example, one finds in the World War I era, and eras before that and eras after that, arguments that women are to be the saviors of humanity, with pacific motherhood cast as the harbinger of future order. One finds many contemporary spokeswomen contrasting masculinism, patriarchy, violence, and disorder with feminism, matriarchy, nonviolence, and harmonious order. We are told that when feminists seize power it will appear only in its healthy form, as holistic understanding, which leads naturally to cooperative and nurturing behavior. Ironically, this feminist variant on pure peace requires its dialectical opposite, pure war, to sustain itself; it defines itself with reference to its other.

Just as there are visions of realism that back away from pure war, there are visions of peace that eschew pure peace contruction. There are stories of peace neither as perfect order nor perfect confidence in the human capacity to fashion on this earth a way of life that looks something like the vision we have of heaven. I refer here, not to celebrations of harmony and wholeness, but to arguments about how one might go about fighting. Rather than assuming absolute disorder and hoping for absolute order, one struggles to fashion a world of relative order and stability that makes room for and accepts the possibility of conflict. The question is how one responds to conflict, what brings conflict about, what ways of fighting may preserve our human commonalities rather than setting others up as entities to be obliterated into nonexistence or to be embraced into nonexistence so that no distinctions finally remain.

Pacifism as a way of fighting is associated, of course, with Gandhian *satyagraha,* with Martin Luther King's Southern Christian Leadership Conference, and so on. Here we find, not the projection of a world of total order but an insistence that disorder, fighting, and struggle can take a form that doesn't make absolute enemies out of others. In this way people transform themselves through participation in struggle. This alternative to pure peace involves an oppenness to suffering, including the possibility of drawing upon yourself the violence of others always in the hope that they might forebear and in the belief that they — ones' opponents — are open to moral example.

We are here inside a moral universe of real but limited goods and exigencies. It has none of the grandeur of the universe of pure force, the universe of Kurtz in *The Heart of Darkness;* nor the universe of Kant, a world of perfect harmony. Instead, it is a sphere of partial achievements, of struggle that eschews violence and that accepts the possibility and even the necessity for disorder. It is this view of peace that makes contact with just war thinking. So, at long last, it is to just war for our time that I will turn. What sort of civic philosophy does just war offer? Is it within our capacities to endorse that civic stance, is it within the repertoire of our own possibilities? We cannot make just war thinkers of ourselves or others if neither we nor they cannot find within our own histories and identities possibilities that might be called forth in the form of just war considerations and just war purposes.

The Vatican II document on the church in the modern world, *Gaudiam et Spes,* stated that Christians, even as they strive to resist and prevent every form of warfare, should have no hesitation in recalling that in the name of an elementary requirement of justice: a people has a right, even a duty, to protect its existence and freedom by *proportionate* means against an unjust aggressor. This is not an obscure or abstract statement: it is a straightforward insistence upon a right to self-defense as an elementary requirement of justice. However, that right cannot and must not take the form of total or holy war; it must be proportionate to the nature of the threat.

As a theory of war fighting and resort to war, just war thinking is a cluster of injunctions: what is is permissible to do, what it is not permissible to do. For example, that a war be the last resort, that war be openly and legally declared, that means be proportionate to ends, that a war be waged in a way as to dintinguish between combatants and noncombatants. The just war thinker, whether in his capacity as someone evaluating the resort to arms or evaluating the bases and nature of internal order, makes certain presumptions. One is a belief in the existence of universal moral dispositions. The other is an insistence on the need for moral judgements, for being able to figure out who in fact in this situation is more or less just or unjust, more or less victim or victimizer, along with an insistence on a particular form of power, the power of moral appeals and arguments.

Just war thinking, as I argued in *Women and War,* requires much of us. It demands deep reflection by all of us on what our governments are up to, which, in turn, presupposes a self of a certain kind, one attuned to moral reasoning and capable of it, one strong enough to resist the lure of violence's seductive enthusiasms, once laced through with a sense of responsibility and accountability, in other wwords, a morally formed civil character. Alas, much just war thinking in the modern era, on the one hand, and civic philosophy understood as that which can actually be thought by citizens in this society or that at this point in time and none other, on the other, pass one another by.

For contemporary just war argumentation is often enormously abstract, featuring cheese paring, extraordinarily recondite discussions about double effect, collateral damage, and so on. Whatever importance this mode of argumentation may have for moral theologians and ethicists of a formal sort, it fails to make contact with genuine civic possibilities. We don't think like that, in and through such complex systematizing. We think in terms of horror and injury, and, yes, just and unjust. What we bring to bear in terrible circumstances will be shaped by whether what is foremost in our minds at a given moment is the suffering of an individual child, say, or a threat to the autonomy of our state. It will depend upon whether one has constructed oneself as a civic being within a frame of aggressive, outward-looking claims or more defensive civic concerns.

Just war thinking easily becomes utopian if it relishes the hope that statesmen and stateswomen, as well as men and women in their everyday lives when they put their minds to it, will be attuned to and be able to insert themselves within the abstract arguments of moral theologians. That's not only unlikely, the weight of historic evidence is against it.

What just war thinking as a civic philosophy does have to offer is this: that which is an expectation requiring little justification for the realist, namely, war, violence, the resort to force, requires explanation and justification for the just war thinker. An additional strength of just war thinking in our time is that it pictures the individual within a framework of overlapping communities and commitments and loyalties: families, civil society, state. We each carry a set of legitimate expectations about what these overlapping institutions and social relations mean and the ends they might serve. We also, on a gut level, react to injustice.

This sort of populist moral concern is assumed by just war thinking, required by it, and necessary to it. For just war is not *just* about war, it is an account of politics that aims to be nonutopian yet to place the political within a set of moral concerns and considerations, within an ethically shaped framework. Once one spells out the implications for a just war position, the possibility of sustaining the moral ethos necessary to support such a position easily seems overwhelming, beginning with the fact that people may be enjoined to die rather to kill (see Hauerwas, 1985: 132–155). And that's only the beginning. In addition, in recent years, Pope John Paul II, the American Catholic bishops, and others have proclaimed peace a value that cannot coexist with injustice. Peace is not the mere absence of conflict, it is a kind of completeness, a *tranquilitas ordinis;* hence, injustice, any kind of injustice, creates moral disorder. For example, Pope John Paul II has called upon various peoples to form transnational orders based on the basic needs of humanity. He emphasizes peoples rather than states, stressing the possibilities for reconciliation and justice such that what is for the common good of a nation can be for the common good of the family of nations.

The stakes in all of this are high. There is an emphasis on the dignity of the human person, an insistence on the primacy of dialogue as a means to change, a commitment to deconstructing a lust for power in order to create space for alternatives, a stress on sin as a form of moral disorder and division.

I share these concerns; hence, I think it is important to see just war thinking in its full elaboration as a theory of international *and* domestic politics. It gives us leverage that we might otherwise lack to evaluate the way the inner determination of state systems may deform the dynamic of the relations between and among states. The broader definition of a violent order as not just the absence of war but a false and unjust peace in which we see, for example, "the exploitation of labor, imperialism, and injustices of the field of the spirit" contributes to an overall theory of society and its goods. Such formulations place a heavy dignity on the possibilities of achievement in the temporal realm, its worth, its value, and its capacity to attain justice. Is there not a possibility, however, that the very persons from whom the just war thinker draws his constituency — religious persons whose dispositions are specifically Christian or, to a certain extent, Christianized — are thus placed under a temptation to re-sacralize or to sacralize the secular order or our attempts to reform it, thereby losing what was essential to just war in its inception, a vision of a perfect order *beyond* our reach that we can use to assess an imperfect earthly order? In this scheme, we must never make the mistake of believing that we can bring this vision to pass fully and completely on earth. For to do so is to lose just war as a potent way to describe, assess, and understand the City of Man. It is, instead, to turn it towards utopian aspiration, but there is, within historic just war, a powerful brake to chasten such urges to sacralize — it is called St. Augustine.

We are well advised to make our own turn or return to St. Augustine. Recall Book 19 of *De Civatate Dei,* of *The City of God.* Augustine has already rebuked the *Pax Romana,* that false peace, in which peace and war had a contest in cruelty and peace won the prize. Let us not be taken in, he warns, by the empty bombast that blunts the edge of our critical faculties with high-sounding terms like honor and civic glory. What the Romans have done is not unlike what the pirate does with this tiny craft, but because the emperor does it with a mighty navy he is called an emperor rather than a pirate.

Unpacking the lust for domination, Augustine is devastating in his irony. The Romans, he claims, should have worshipped foreign aggression, *eniquitas aliena,* as well Victoria as a diety, because they claimed all their wars were defensive. Peace, he admits, can be a term used to describe a coercive order. It is called peace, and people acquiesce in this definition because they do not want their repose disturbed. For peace is an instinctive aim of all creatures, even as it is the ultimate purpose of war. There is, then, a peace of justice and a peace of injustice. Yet even the peace of injustice is worthy of the name of peace as a fragile human achievement. It provides some partial order to the universe, some appropriate object of desire. It is dear to the hearts of humankind even when it is not a situation of perfect justice.

This is the language just war thinkers should recall. Both a denunciatory language, and a language of the delight, of the longing, the yearning for peace as a real but limited good. Augustine writes that even the savage beasts safeguard their own species by a kind of peace. What tigress does not gently purr over her cubs and subdue her fierceness to caress them. How much more strongly is a human being drawn by the laws of his nature to enter upon fellowship with his fellow men and women. For even the wicked, when they go to war, do so to defend the peace of their own people and desire to make all men their own people, if they can, so that all men and things together might be subservient to one master. War, paradoxically, often emerges from an overly robust yearning for peace as perfect order or dominion.

Augustine reminds us of our mortal natures, of what gets stirred up in us through civil strife, the temptation to ravish, to murder, and to devour in order to insure peace. This is a language, at once evocative, morally evaluative, and rhetorically potent, that we must recover if we are to make just war a real possibility for our own time; if we are to encourage people to think in and through its terms. To seek peace as a worthy longing and then to think about what is worthy of the name of peace. To ask how much we are prepared to forfeit in order to retain the kind of order or peace that does not, by any means, represent a wholly just order? What price are we willing to pay in order to alter this imperfect harmony by aiming for a more perfect justice that may require a period of disharmony, disorder, even violent disorder, in order to come into view?

Augustine enables us to see that a lust for domination is at work in all human affairs as is dutiful concern for others. That pride in taking precedence over others is at work, but so is compassion. He elides the distance between grand moral philosophy and ordinary moral reflection. He offers up a theory of civic possibility and of statescraft, reminding us of the problem of dirty hands within the *saeculum,* the realm of worldly affairs. He urges us to recognize with the realists that we live in a world of constraint and of unpredictabilities but that we need not endorse the pure war conviction that we are surrounded on all sides by enemies. What we are surrounded by is autonomous actors, not necessarily hostile enemies, but strangers, sources of independent action that may affect us. Such entities are potential enemies or allies, thus, we are urged to forge lasting alliances with to preserve our independence yet make commonalities possible.

Just war thinking is a cautionary tale of internal and domestic order, a story of the systemic requirements and purposeful uses of power and order. It is a product of Western ethics, but it is also a proposal concerning the nature of the international system. If we think of just war in this way, we can more readily urge its consideration upon those who do not share our own tradition.

At the conclusion of *Women and War,* I argued that we must break the deadlock of war's mobilized language; I might have said the language of war *and* peace. I argued that a politics beyond war and peace refuses to see all right and good on one side only. Such a politics offers values for which one might die but not easy justifications for the need to kill. The political embodiment of this attitude is a character I call the chastened patriot, one who has no illusions, who recognizes the limiting conditions internal to international politics, who does not embrace utopian fantasies of world government or total disarmament.

Chastened patriotism evokes and calls up compassion and concern for country, civic involvement in country, always with the recognition of the love and concern others bear for their countries. One's own actions are limited, not in spite of but because of one's loyalty to one's own particular polity. The chastened patriot has learned from the past. The chastened patriot is someone committed and detached, someone who can reflect about civic ties and loyalties. The only way we can do that is if we have multiple ties and loyalties, to our families, our friends, our religious communities, our voluntary associations as well as our polity. Recognition of our multiplicity is, as I already indicated, one strength of just war thinking. Diversity and commonality are not only tolerated but cherished. A view of ourselves devoid of all utopian and universalistic pretentions, a view that takes account of the element of relativity in all antagonisms and friendships, that sees in others neither angels nor devils, neither heroes nor blackguards, is extolled (see Elshtain, 1987:252–258).

How does one simultaneously animate and chasten civic impulses? If there are any real possibilities open to us at the present moment along these lines, I believe they will come from a reconstructed just war tradition, which makes room for patriotism even as it offers a critique of aggressive nationalism and imperialism, which makes room for internationalism even as it offers a principled rejection of an ideal of one world or one state.

The final word shall be Augustine's. From Book 19, chapter 11, *City of God:* "For peace is so great a good that, even in relation to the affairs of earth and of our mortal state, no word ever falls more gratefully upon the ear. Nothing is desired with greater longing, in fact nothing better can be found. So if I decide to discourse upon it at somewhat greater length, I shall not, I think, impose a burden on my readers not only because I will be speaking of the end of the city which is the subject of this work, but also because of the delightfulness of peace which is dear to the heart of all mankind."

References

Elshtain, Jean Bethke
1987   *Women and War.* New York: Basic Books.

Hauerwas, Stanley
1985   *Against the Nations: War and Survival in a Liberal Society.* Minneapolis: Winston Press.

Howard Michael
1984   *The Causes of War.* Cambridge, Mass: Harvard University Press.

Kant, Immanuel
1983   *Perpetual Peace and Other Essays.* Trans. Ted Humphrey. Indianapolis: Hackett.

New York Times
1988   "Hamlet, a Mirror of the Times."

Part V

Concluding Reflections

13

On Thinking about Systems: Some Implications for the Study of Religion in the World Order

W. Barnett Pearce

"The search for an essence" of religion, Ninian Smart (1989:11) reported, "ends up in vagueness." To make sense of the variety of the world's religions, he proposed a series of seven "dimensions": practical and ritual; experiential and emotional; narrative or mythic; doctrinal and philosophical; ethical and legal; social and institutional; and material.

An unresolved tension between apparently incompatible perspectives is deliberately embraced in Smart's list of dimensions. Religions are seen as both hermeneutic (the first five dimensions) and materialistic (the last two dimensions).

Pairing the terms *world order* and *religion* in the title of this book is not neutral with respect to this tension, and with it the study of religion. By focusing on the nomothetic (*world* order) rather than ideographic, and by focusing on impersonal structures (world *order*) rather than the apparent cacophonies of lived experiences, it biases the conceptualization of religion toward materialistic factors (e.g., religion as aggregate patterns of behavior, political or military forces, economic entities); away from religion as hermeneutic (e.g., people who tell themselves stories to make the particularities of their lived experiences interpretable and tolerable and who act in ways informed by those stories); and toward unitary explanatory principles rather than case studies and pluralistic explanations.

Robert Wuthnow (in this volume) asked, "What do we gain, if anything, from adopting a theoretical perspective that specifically attempts to take into account the forces of some social unit larger than the society itself?'' In the spirit of that question, I want to investigate where such a perspective leads, and to go beyond the first, obvious level of implications.

The term *world order* emerges from a larger discourse, which lauds the analysis of material forces as the ''real'' source of the dynamic of social history (and which continues the Englightenment project of replacing ''the merely verbal sciences'' (Rodgers, 1987, p. 17) with more positive [statistical] descriptions of functional relations). The political economy, not the narratives, stories, or practices of personal piety, is described as the structure of the system comprised by the pattern of interconnections within the world. The doctrines or interpretations of current events offered, e.g., by Muslim fundamentalists, Buddhist monks, and liberation theologians, according to this view, are part of the ''superstructure''; ephemeral and impotent in comparison to more objective economic forces.

One line of criticism of such analyses of the world order sets the importance of understanding the lived experience of individuals against the values derived from treating religious groups as economic or political aggregates. Such arguments often begin with the uncontroversial observation that a theoretical discourse whose terms describe patterns in the production and exchange of goods and services (e.g., centers and peripheries) is not particularly powerful in describing or accounting for either singularities in the lived experience of individuals or for the meanings by which individuals and groups account for their own histories and futures. As a result, the hermeneutic aspects of religion are either ignored or derogated.

In this paper, I wish to focus my argument in just the opposite way. Rather than arguing that one should not do materialistic analyses of religion because too much is lost, I claim that if the world order is examined with sufficient vigor, it must inevitably lead to a stance that foregrounds hermeneutics. By looking more deeply at the systemic structure of the world order, the hermeneutic aspects of religion are seen as central.

Two questions direct this inquiry. First, what type of system is the world order? Second, in what language can we describe the organization of that system?

Ultimately, the answers to these questions suggest that they are not independent, and lead to a surprising recognition of the importance for developing a language, which can direct attention to the manner in which the stories of various persons and groups (including theorists and researchers) intermesh in conjoint social practices and in which these practices (re)construct those stories. Although it does not now loom large in the literature, I suggest *eloquence* as a nonpejorative term describing what such a language affords.

What Type of System is the World Order?

As far as the world order is concerned, academic interest has followed economic reality. In the second half of the twentieth century, advances in communication, transportation, and economic and political infrastructures have permitted the development of transnational corporations and an unprecedentedly integrated world economy. Information, raw and processed materials, services, and people (immigration and tourism) move among nations in powerful patterns, which comprise the structure of the world order.

Many scholars passionately believe that this structure, invisible from the intellectual perspectives of pre-World War II social theory, is a powerful explanatory principle for understanding the contemporary world. Among those championing analysis of the world order are Wallerstein (e.g., Hopkins and Wallerstein, 1982) and his colleagues in the world systems analysis project; Robertson's (1985) emphasis on globalization in understanding secularization and religion; various dependency theorists (e.g., Rodney, 1982) who describe the process by which much of the world has been underdeveloped; and various political advocates and scholarly analyses of what is called the "new world information order," which describes how patterns of information and data-flow among nations reproduce the hegemony of the former colonial powers over the former colonies (Smith, 1980).

Having decided to study the world — that is, to take a perspective that focuses on relationships which transcend the boundaries of nations — the task becomes that of determining what kind of order exists in the world. The nature of this order is not at all obvious, and new vocabularies have to be developed to describe it.

The most powerful set of concepts for describing patterns of interrelated components is systems theory. However, there are several versions of systems theories, and most systems theories contain important distinctions among types of systems. These distinctions provide a vocabulary in which we might answer the question of the kind of order that exists in the world. In addition, systems theory has developed some useful maxims, which function as theorems about systems per se.

Boundaries

Systems may be open or closed with respect to substances and to information. If open, then the organization of the system can be changed by that which enters the system from outside the boundary.

For theoretical purposes, this distinction is crucial because only closed systems are determined by their organization. Among other things, this means that deterministic concepts and finite mathematical models work only for the subset of systems that can be treated as closed. Open systems, on the other hand, change their patterns of organization as the result of ingesting new information or substances. As such, open systems are inherently, at least partially, undetermined.

In more complex systems, as discussed below, the distinction between open and closed systems fades. Sufficiently complex systems — which observe themselves and other systems—generate information that changes their organization. As such, they are not only (to some degree) undetermined but (to some extent) autonomous.

Organization

The most basic concept in systems theory is that of organization. All systems theories differentiate a system from a heap on the basis that the former is organized in a way that the latter is not. The first theorem of systems theory is that *the whole is something other than the sum of the parts*. The something other is the organization that enables the system to function in a manner in which none of its components, taken singly or as a heap, cannot.

This apparently straightforward theorem has drastic implications for the perspective of a systems theorist. The bulk of Western scientific thinking has always focused on the knowable, invariant relations among discreet entities. Harré (1972) called this our "corpuscularian" tradition, which reached its culmination in Newton's vision of a mechanistic universe and whose influence in the rhetoric of satisfying explanations persists despite, e.g., Darwin, Einstein, and Freud's assaults on its fundamental tenets.

By focusing on the organization of systems, we are quickly led into a boldly noncorpuscularian world in which systems are not simply aggregates of their components. Systems are themselves entities whose components do not necessarily reflect the emergent properties of the whole, and which have powers that are not possessed by any of their components. The practices of reductionism, which analyzes complex entities by examining their components in isolation, is antithetical to the first theorem of systems theory; and the "covering law" form of explanation depends on assumptions contradicted by this basic notion of systemic organization.

The organization of a system constitutes its identity and function. The second theorem is that *the system is its own best explanation*. The dynamics that govern the way the system functions are those which structure it. Rather than looking at outside causes for the states and changes of a system, one should focus on the structure of the system per se. Contradicting the Aristotelian and Newtonian principles of efficient causation (in which like causes have like effects), systems frequently respond to stimuli in ways which have more to do with their own organization than to the stimulus itself. To describe these phenomena, some theorists use the term *perturbations in the environment* rather than stimulus or cause; others speak of *equifinality* to describe how the organization of a system can produce the same effect from many different causes and *multifinality* to describe how the organization of a system can produce many different effects from the same cause.

Systems are comprised of organized components, but these components are often systems themselves. From the perspective of systems theory, the world consists of various patterns of organization, including systems which themselves are wholes and, simultaneously, components of larger systems. For such systems, the first two theorems have opposing force: as whole systems, their own organization is the best explanation of their function; as a component of a larger system, they function in a manner which is not the summative product of their own organization. This tension is described in the third theorem: *Different explanatory principles are required at different levels of systemic organization.* Similar to Heisenberg and Bohr's principle of complementarity in quantam physics, this theorem suggests that a satisfactory description of complex systems must employ several vocabularies simultaneously, each of which accounts for the structure of various levels of the system.

From this perspective, an analysis of a religious practice (e.g., a Bible study meeting) in a base community in Brazil would employ different explanatory principles to account for 1) the function of this practice in the lived experience of one of the participants; 2) the way this practice reproduces the structure of the community; 3) the meaning which the community ascribes to this practice; 4) the way this practice fits into the larger events of religion and politics in Brazil; 5) the relationships among community empowerment, liberation theology, and the development of the Catholic church worldwide; etc. Rather than being seen as a problem to be resolved, the complex and perhaps contradictory relationships among these explanatory principles are themselves markers of the complex systemic structure of the event being studied.

Types of Organization

There are (at least) three types of systemic organization: simple, cybernetic, and second-order cybernetic.

Simple systems. Designating something as a simple system merely states that the components are interrelated. Simple systems may be adequately described in a vocabulary that 1) records the inputs and outputs of the system; 2) describes its structure (It is assumed that the structure is unchanged by the movement of substances and information across the boundary.) and 3) relates 1 and 2, perhaps using a "path model" analysis.

Systems that have simple structures may display complex patterns of behavior, including cycles and trends. For example, the growth of bacteria colonies in petri dishes show distinctive patterns. Their growth produces (as output) toxins, which ultimately accumulate past a threshold and then become input, which poisons the colony, killing off most of the individual bacteria, reducing the proportion of toxins, etc.

If this is the kind of system we see in the world order, then studies of religion may look for more or less determinant relationships between what happens at various places within the system. Such research may disclose, for example, otherwise undetected correlations between patterns of religious activity (e.g., charismatic healing) and economic conditions or perhaps explain the processes by which certain forms of religious activity (e.g., political activism) follows particular cycles.

If the world order is a simple system, we need no hermeneutic conceptualization of religion or hermeneutic account of the place of religion in that order.

Cybernetic systems. Designating something as a cybernetic system involves an additional claim about its structure: that it possesses some mechanism by which it monitors and adjusts its own behavior according to some preset goal state. Derived from the Greek word for the person who steers a boat, the most common illustration of a cybernetic system is a thermostat (a monitoring device) coupled to both a heater and air conditioner (effector devices), which can keep the temperature in a building between the upper and lower limits (the goal state) established for it.

If the world order is taken to be a cybernetic system, an adequate explanation requires a description of the goal state, the monitoring apparatus, and the effector devices. This reintroduces the old Aristotelian notion of "teleological explanation" in which purposes or "goal states" replace the eighteenth-century notion of cause as the explanation for why the system works as it does.

Teleological explanation has been out of fashion for a long time, but *when accounting for cybernetic systems,* such descriptions of the goal state, the monitoring device, and the connection to the effector mechanisms are much more parsimonious than, e.g., a series of graphs showing the fluctuations of temperature in a building.

However, in practice, researchers may have access to data describing patterns of performance, perhaps a recurring cycle of activity, and be testing the hypothesis that the system is cybernetic rather than simple. The third theorem of systems theory comes into play here: the nature and function of cybernetic controls may be inferred from descriptions of cycles and trends but cannot be explained in a vocabulary that is limited to such descriptions. A jump from one vocabulary and explanatory principle to another is required to account for the structure and functioning of a cybernetic system.

Just this decision seems at issue in Wuthnow's (1980) study of the correlations of patterns of religious activity and states of the world economy. The principle that a system is its own best explanation suggests that a description of the organization of the world system is the best way of accounting for the process by which economic conditions affect religious behavior.

In the 1980 paper, Wuthnow offered little description of the structure of the world order other than the correlations themselves. This level of data analysis is consistent with the hypothesis that the world order is a simple system, and might have been further elaborated by citing aspects of the function of the system that brought about changes in religious behavior. For example, perhaps there is a threshold percentage of impoverished (or newly enriched) people within a community, which provides a constituency for certain types of leadership.

However, it seems unlikely that this approach will get very far without including what I characterized as hermeneutics. Particularly when dealing with the religious activities of human beings, it is at least plausible that we are dealing with a system open to information such that, e.g., changes in economic states are compared to a goal state defined by stories about what is true, good, and possible, and that flagrant discrepancies between the state of the system and these stories cause activation of various effector mechanisms intended to return the system to its proper state.

Without questioning the accuracy of Wuthnow's data, note what can and cannot be said in the vocabulary that presupposes that the world order is a simple system. In the vocabulary of simple systems, Wuthnow cannot account for the lived experience, intentions, rhetorical feats of persuasion, agonies of conscience, fantasies, midnight strategy planning meetings, etc. of the various elites and cadres whom he identified as engaging in religious activity. By its conventions of naming and explaining, this vocabulary treats the system as if its structure is unchanged by information, simply activated by it; it treats people who act in ways which it calls religious *as if* they were insensible components of a simple system, devoid of intentionality, responding to economic forces of which their understanding is irrelevant, and whose actions affect the system of which they are a part more like the toxins in a petri dish than the scientist's decision to end the study and sterilize the equipment.

In a later paper, Wuthnow (1987) wrote in a vocabulary that named the rhetoric and stories of the people whom he studied. Whatever else might be indicated by this shift—whether a methodological whim or shift in his interests — this vocabulary affords the opportunity to treat the world order as containing (even if not fully determined by) cybernetic processes.

To the extent that a goal state is an intention comprised by a story of what should be the state of a system, the hypothesis that a system is cybernetic requires a hermeneutic explanatory structure. This may lead to a very thin hermeneutics, however. The story told by the thermostat that keeps a building within a specified temperature range is not particularly rich, and it may well be that the stories told by prophets and revolutionaries embody profound mystifications of the real processes that govern the functioning of the system.

If the world order is a cybernetic system, there must be some element of hermeneutic interpretation of its function, and religion may be usefully conceptualized in terms of people's beliefs, stories, attributions, and all the rest. However, it is possible to define the hermeneutic aspect of religion as relatively unimportant, profoundly misguided with respect to an explanation of the dynamics and structure of the world order, etc.

Second-order cybernetic systems. If the world order is understood as a second-order cybernetic system, on the other hand, there can be no coherent explanation that does not foreground hermeneutics. That which people believe and believe that other people believe, and how they interpret what they and others do, matters, and matters greatly, because it is a component of the structure of second-order cybernetic systems.

Second-order cybernetics deals with systems that observe themselves and other systems, rather than — as with simple and cybernetic systems—systems that are observed from somewhere outside them (Maturana and Varela, 1980; Winograd and Flores, 1986; Kenny and Gardner, 1988). If a thermostat is a cybernetic, self-regulating system, a second-order cybernetic system is the homeowner who lives in the house, both monitoring the level of comfort and the amount of the fuel bills. The hermeneutic processes engaged in by this system are considerably more complex than that programmed into the thermostat.

Again referring to Wuthnow's research, to treat the world order as a second-order cybernetic systems leads to a conceptualization of local elites in peripheral societies not just as responding, on the basis of their programming, to changes in economic conditions, but as self-aware entities who take note of themselves responding to economic conditions and set themselves to change those conditions. This description of the system must be done in a vocabulary that permits description of how elites note changed conditions, "take note of themselves responding" to those conditions, and "set themselves" to a strategy that will bring about, e.g., the changes described in Wuthnow's 1980 paper.

The fourth theorem of systems theory states that *systems appear differently depending on the perspective from which they are viewed.* A first corollary of the theorem is that *systems look very differently depending on whether one's perspective is inside or outside the system.*

At first blush, this corollary seems to reinstitute the earlier concern with the boundaries of a system; in fact it provokes a much more radical revision of ways of thinking. Viewed as an epistemic problem, this corollary leads to a series of humbling questions: If the world is systemically organized in often subtle and nonobvious ways, how can one know where to draw the boundaries of the system? Given the by now well-known relationship between the knower and the known, how sharply can one identify a boundary between the observer and the observed system?

Once posed, however, these questions require movement from a self-effacing narrative about relations among components of the system to a self-reflextive narrative about the relation among narratives. Rather than the unanswerable epistemological questions of "where do the boundaries *really* exist?" or "how can I *know* the real boundaries?" the implications of this corollary are best understood as making salient a different set of questions, more readily answerable and best understood as ontological.

Every researcher and theorist must confront the question, "what system do you have in view?" This question is ultimately biographical. It is elaborated in such probes as "When did you first start to draw the boundaries so that they included (excluded) yourself?" "What do you think you would lose by redrawing the boundaries to include, e.g., supranational entities?" "What led you to postulate that the system has the level of organization that you now believe that it has?" "What difference would it make if you thought that the system had a higher (lower) level or organization?"

Descriptions of second-order cybernetic systems focus on their function as observing. As such, the fundamental explanatory principles involve dynamic processes of change and relations among systems rather than static states of a single system. Any account of an observing system must include a vocabulary capable of dealing with the perceptions, intentions, interpretations, fantasies and strategies of the self-aware components of the system. Without making the mistake of assuming that the narratives of a self-aware system are identical to the behavior or structure of the system, the relation between these narratives and the system's functioning mubt be taken into consideration. If there are more than one such self-aware components, one must also deal with the manner in which the narratives of various groups intermesh.

Is the world order a second-order cybernetic system? Certainly! Like Descartes's inability to doubt that he was thinking, this is the kind of issue in which the ability to raise the question provides the answer. The authors included in this book are *in* the world order, and their thoughts and writing *about* the world order are parts of it. They are drawn from a class of people who produce scholarly narratives about the world order, raising consciousness about the interrelatedness of it all, providing vocabularies (e.g., *local elites*) in which to talk about that organization, deconstructing and reinterpreting concepts such as underdeveloped, and sensitizing people to patterns of oppression and domination.

There are other self-aware components of the world order as well. Chief among them are self-designated leaders in religion, politics, and academia. Each of these leaders produces narratives, which may be read as describing themselves in relation to other components of the system, the state of the system in relation to a vision of a desired condition (e.g., Islamization; nirvana); and a set of plans by which the present state can be transformed into the desired state.

Still another component of the system that marks its nature as second-order cybernetic are those strangely disembodied "hegemonic ideas and . . . the opposing ideas defining them," referred to by Hopkins and Wallerstein (1982:137).

In What Vocabulary Can We Describe the World Order?

I believe that much is to be gained from an analysis of religion, which looks to patterns of organization which transcend national and cultural boundaries. However, a sufficiently rigorous analysis of the world order requires the development of a conceptual and methodological vocabulary, which differs radically from that based, e.g., on Newtonian physics.

In my judgment, such a vocabulary is not now available, and its absence is shown by the struggles of those who have led the attempt to come to grips with a systemic view of the world order. Robertson's (1985:348) definition of globalization conflates two quite different concepts of system. Globalization, he writes, "refers to the processes by which the world becomes a single place, both with respect to recognition of a very high degree of interdependence [a simple system] . . . *and* to the growth of consciousness pertaining to the globe as such [a second-order cybernetic system]."

Whose consciousness is being referred to here? Theorists? Elites? Ideological leaders and spokespersons? The masses? All of the above? Is this consciousness in or outside the system?"

Similarly, Wallerstein's more general characterization of the world system, that it combines wholeness and unevenness, is insufficiently precise to differentiate among dissimilar types of systems. World system analysis is presented in a vocabulary that is self-reflexively aware of the interconnections of various forces, but is apparently outside the system, because it describes these relations as contradictory insensate forces inherent within capitalism as they create a simple system. (There is rich irony in the use of the term *contradictory* — to speak against — to refer to nonverbal economic forces!)

To their credit, world systems analysts have been uncomfortable with their ability to specify what kind of system the world order comprises. Bach (1980:165) felt that the claims of world systems analysts were being read as less radical than their theory supported. The maxim "the whole is greater than the sum of the parts," he reminded, is not so much a quantitative statement as a description of a perspective, which transforms the types of questions and the interpretations of answers with which one is concerned.

Toward "Eloquence" in Understanding the World Order

I do not have a fully developed vocabulary to offer which better accounts for the world order as a second-order cybernetic system. Hopefully, such a vocabulary will be developed as theory and data are woven into discourse. However, I offer the following as suggestions, which seem to me useful in understanding at least some aspects of religion in the world order.

Hermeneutics

The claim that the world order has the properties of a second-order cybernetic system implies that hermeneutics—that which is variously referred to as "actors' meanings," "narratives," "discursive economies," "discourse"—should be foregrounded. In second-order cybernetic systems, such factors comprise the function of observing, which is the criterial state of the system; in this type of structure, hermeneutics are not merely superstructural ideologies masking or diverting attention from the real forces at work in the world order (Harland, 1987). Even though ideologies may be quite at variance with other aspects of the system, they are in the system rather than outside it and are a part of its structure.

Disorder, diversity, and conflict. The legacy of Darwinian evolution and structural/functionalism has taught us to reason backwards. Whatever is, we reason, is an evolutionary solution to a problem, or serves a function within an existing, ergo evolutionarily viable system. As a result, we tend to focus on patterns of order when we look at the larger structure of the world.

One of the great contributions of the study of comparative religion leads us in just the opposite direction by celebrating the diversity of human responses to the environment, the incommensurate worldviews developed in different times and places, the mutually opaque customs and rituals of various cultures. This aspect of religion suggests that the world order is not very orderly: it includes conflict, disorder, and irreducible diversity.

I suggest a radical departure from the notion of order. The components of the world order (the people whose labor, interpretations, and actions comprise the human world) have the capacity but not the necessity of acting as second-order cybernetic systems. By habit or choice, they often act as simple or cybernetic systems and sometimes as second-order cybernetic systems; that is, they often respond to situations *as if* the situations were stimuli and their behavior the response, but they do not have to. Sometimes they reflect on situations, transforming them into powerful, complex narratives in which their actions change the world.

This conception of the world system suggests that, in addition to the inherent contradictions of capitalism (Wallerstein, 1982:112) and "a population's place in the larger world order" (Wuthnow, 1980:60), the world order consists, simultaneously, at each of its points, of multiple narratives whose manner of intermeshing, embodied in particular events and lives, comprises an important part of the structure and determines the functioning of the system.

Eloquence. As I am using it here, eloquence pertains to theorists and researchers who would give an account of such a disorderly, complex system, remembering always that they are observing that system from inside it and that their descriptions become, at the moment of utterance, a part of the system. Is it possible to "do science" under such conditions? What form of knowledge is possible? In what language can we speak and write?

There is a pernicious myth abroad in the land. The fact of multiple, incommensurate discourses is taken to imply the inevitability of relativism, the impossibility of communication, and the end of rationality. The

Enlightenment project of bringing the whole world under the common mantle of reason seems to be undone, supplanted by a vision of hegemonic processes joining but not uniting mutually opaque discourses in a carnival of cacophonous polysemy (cf. Tyler, 1987).

The fact is that there are far more antirelativists opposing the drift toward intellectual anarchy than relativists who have so drifted (Geertz, 1984). The specter of relativism frightens most of those who are insufficiently emancipated from the "Cartesian anxiety" of harboring a doubtful premise (Bernstein, 1983) — a condition which appears quite quaint given the characterization of the world order previously mentioned.

Once past the unreasoning fear of relativism, the new sensitivity to the multiplicity of incommensurate discourses defines the nature of communication within and thus about the world order rather than precludes its possibility. We now know that one cannot communicate *about* complex systems or *among* incommensurate discourses *within* the rhetorical resources of any of these discourses, but we can construct *new* vocabularies, discourses, and resources. Eloquence within a disorderly second-order cybernetic system consists of the ability to discover and create the possibility of communicating among incommensurate discourses and of representing the (temporary) levels of functioning of various components within the system (Pearce, 1989).

My attempts to understand religion in the world order have taken the form of case studies of conflicts among various groups. For example, the discourse of Islamization poses a threat and opportunity for the political and ethnic groups in Malaysia. Mess and Pearce (1986) analyzed how some of these groups acted, how they interpreted their own actions and those of other groups, and the ways in which these sequences of actions comprised logics, which sometimes lead to unwanted repetitive patterns in which the participants felt inextricably enmeshed. Although each of the groups we studied had its own account of what was happening and why, we took these as components of a disorderly second-order cybernetic system; eloquence consists of finding/inventing a discourse in which we could describe how these incompatible human worlds fit together.

The heated conflict between the new Christian right and the secular humanists in the first part of the 1980s in the United States is particularly rich as a place where multiple, incommensurate discourses clashed, producing a disorderly second-order cybernetic system. The sequence of events was fueled by the repeated attempts of spokespersons for each side to explain themselves. Each explanation, however, was heard by the other as further proof of the insincerity, foolishness, and depravity of the other, leading to an escalation of the conflict (Pearce, Littlejohn, and Alexander, 1987). A pivotal event consisted of Senator Edward Kennedy's speech at Liberty Baptist College, the stronghold of the moral majority. Kennedy deliberately and strategically sought to transform the context in which secular humanists and moral majoritarians acted and understood each other; he offered a speech which demonstrated that there was a discourse in which both he and Jerry Falwell could remain faithful to their commitments without stridency (Branham and Pearce, 1987).

Important questions remain about the extent to which a vocabulary that permits eloquence is transferable across particular situations or whether it must be developed specifically for each new application. (I am presently impressed by the demands of specific situations.) To what extent will eloquence address the interests of those who are now focusing on the political economy of the world order? How will the explanatory eloquence of researchers affect the world order? (Part of my interest is the hope that such creativity might be useful in averting repetition of dysfunctional conflicts.) While these are open questions, I believe that an adequate account of these particular events in which religions conflict or in which particular individuals reconstruct the context in which some conflicts occur requires eloquence on the part of the theorist and researcher.

Conclusion

The development of eloquence among those who study religion in the context of the world order has much to commend it. It is the place where is found the ability to transcend the familiar patterns of domination and exploitation, which have characterized the old world order; it requires a theoretical ability to take into account the functioning of the system (at least locally and temporarily) as a second-order cybernetic system; it is much more interesting than charting the collision of blind economic forces. If religious activity is something other than a manifestation of economic circumstance, eloquence is a place marker for the kind of study that distinguishes religion from, for example, patterns of economic consumption. In a disorderly second-order cybernetic system, religion can be taken, as Smart suggested *and for scientific purposes*, as practical, experiential, narrative, doctrinal, and ethical as well as social and material.

References

Bernstein, Richard
1983   *Beyond Objectivism and Relativism: Science, Hermeneutics, and Praxis.*
    Philadelphia: University of Pennsylvania Press.

Branham, Robert J., and W. Barnett Pearce
1987 "A Contract for Civility: Edward Kennedy's Lynchburg Address." *Quarterly Journal of Speech* 73:424–443.

Geertz, Clifford
1984 "Anti anti-relativism." *American Anthropologist* 86:263–278.

Harland, Richard
1987 *Superstructuralism: The Philosophy of Structuralism and Post-Structuralism.* London: Metheun.

Harré, Rom
1972 *The Philosophies of Science.* London: Oxford.

Hopkins, Terence K., and Immanuel Wallerstein
1982 *World-Systems Analysis: Theory and Methodology.* Beverly Hills: Sage.

Kenny, Vincent, and Georgiana Gardner
1988 "Constructions of Self-Organizing Systems." *Irish Journal of Psychology* 9:1–24.

Maturana, Humberto R., and Francisco Varela
1980 *Autopoiesis and Cognition: The Realization of the Living.* Dordrecht: Reidel.

Mess, Zulkarnaina Mohd., and W. Barnett Pearce
1986 " 'Dakwah Islamiah': Islamic Revivalism and the Politics of Race and Religion in Malaysia." In Jeffrey Hadden and Anson Shupe, eds., *Politics and Prophetic Religions,* 196–220. New York: Paragon Press.

Pearce, W. Barnett
1989 *Communication and the Human Condition.* Carbondale: Southern Illinois University Press.

Pearce, W. Barnett, Stephen Littlejohn, and Alison Alexander
1987 "The New Christian Right and the Humanist Response: Reciprocated Diatribe." *Communication Quarterly* 35: 171–192.

Robertson, Roland
1985 "The Sacred and the World System." In Phillip Hammond, ed., *The Sacred in a Secular Age: Toward Revision in the Scientific Study of Religion,* 247–358. Berkeley: University of California Press.

Rodgers, Daniel T.
1987 *Contested Truths: Keyword in American Politics Since Independence.* New York: Basic.

Rodney, Walter
1982 *How Europe Underdeveloped Africa.* Washington, D.C.: Howard University Press.

Smart, Ninian
1989   *The World's Religions*. Englewood Cliffs: Prentice-Hall.

Smith, Anthony
1980   *The Geopolitics of Information: How Western Culture Dominates the World*. London: Oxford.

Tyler, Stephen A.
1987   *The Unspeakable: Discourse, Dialogue, and Rhetoric in the Postmodern World*. Madison: Wisconsin University Press.

Winograd, Terry, and Fernando Flores
1986   *Understanding Computers and Cognition: A New Foundation for Design*. Reading: Addison-Wesley.

Wallerstein, Immanuel
1984   *The Politics of the World-Economy: The States, the Movements, and the Civilizations*. Cambridge: Cambridge University Press.

Wuthnow, Robert
1980   "World Order and Religious Movements," In Albert Bergesen, ed., *Studies of the Modern World-System*, 57–75. New York: Academic Press.

Wuthnow, Robert
1987   "America's Legitimating Myths: Continuity and Crisis." In Terry Boswell and Albert Bergesen, eds., *America's Changing Role in the World-System*, 235–256. New York: Praeger.

14

World Order and Religion: A Match Made in Heaven or a Marriage of Convenience?

Rhys H. Williams

The scope, diversity, and originality of this collection of essays is quickly apparent. Indeed, given the amount written on religion, and how little of it focuses explicitly on the relationship of religion to concepts and processes related to the world order, this should provide grist for many mills—a provocative collective push. However, it is not difficult to notice how many directions this collection goes at once; there is nothing approaching a single paradigm. So even at this early point, a little stock-taking is in order. What does all this mean for the analysis of religion? As we go from the "misty world of theory" to the "messy world of application," have we gotten anywhere? Is there anything more here than a marriage of convenience between two only distantly related scholarly idioms? To open this discussion, let us start straightforwardly: what exactly are we talking about when we speak of world order and religion?

At this stage in the life course of any scholarly idiom, there are multiple foci for analytic attention. The articles collected herein demonstrate that. Some call for understanding religion as a world-historical force, influencing immigration patterns, national foreign policies, and transnational cultural exchanges, in addition to influencing the course of internal developments within nations. Others focus their attention on the impact global level events have on religion, and *American* religion specifically; conversely, some examine how American religion has influenced the world—either directly or indirectly, through its many roles in the United States politics.

Finally, several chapters call for the incorporation of religion and the analysis of religion into current world-systems models. That is, given an increasingly integrated world—the much heralded global village—the primary units of social analysis should be global rather than national. While this type of analysis is already common within economics, many of the included papers argue for its relevance to the study of religion. This last point offers the most reaching theoretical challenge, and in my esti- mation, the most problematic as well. Thus, a bit of unpacking of some of the issues involved here seems in order.

Systems-level Assumptions

First, it is the basic assumption of this volume that the study of re- ligion requires a more global perspective—a broadening of context. This is intended to mean more than merely additional comparative research, studying similar phenomena in different cultural and political settings. It implies a level of analysis, and perhaps a level of social reality, beyond that of the inclusive society. A global or world-systems perspective may also imply that the theoretical schemes that currently account for na- tional-level processes may not be adequate for this more macro level.

Yet, there is also within this collection a consistent call for more at- tention to local diversity, indigenous traditions, and cultural pluralism. This could involve either exploring the terrain of "local knowledge" (Geertz, 1983) or using what Eleanor Scott Myers calls "radical local- ism" as an analytic point of departure. In any case the accent is on mul- tiple discourses, multiple, specific, and perhaps unique expressions of re- ligious and political life, and the ability of cultures—even those outside the core of the globalization process—to create and interpret their own worldviews.

Concern about a developing cultural hegemony of the West is at the base of this perspective. Thus, in addition to a world-systemic compo- nent, that is, a macro aspect focusing on dominant global processes, there is a simultaneous call for a more constructionist or interactionist perspective that can highlight the multivocal aspects of cultural interpre- tation. The latter would also focus more or less explicitly on possible cen- ters of resistance to just those world-dominating (or world-integrating, depending upon one's perspective) processes that world-systems ana- lysts view as primary.

It is not impossible to justify either of these two directions, but their theoretical and research implications seem to run in opposite directions. If the world is ever more tightly integrated into a coherent system, if pro- cesses that circle the globe are all the more pervasive, then local con- struction and subsequent resistance become mere side pools and eddys in the stream of history. On the other hand, if the creative and indetermi- nant aspects of local cultures are the more significant foci for analysis, then perhaps the world system and its attendant global village are primarily convenient analytic categories rather than empirical realities.

These countervailing tendencies are apparent in recent writing on the globalization of culture, religion, and theological education. There seems to be the simultaneous assumption that both processes of core domination and peripheral resistance are the primary locus of social vitality. Of course, it is unfair to imply that this tendency is apparent only in the papers collected here. Almost all social analysis with a liberal-left persuasion is caught wrestling with the apparent conflict between claims that, on one hand, social structures create and limit humans and their life options, pressing them into predetermined molds, while on the other, humans create society and its structures, and thus these structures are available to human will for manipulation and change. When the level of analysis becomes as encompassing as the world system, these twin claims become all the more difficult to keep in balance.

Granted that we wish to add a global or world-systemic component to the analysis of religion, the question then turns to discerning the ways in which we want to consider the impacts of supranational forces. Wuthnow's chapter provides two broad options: a) graft global or world-systems variables onto present explanatory schemes, thereby adding some context; or, b) make a systems-level jump to a different level of analysis, one that requires radically different explanatory principles for its different order of phenomena.

The more appealing theoretical response is to opt for the second approach, even though it is the first which is more often, and easily, accomplished. Simply adding context does not seem to account adequately for the additional complexity of global-level processes. Indeed, one can envision, with some horror, regression equations containing variables from the global, national, regional, group, and individual levels, all stacked upon each other. This does not seem to be the most promising new direction for research.

Better to research the world order on its own terms — that is, after all, an implication of the often cited paradigm shift. As Pearce notes, a world-systems theory generally contains the claim that the world system is not just a simple system of relationships but is rather a cybernetic system that includes a monitoring function as an inherent systemic property. There is a logic to the entire system's operation that is analytically distinct from the logic guiding the constituent parts, and it can only be explained on its own terms.

Included in the research implications of this theoretical approach is a test of the very concept of "systemness" itself. Is there a single world system? If so, what type, or level, of system is it? Perhaps most importantly, is the world system an ontological level experienced by actors themselves, or rather, an epistemological level of the analysts? In other words, whose categories are these anyway? This tension, that between actors and analysts, holds the key for the divergent research implications emanating from these papers. Before turning to this subject, it will be helpful to focus on both halves of our title: world order, and religion.

World Order

Taking this shift in the levels of analysis and abstraction into account, one notices a variety of meanings bound up in the phrase *world order*. Without trying to subject the current authors to either critique or theoretical hegemony, the theoretical and empirical implications should be considered. Four different terms predominate: international; globalization; world system; and world order. Each evokes a separate meaning and contains within it different preferred directions for research.

International is most common: an international focus considers interactions and relationships between more or less autonomous nation-state actors. Its basic epistemological assumption is that the world is composed of nation-states; that is, it assumes that what happens at the world level of analysis happens between nations. The whole, in other words, is some sort of aggregate of the self-contained parts, and transnational phenomena should be conceived as composed of unit interactions.

Bergesen (1985) has noted that this conception of the world order is a macro version of classical liberalism's theory of society. The world is an international phenomenon in the same way that a society is basically an interpersonal phenomenon. Self-constituted and autonomous units come together and through their actions toward each other, form another level of analysis. Further, the analysis of social phenomena within each unit is distinct from, and often only indirectly affected by, similar analysis of phenomena between units. Finally, it implies that the units, in this case nation-states, precede the whole, both theoretically and empirically.

However, the importance of transnational organizations, in particular the Roman Catholic church, and the cultural universalism of Christendom, both of which preceded the rise of the capitalist nation-state, should prevent a too easy assumption of temporal and theoretical order:

> From the early state conferences being part of the later Councils of the church, to the presence of an extra-state language for diplomacy, to the heridary linage of princes, there was an international order which arose at the same time as states, such that one cannot

separate out the state as coming first and the international system as second. In fact, this international culture often preceded state action, and certainly made it possible, such that what Durkheim noted about the utilitarians that contractual order was not the source of society, but society the source of contracts, must now be applied to international relations. (Bergesen, 1985:10)

Thus, international seems to be of only limited utility in expanding our understandings of religion's interactions with entities and processes beyond the level of the nation-state, partly for the very reason that it only goes a short theoretical distance beyond nation-states themselves. While it is often important to understand international relations on the political level, the fluid nature of cultural borders, and the inherent universalizing tendencies of many religions, make it less germane to the analysis of world religious processes.

Globalization, as a concept, avoids these pitfalls that adhere to an international perspective. As used by Robertson (1985; Robertson and Chirico, 1985) it denotes a process of integration and interdependence at a level beyond the nation-state. As such, it includes the imagery of coherence and organic development that has characterized the modernization school of economic development (e.g. Eisenstadt, 1966). That is, the process of the transformation from traditional to modern, *gemeinschaft* to *gesellschaft,* mechanical to organic solidarity, is basically a unitary one, experienced in more or less similar terms across place and time (see, for example, Jaffee's (forthcoming) analysis). In this case, the global order relates to the rise of nation-states dialectically, itself developing as it is in turn the context for the development of its component parts. Certainly the integration fostered by the rise and dispersion of a truly global communications network lends credence to this perspective.

It is, however, important to note that much of the impetus for developing a focus on multivocal and local cultural discourses arose as critical response and reaction to the overly unitary conception of modernization theory. Much of the economic modernization literature posited specific cultural values as prerequisites for economic development and political democracy. Not only was this rather dubious as empirically grounded causal relationships, but the political implications of cultural hegemony were anathema to many scholars. One response of scholars influenced by critical theory has been to demonstrate the relative plasticity of dominating traditions, thus making a case for the cultural resources of resistance available to locals.

While globalization and modernization are not identical concepts, they are closely related. Indeed, Robertson and Chirico refer to a sense of wholeness or unity in the concept and describe it as "the phenomenon of globality, which we see as a generalization and extension of the older gemeinschaft-gesellschaft problem" (1985:240). In another place, they speak of globalization as having an "element of directionality involved in the realization of the global-human condition" (1985:238). A major aspect of this condition is the possibility of shared values at the global level. Thus, while they are conscious of variation, their approach to globalization is predicated upon its coherent, universal, and integrating characteristics. While this may well account for the dispersion of cultural messages throughout a global communications network, it does not offer developed conceptual tools for understanding the multivocal nature of discourse.

A response to the perceived shortcomings of the international, and modernization perspectives is the body of work known as world-systems theory. Wallerstein (1974) is credited with its formative statements, but it has blossomed into a many-faceted outlook. The basic contours are consistent; in brief, it charts the rise and development of a world economic system with the development and extension of the European capitalist economy from the sixteenth century. Its fundamental proposition is that there is basically a single world system, knit togeter by capitalist political-economic processes. Whether the world-encompassing aspect is a necessary or contingent part of capitalist development is the source of some debate, as is the degree and impact of relative integration of various parts of the world into the system. Nonetheless, it is a theoretical perspective that truly uses the world as the basic unit of analysis, its component parts both systematically and systemically related. Further, its central metaphor of dividing the world into core, semiperiphery, and peripheral states has great intuitive appeal.

This perspective is not without its critics, however. In the first place, its central claim is that events in different parts of the world are related systemically. This is, of course, an elusive claim to document. It is one thing to demonstrate that similar social processes were happening more or less conterminously in various parts of the world. That alone does not mean that they are related components of the same system; every transnational event or process is not necessarily world-systemic.

A critique of world-systems theory particularly relevant for this collection is the extent to which the perspective's foundations in Marxian theorizing limits its usefulness to political-economic analysis. The theory is centered on the production, distribution, and consumption of economic goods and services — it is an inherently economic, not a cultural, model. Moreover, because it is a Marxian economic model, culture and religion are often treated as marginal, if not epiphenomenal, spheres of life. The best known example of this tendency comes from the oft-noted first volume of Wallerstein's work: in an entire book on the sixteenth century, the Protestant Reformation garners but a handful of paragraphs.

Some critics have challenged the accuracy of this aspect of the world-systems perspective. They have noted that the present world economic order and modern religions are both products of colonial period, and thus have both inherent and contingent relations that must be considered when examining the impact of any locale's placement within the system. Peter Smith's (1986) provocative, if problematic, article is just such an example, as are the several works in this volume that relate religion in Latin America to the dependency-based economic relationships between the North and South.

Robertson (1985) finds within the writings of world-system research a theoretical space for the role of ideas and culture, and by implication, religion. While the approach is secular at its base, it can be accommodated to considerations of the sacred without stretching the perspective beyond recognition. On another occasion, however, Robertson and Chirico are critical of world-systems theory due to its tendencies to see all relations between societies as primarily economic and political, with cultural events being only "*intra*-societal outcomes of *inter*-societal relations" (1985:223). Bergesen also criticizes the economistic tendencies of world-systems research. In the conclusion of the passage just cited, he continues:

> ... must now be applied to *international relations and world-systems theory*. There is a cultural foundation of global order, one that made it possible in the first place and that continues to make its existence possible today. (1985:10; emphasis added)

Finally, speaking of a world order brings a sense of order and stability to the globe that is not necessarily present when one speaks of a world system. Systems can operate smoothly or not, they are merely consistent relationships between interconnected units. Indeed, world-systems researchers are usually faithful to their Marxian roots in that the contradictions inherent in the system are seen as enduring, if variable, sources of disruption. Wuthnow (1983) uses the phrase *global social systems,* but very modestly, noting that a system consists only of relationships, and should not be conflated with consistency. The "systemness," he claims here, is the construct imposed by the observer.

World order, on the other hand, implies less attention to systemic functioning, and more on the features of the resulting order. Order is a double-edged sword, however. While it may begin as only a convenient conceptual handle reminding us that there are patterns in social life at any level of abstraction, it, too, often becomes either reified, normative, or both. In the same way that a world system becomes a property of empirical reality, the world order can become a normative assumption concerning stability, integration, and stasis. This can miss the extent to which a focus on a global level of order masks the tensions and contradictions within societies.

However, it is also the case that the term world order is not associated with a particular theoretical school, as is world system, or to a lesser extent, globalization. Thus it does not call to mind an entire cluster of other concepts and assumptions. Its relative openness to interpretation makes it the most appropriate for characterizing this collection—as well as calling for a new direction in the analysis of religion without specifying what it should be. It is often the case that studies of economic, political, or social order portray that order as an end state rather than a process (or collection of processes). With that caveat in mind, world order does indeed seem like a suitably flexible term.

Theoretical and Empirical Congruence

Theoretical openness may well be necessary here because the diversity and the seeming contradictions of recent world events makes the coherent explanatory schema of the globalization and world-systems perspectives less than satisfying. Several of these very issues are pursued in these chapters. For example, George Thomas discusses the folk ontologies that create moral boundaries between different spheres of life. He notes that political movements the world over have taken on religious casts, and these moral boundaries are the very focus of the politicized activity. The folk ontologies that separate economic, political, moral, and religious institutional life are being strained, attacked, and rearranged. Further, he connects increasing density in the world system to its intuitive opposite—an increased focus on individuals, individualism, and an atomized conception of human rights. In contrast to Thomas' religio-political ferment, James Davison Hunter's comparative study argues for a marginalization of religious elites, at least at the national level.

Certainly many observers of the contemporary United States point out that there seems to be an increasing boredom with conventional politics at the same time that more issues once considered private are becoming public and politicized. A related phenomenon, and another seeming empirical anomaly, is that few of the religio-political movements sweeping contemporary society are doing so under the banner of liberal Protestantism, once the cultural standard-bearer of Anglo-American society. It is possible to argue that America's liberal religious tradition has lost its capacity to mobilize political movements around its symbols precisely because they have become institutionalized, globalized, and hence, invisible — more background than "figure." What were once the sectarian properties of a particular tradition are now understood as general cultural assumptions that have a truly global dimension and impact — carried by both missionary activities and modern communication networks. Yet this very development has made them less potent in shaping the sociopolitical environment of their home domain. As Jay Demerath has noted on several occasions, liberal Protestantism's cultural victories may have led directly to its structural marginality.

It is impossible not to notice that the tide that has passed liberal Protestantism by as a sectarian world-historical force is also correlated with challenges to the centrality of the Anglo-American world in the global political economy. Connecting these two trends with some type of empirical and theoretical mechanism is one of the challenges posed by this collection. A key point here, for both theoretical consideration and empirical work, is that documenting a global communications network of organizational linkages, or a world economy powered by institutional and national elites, is insufficient if the questions being asked concern the meanings, interpretations, and uses to which the globe-spanning messages and processes are put. It is my contention that the cultural analysis required for an understanding of religion in the world order will not work best using the models of economic and organizational exchanges developed by world-systems theory. Again, this discussion must be postponed briefly while we unpack the second half of our title.

The Case of American Religion

American in this context is primarily concerned with the United States, although why this should be so goes beyond the national identities of most of the current contributors. American religion is often taken as a particularly important case of religion as a world-historical force for two reasons, that (again) seem to run in counter directions. First, in contrast to most industrialized Western nations, in the United States many of the behavioral dimensions of religiosity (e.g. membership, attendance at services) have remained strong and fairly stable. Without retreating into an argument resting on American essentialism, it is important to note this behavioral and cultural vibrancy as a critical component in American culture and politics, including foreign policy (see, for example, Tiryakian, 1982).

Second, the form of Christianity that is the cultural hallmark of American religion, so-called liberal Protestantism, is often considered a

bellwether for changes that all forms of religion experience in their deal-
ings with modernity. Liberal Protestantism as test case undergirds some
of the most basic theoretical writings in the sociology of religion (e.g.
Berger, 1967; 1979); Hunter's (1983) study of conservative Protestantism
plays off that theme as well. George Thomas' (1989) study of nineteenth-
century revivalism (which was not, it should be noted, the liberal Protestantism of its day) specifically uses United States religion as an illustrative case to tie together general theoretical statements about religious
movements with specific historical interpretations of cultural change.

These two approaches echo the opposing tendencies in social
analysis described above: American religion as either unique historical
phenomenon or as illustrative of transnational processes and change —
local meaning versus global dominance. It may be, however, that American religion offers just the historical force to allow the transcendence of
these apparently opposed perspectives. Thomas (1989), while using the
United States as an illustrative case, connects revivalism's attempt to re-
figure the culture and polity to the nation's changing relationship to the
world economy in what is a very promising marriage of global context and
American religion. Other works, some of them in this collection, also
show the beginnings of an understanding spanning several levels of analysis.

For example, American religion's historical concerns with missions
is an important dimension in tying national religious arrangements to
global processes. As Andrew Walls notes, the United States became the
world's leading evangelizer after having been evangelized. This was not a
transplanted European church, but a church for the New World, "essentially societal rather than ecclesiastical," and in many ways it was an essentially frontier society. The ambiguity and open-endedness of the organizational forms that accompanied nineteenth-century American
society allowed its penetration into many world markets, both economic
and religio-cultural. This is an important point in Lamin Sanneh's chapter and is demonstrated convincingly in a superb work by Fields (1987) on
colonial central Africa. While the processes that spread American religion were certainly interwoven with other global forces, the autonomy
and variation of local interpretation should not be underestimated.

Further, Burdick and Hammond's analysis of Protestant foreign
missions makes it clear that cultural and political dominance are not necessarily related to numerical advantage, lending an uncertainty to the
whole idea of an establishment religion. Any mechanism that attempts to
link a nation's placement in the world economic order with its internal
cultural arrangements is fairly indeterminant. Wuthnow (1983) makes
that point clearly. While he analyzes several world-systemic patterns and
correlate processes within nations, he also notes that the outcome of in-

corporation in the world system is not complete absorption and dominance on the cultural level but the promotion of new cultural forms "that
differ both from tradition and from the culture of core areas" (1983:66).
Economic modernization, far from being a "universal solvent" producing cultural convergence, has other effects. Wuthnow concludes:

> We can, therefore, reconcile the fact of economic modernization
> with the obvious persistence of a local and regional cultural differ-
> ences, for they are elements of a common process. (Ibid)

George Thomas' work also makes this point; world-level processes,
particularly those incorporating peripheral areas into world economic
processes, are intimately tied to local variations in interpretation and cultural construction. The two are intrinsically related and contradictory
tendencies, not mutually exclusive.

Theoretical and Empirical Integration

Where a theoretical problem develops is in trying to establish a single world system. The study of culture, and with it the study of religion,
is moving toward the analysis of multiple discourses, which in turn implies multiple theories of reality undergirding social practices. The polit-
ical-economy approach, which can chart the flows of goods and services,
cannot take into consideration the multiple and complex levels of meaning, logic and practices, that exist simultaneously in any cultural setting.
As Pearce notes, culture and religion are different analytic levels than
that assumed by world-systems theory. While it is absolutely imperative
to document the interaction of different cultural forms and discourses —
and in that sense a global perspective is necessary—merely documenting
interaction does not reveal or explain the resulting "webs of meaning"
(Geertz, 1973). There is a world system of connections, but not of invariant meanings. While some recent cultural theory calls for abandoning
the quest for meaning (Wuthnow, 1987), my point here is not a brief for a
radical subjectivism. Rather, it is my contention that the processes of appropriation, interpretation, and reconstruction at the local level are as important as the objective connection and interactions between system-
level units. Understanding one does not reveal the other.

The empirical task, then, begins with the texture and multivocal nature of multiple discourses. Taking culture seriously as a discourse demands such attention to localness. The coherence of these many discourses is one starting point for research. Although I have argued for a
theoretical position that preserves the autonomy of local interpretation,

the degree to which transsocietal cultural forms are manipulated is an empirical question. The extent to which they are reconstructed, and the consequences of that cultural work, is an important issue—and one that can only be grasped when the global flow of objective culture is incorporated into the explanation.

From that point, it is important to remember that culture has carriers as well as content. So an examination of the primary carriers of transnational culture is a critical next step. The analysis of religion and culture cannot be divorced from questions of social power. If culture is indeed a tool kit (Swidler, 1986) with indeterminant rules about how the tools are to be used, it is nonetheless important to know whose tools they are in the first place. Interpretation may be a relatively open process, but some interpretations are more, and less, likely. Thus, whereas nineteenth-century American religion was very frontierlike, it is significant to note that the structure of contemporary American religion is bureaucratic. The expansion of these forms into Third World areas, particularly in situations where other spheres of life are less bureaucratically organized, is perhaps the colonial question of our age.

Or, for example, those of us who watched the events in Beijing's Tiananmen Square know the worldwide power and resonance of such religio-political concepts and symbols as democracy and liberty—and yet the local constructions of their meaning is the key to understanding both the movement's participants and opponents. The tendency for the American media to interpret China in terms of American categories did not make those events any clearer. Moreover, anyone who noticed that the Chinese students' banners were inscribed in both Chinese and English could only marvel at the transnational reach of the media—world politics is truly becoming interactive. It was a time, perhaps the most dramatic in recent years, that called for wedding our understandings of both global-level processes and local-level interpretations.

Another example of the fascinating interplay of politics and religion on a world stage is currently developing in the tragic land of Cambodia. As the Vietnamese withdraw their armies (September, 1989), the indigenous government they leave behind attempts to revive a somewhat flagging nationalism to fend off the expected onslaught of the Khmer Rouge guerrillas. One of the ways they hope to nurture this nationalism is the removal of restrictions on Buddhist practices, beliefs, and religious personnel. That traditional Cambodian Buddhism, a thoroughly peaceful set of beliefs and practices, may be a political tool for a Vietnamese-supported Cambodian government in its struggle with a Khmer-based insurgent army, is a political event too complex to grasp without sensitivity to both world geopolitics and local history.

We must also consider the reverse case and study American religion in terms of the world order. One of the issues most crucial to current American cultural life is the viability of the notion of the public sphere. While studies of American religion often point out the changes in *who* is primarily responsible for defining the public sphere, it is also the case, I believe, that there is a change developing in the *way* it is being defined. Not just who is in and out, but *how* it is re-created and defined. The conventional research project would be to connect the fortunes of those social groups whose symbol systems control our national public sphere to the nation's location in the world order. I propose a different task. For example, the relationship of national and international politics to the global media is changing and what this means for our nation's public life and self-understanding is far from settled. Increasingly, primary groups are being replaced by society-wide institutions as the conduits for our most essential political and moral concepts — that is, such ultimate political notions as freedom, justice, and democracy.

In such a situation it is imperative, in both scholarly and political terms, to understand the differences between the "politics of imagery" and a public forum of viable motives and cultural resources. These concepts are "essentially contested" (Connolly, 1983). They are powerful, resonant, descriptive, and moral, all at once. Religious organizations have played, and continue to play, a historical role in their formation and interpretation. A clear empirical task is to understand how processes and events around the globe affect these resources for shaping our public sphere.

For example, one often hears the phrase "the personal is political." This has been a powerful attack on the moral boundaries between public and private, the realms of collective and individual responsibility. It uncovers the intersection between these two spheres of life and makes possible a questioning of why they should be arranged as they are. Conceptually, it expands both notions of public and private; yet at the same time it undermines the autonomy and hegemony of both within their own realms. While the phrase was first used by feminists in order to open the previously closed doors of private life to the analysis of power, discrimination, and politics, there are other possible readings. Recent Supreme Court decisions on issues surrounding gay rights have used a version of this logic in order to justify the intrusion of political authority into the most intimate realms of interpersonal relations. Indeed, a hallmark of totalitarianism is the completely illegitimate status of a private life. Thus, this phrase, like any religious or political symbol, can get away from its originators through the natural processes of cultural interpretation and re-creation.

In sum, our national public life is experiencing a changing cultural vocabulary upon which it can draw. The meanings we *can* draw from these resources, and what we are *likely* to produce, are questions of utmost importance. That American religion has had a large role in this process, both historically and currently, is beyond question. That global economic, political, and cultural processes, and the United States' location within the resulting orders, also condition these processes of appropriation and interpretation, is clear. Our task is to unpack the various meanings, images, and constructions while being sensitive to both the global and the local dynamics involved. While the world must be one level of analysis, those primarily concerned with a particular locality must also keep that level of analysis firmly in view.

As I consider the necessary coexistence of tendencies that are at least superficially contradictory, I am reminded of the bumper sticker common among 1980s social activists: "Think globally, act locally." Our charge may well be a version of this, that is: "Theorize globally, research locally."

References

Bergesen, Albert
1985   "Religious Studies and World-System Theory." Paper presented to the American Sociological Association, Washington, D.C.

Berger, Peter L.
1967   *The Sacred Canopy*. Garden City, N.Y.: Doubleday-Anchor.
1979   *The Heretical Imperative*. Garden City, N.Y.: Doubleday-Anchor.

Connolly, William E.
1983   *The Terms of Political Discourse*. Second Edition. Princeton, N.J.: Princeton University Press.

Eisenstadt, S. N.
1966   *Modernization: Protest and Change*. Englewood Cliffs, N.J.: Prentice-Hall.

Fields, Karen
1987   *Revival and Rebellion in Colonial Central Africa*. Princeton, N.J.: Princeton University Press.

Geertz, Clifford
1973   *The Interpretation of Cultures*. New York: Basic Books.
1983   *Local Knowledge*. New York: Basic Books.

Hunter, James Davison
1983 *American Evangelicalism.* New Brunswick, N.J.: Rutgers University Press.

Jaffee, David
Levels of Socio-Economic Development Theory. New York: Praeger, forthcoming.

Robertson, Roland
1985 "The Sacred and the World System." In *The Sacred in a Secular Age,* P. Hammond, ed. Berkeley: University of California Press.

Robertson, Roland and JoAnn Chirico
1985 "Humanity, Globalization, and Worldwide Religious Resurgence: A Theoretical Exploration." *Sociological Analysis* 46 (3):219–242.

Smith, Peter
1986 "Anglo-American Religion and Hegemonic Change in the World System, c. 1870–1980." *British Journal of Sociology* 37 (1):88–105.

Swidler, Ann
1986 "Culture in Action: Symbols and Strategies." *American Sociological Review* 51:273–286.

Tiryakian, Edward A.
1982 "Puritan America in the Modern World: Mission Impossible?" *Sociological Analysis,* 43 (4):351–368.

Thomas, George M.
1989 *Revivalism and Cultural Change.* Chicago: University of Chicago Press.

Wallerstein, Immanuel
1974 *The Modern World System.* New York: Academic Press.

Wuthnow, Robert
1983 "Cultural Crises" In *Crises in the World Order,* A. Bergesen, ed. Beverly Hills, Calif.: Sage.
1987 *Meaning and Moral Order.* Berkeley: University of California Press.

Contributors

Michael A. Burdick is a lecturer at California Polytechnic State University at San Luis Obispo.

James H. Cone is Briggs Distinguished Professor at Union Theological Seminary in New York City.

Jean Bethke Elshtain is Centennial Professor of Political Science at Vanderbilt University.

Phillip E. Hammond is Professor of Religious Studies and Sociology at the University of California at Santa Barbara.

James E. Hawdon is a graduate student in sociology at the University of Virginia.

Graham Howes is a Fellow at Trinity College, Cambridge University.

James Davison Hunter is Professor of Sociology at the University of Virginia.

Juan Carlos Navarro is a writer living in Alexandria, Virginia.

W. Barnett Pearce is Professor of Communication at the University of Massachusetts at Amherst.

Wade Clark Roof is J.F. Rowny Professor of Religion and Society at the University of California at Santa Barbara.

Lamin Sanneh is Professor of Missions at Yale Divinity School.

Ninian Smart is J.F. Rowny Professor of Comparative Religion at the University of California at Santa Barbara.

Max L. Stackhouse is Professor of Christian Social Ethics at Andover Newton Theological School.

George M. Thomas is Associate Professor of Sociology at Arizona State University.

Andrew F. Walls is Director, Centre for the Study of Christianity in the Non-Western World at the University of Edinburgh.

Rhys H. Williams is Assistant Professor of Sociology at Southern Illinois University.

Robert Wuthnow is Professor of Sociology at Princeton University.

Index